PRAKṚTI
The Integral Vision

VOLUME 2
Vedic, Buddhist and Jain Traditions

PRAKṚTI

The Integral Vision

General Editor

KAPILA VATSYAYAN

VOLUME 2

Vedic, Buddist and Jain Traditions

Edited by

Baidyanath Saraswati

Indira Gandhi National Centre for the Arts
New Delhi

D. K. Printworld (P) Ltd.
New Delhi

Cataloging in Publication Data — DK

Prakṛti : the integral vision / general editor,
Kapila Vatsyayan.
Includes bibliographical references.
Includes index.

1. Nature. 2. Cosmology. I. Vatsyayan, Kapila, 1928-

ISBN 81-246-0036-8 (set)
ISBN 81-246-0038-4 (vol. 2)

First Published in India in 1995

Publishers
Indira Gandhi National Centre for the Arts
Central Vista Mess, Janpath, New Delhi - 110001

D.K. Printworld (P) Ltd.
Regd. office : H-12, Bali Nagar, New Delhi-110015

Printed at : D. K. Fine Art Press (P) Ltd., New Delhi

आसीदिदं तमोभूतमप्रज्ञातमलक्षणम्।
अप्रतर्क्यमविज्ञेयं प्रसुप्तमिव सर्वतः।
ततः स्वयंभूर्भगवानव्यक्तो व्यञ्जयन्निदम्
महाभूतादि वृत्तौजाः प्रादुरासीत् तमोनुदः।।

(मनु स्मृ. 1. 5-6)

Foreword

In 1986 when the first of the Multidisciplinary and Cross-cultural Seminars was held under the aegis of the Indira Gandhi National Centre for the Arts, there was a trepidation. In my Introduction to the Volume on ***Concepts of Space : Ancient & Modern*** I have shared with the readers the sense of challenge as also of gratification. Then, it was not easy, nor has it been easy in the subsequent years to bring together people from different parts of the world of diverse disciplines and levels of society to speak through a multiplicity of languages to reflect and converse, and have a meaningful dialogue on the fundamental concerns of humanity in the past or present, in science or religion, philosophy and the arts, in civilizations as far apart as Egyptian, Chinese, Greek and Indian, permeating expressions through the written or the oral word, generating a language of myth and symbol which communicates across cultures.

The gathering, the dialogue and the discussion on a single concept of **Space** (*ākāśa*) made it evident that the more fundamental and universal the concept, the greater the probability and possibility of diverse interpretations at multiple levels. The single concept of **Space** had taken us through the journey of the concepts of cavity, cave, aperture, fountainhead, body, air, sky, vacuity, cipher, point and much else. The scientist and the technologist explored the concept through their method of empirical investigation, the philosopher and the metaphysician, artists and the sociologist through perennial questioning and speculation. The two approaches and methods we learnt were complementary and not in conflict. The arts, architecture, sculpture, painting, music and dance enclose, embody and evoke space. Poetry creates vast edifices of space as spatial situations, and evoke the experience of outer and inner space.

The concern with **Space (*ākāśa*)** could not be dissociated from the concern — the concept of **Time (*kāla*)**. Two years later, a similar gathering with many familiar faces (who communicated with one another with greater ease) gathered to deliberate upon the many dimensions of **Time** (*kāla*). Once again, the discussions at that Seminar revolved round the micro and the macro levels of the single concept, from molecular time to the cosmic time, from the time of biologists to the time of astronomer, from the time of the seer and meditator —

to the time of the architect, sculptor, musician, dancer and the poet. Besides the familiar faces, there were others who had joined the family of the IGNCA. The enlarged family gave this Seminar a depth and richness, unique and unparalleled. The experiences His Holiness The Dalai Lama articulated in words lucid and resonant, were juxtaposed with the precision and meditation of a scientist — the late Professor D.S. Kothari. The depth of the experience of **Time** in religious traditions, Islamic, Christian, Hindu, Buddhist, Jain and Hebrew, and the embodiment of inner and outer **Time** in poetic language was shared through rapt silence through the voice of the Poet Kathleen Raine.

Logically and naturally, from these two fundamental and universal concepts the next step in our quest for exploration of a single universal theme through diverse paths recalling the Ṛgvedic Verse, **Truth is one; man knows it by different names**, was to explore the concept of the primal elements (five or four) in different civilizations which have governed and determined the evolution of civilization and culture. Perhaps, the first conscious awareness of Man was the fact that his life depended on water, Earth, air, fire and, above all, space. Understandably, in all civilizations, at the most sophisticated level as also at the simplest level, the recognition that the primal elements were primary and indispensable for Man, is universal. Myths of the origin of the universe, creation, cosmology and cosmogony, have been developed on the concept of the elements which are four or five. There is a vast body of primary sources and equally extensive and complex a history of critical discourse on the nature of primal elements and their indispensability, not only for Man but for all life on Earth.

The subject was too vast and too monumental to be taken up in a single Seminar. Organizationally, therefore, this time it was decided to hold five successive but interlocked Seminars, one leading to the others, so that they could all culminate in a final international cross-cultural multidisciplinary Seminar. Since cultures, disciplines, and levels of society are not completely autonomous and insulated, there was a planned and understandable overlapping between one Seminar or Workshop and another.

The five Seminars were divided more for facility than the autonomous nature of each area or field. The discussions, therefore, at one Seminar were taken up and did interpenetrate into the next.

Logically, the first of these Seminars focused attention on the articulations of cohesive communities in the world who have lived in harmony with nature and who have communicated with the five elements in a continuous unceasing dialogue. To them the nature of the five elements — water, earth, air, fire and space — is not a matter of intellection or breaking down into separation and divisions of totality or a whole; instead, it is a question of life here and now. This is manifested in ritual practices which sacrilize nature so that man can live as an integral part of the universe, the rhythmic movement of the changing seasons, and the symmetrical punctuation and cycle of seed sprouting, growing, flowering, fruiting, decaying and renewing. In modern discourse this is understood as the need for man to live in harmony with the environment for an evolution of socio-cultural systems and methodologies for ensuring the maintenance of ecological balances. The lives and lifestyles of these cohesive groups have begun to acquire renewed validity on account of what man has done to pollute, contaminate, desacrilize and desecrate the very fundamentals that sustain him and make it possible for him to live on earth. The first Volume is based on the papers submitted at this Seminar.

The second Seminar moved the emphasis to the textual traditions. There is a vast body of literature in Greek, Chinese and Indian sources where philosophic discourses have been held on the nature of the universe, the nature of matter, the elements and the possibility of transmutation of the gross to the subtle. In India all branches of the philosophic streams have discussed the nature of the *Bhūtas* and the *Mahābhūtas.* The discussion ranges from the earliest articulation on the subject in the *Ṛgveda* to the philosophic schools of Vaiśeṣikas, Vedāntins, Śaiva and the *Āgamas.* The old system of *Āyurveda* in India, as much of medicine in Greece in a very different way, is based on the concept of the *Mahābhūtas* in the constitution of the body itself. The very conception of the five elements constitutes the body. Texts for Indian astronomy, chemistry, metallurgy are replete with discussions on the elements. This discussion cannot be dissociated from a speculation, and discourse of, the nature of the universe, cosmology, cosmogony. The second Seminar delved deep into each of these aspects specially in the Indian tradition — Vedic, Brāhmaṇical, Upaniṣadic and Tāntric. In addition, there was a consideration of the concept of the *Mahābhūtas* in Buddhism and Jainism. This Seminar unfolded the very complex and subtle aspects of the discourse on the nature of the matter, the fivefold organic matter and the five external objects. It also brought forth the many convergences as also divergences of viewpoint between and amongst these different streams of Indian thought as exemplified in the textual tradition. The Seminar was hosted by the Department of Sanskrit, University of Poona, Pune. The second Volume of this series is based on the papers and the discussions held at this Seminar.

Logically, the third Seminar had to and did explore the discussions as also the manifestations of the five elements in the Indian arts, along with their Āgamic background. As is well-recognized, while the *Upaniṣads* provide the basis for speculative thinking, the *Brāhmaṇas* give the methodology of ritual practice (*Yajña* and *Prayoga*). Parallel is the development in early and later medieval India where the texts on *Vāstu* and *Śilpa* provide the frame-work of the abstract principles of creating concrete structures through different media and in different forms. The *Āgama* is the twin which provide the methodology of enlivening, giving life and breath to the concrete structures and forms of art. If monumental architecture, sculpture, painting, music or dance, poetry or theatre, is created on the comprehension of space and time, they are even more built on the system of correspondences first for embodying and then evoking the five elements. The fascinating and unceasing cycle of the movement from the inner experience to the creation of form, which would incorporate the five elements and the employment of a methodology of ritual, is outlined in the Āgamic texts only to achieve the end experience of the transformation of the gross to the subtle. This was the subject of this Seminar. From different vantage points of the architect, sculptor, painter, musician and dancer, the field was re-opened to examine the structure of the Indian arts at its primal level.

Naturally, theories of aesthetics which have emerged from such a viewpoint had to be discussed and many questions asked. The third Volume incorporates the span of the papers presented and the discussions held at this Seminar.

If the arts deal with the process of transmutation and mutation of the subtle to the gross, and the evocation of the subtle from the gross, in other words, the process of the abstract and the concrete suggesting, stimulating and evoking the abstract, then the astrophysicist deals with the nature of primal matter itself. No discourse on the elements could have been completed by excluding the discussion on modern physics of elementary particles and the most recent developments in microbiology. The fourth Seminar took up the question of the nature and function of matter itself and discussed the theories of the creation of the universe and emergent cosmologies in the modern physics. This was juxtaposed with the consideration on the nature of matter and consciousness. It was obvious that the new developments in science were, perhaps, not all that far remote from the earlier insights in the context of consciousness. The debate between the nineteenth Century mechanistic science and the modern physics was re-opened. This was juxtaposed with speculations and the philosophic discourses in the Indian philosophic schools. If the second Seminar dealt with the textual traditions and the philosophic schools of *Sāṃkhya, Mīmāṃsā* and the *Vaiśeṣikas*, this Seminar looked at these traditions as structuralistic traditions from a scientific point of view. The dialogue created between the method of science and the method of speculation was invigorating. The fourth Volume comprises papers and discussions at this Seminar.

The fifth and the last Seminar was a coming together of cultures as also disciplines. Coordinators of the earlier Seminars presented brief Reports on each of the Seminars which provided the background and the landscape. The international community, comprising scientists, biologists, philosophers, anthropologists, ecologists and artists shared not only the myth and cosmology of their particular societies but also there was a most meaningful dialogue between those who lived in the awareness of the primordial myths of the elements and those who had employed the tools of science to explore the nature of the phenomenon of matter.

The putting together of the deliberations of the five major Seminars, as a single or a multiple-volume, is a daunting task. Through the combined efforts of the Coordinators of each of these Seminars and, particularly, the Chief Coordinator — Professor B.N. Saraswati and his associates — it has been possible to prepare the five Volumes based on the deliberations of these Seminars as also a companion exhibition which was called "**PRAKṚTI: The Integral Vision**".

It is my hope that these Volumes will provide material for further discussion and dialogue. The perennial nature of the theme and its urgent and contemporary validity will, I hope, make these Volumes significant. As I have said earlier in my Introduction, Man stands today at a moment where he is threatened by the pollution, inner and outer, of his own making. The primal elements and the urgent need for purification through austerity and discipline are not the matters of intellectual discourse alone. Their maintenance and sustenance, and the purity of these that are primary and primal, are the objectives of our life, lest death overtakes us.

9th June, 1994 **Kapila Vatsyayan**

Contents

Introduction

India's textual tradition consists of the Vedic musings, Upaniṣadic thoughts, rituals, *Darśana* of various orders, *Jyotiṣa, Āyurveda, Vāstuśāstra* and so on. Each of these texts deals with concepts concerning man and the Universe. The essays compiled in this Volume are based on the IGNCA series of seminars on five fundamental elements. Here the development of the concept of elements is traced through the *Vedas,* the *Upaniṣads,* rituals and other *Śāstras.*

The Vedic section is dealt with by S.K. Lal, Srinivas Madabhushi and Usha Bhise. The earliest musings of the *Ṛṣis* did not specify the five *Mahābhūtas* but have described the creation from *tamas,* from Primordial waters, from *Agni,* from Prajāpati, *Brahman, Ātman, Ākāśa* etc. These elements have been deified in the Vedic *Sūktas,* but the later Upaniṣadic conclusions give a definite shape to these concepts.

S.K. Lal traces from the earliest Vedic period the development of the concept of *Pañcabhūtas.* In the beginning water, fire, air, sun and earth were considered not merely as physical elements, but as a combination of both sentient and non-sentient aspects, which led them to treat these elements as deities, to be propitiated for getting their benevolent gifts and escaping from their ire. This was the result of observation of their pervasive nature in all things, and their creative power.

The Hymns of creation of the *Ṛg Veda* were reflected in the *Sūktas* of *Yajur* as well as *Atharva Vedas.* Srinivas Madabhushi discusses as to how, the *Tamas, Ambhas* and the fire were considered as the Primeval causes of creation and the development of a conscious principle's will — which is called *Brahman* — as the universal cause, comparing them with modern scientific theories.

Usha Bhise underscores the dominant principle of primeval waters which were considered the cause of the universe and they were treated as sentient beings, having a will and how the earth etc., emerged out of those waters. In this description, she points out the role played by the floods in the Indus Valley of those times.

R.K. Mande discusses the *Brahman* concept, the *Trivṛtkaraṇa* of *Chāndogya*, the *Pañcīkaraṇa* based on *Taittirīya*, the spider example of *Muṇḍaka* etc. She further elucidates the concept that the essence pervading all things is same and the ultimate aim of man considered there being the conquering of elements.

T.N. Dharmadhikari traces in the various Vedic rituals, how the deities waters, fire, air and others were worshipped and offerings were given. This again confirms the conviction of Vedic seers that the *bhūtas* were not merely insentient elements but were a combination of both conscious and non-conscious principles.

Pt. N.S. Devanathachariar in his Sanskrit paper gives the arguments of Buddhists for the non-acceptance of *Ākāśa* as a *bhūta* and the counter-arguments of the orthodox school. An English translation of this paper is also provided for the benefit of those who would like to read in that language.

Mahesh Tiwari's paper discusses the Buddhist system which approves of only the four *bhūtas* and how the adjective *Mahā* was added to the name *bhūta* because of their vastness. He further elucidates that all these *bhūtas* are accepted as mere appearances — they exist only in name and form. There is no creation as such in their system and what is appearing as world is a beginningless stream. He further discusses the transition of the term *bhūta* as *dhātu*.

A.M. Ghatage, traces the chronological development of the word *bhūta* in Hindu and Greek traditions — which presupposes a living principle and not merely a dead matter. Just to avoid this double meaning, the Bhuddhist and Jains used the term *dhātu* in later times. The final stage of development as a psychic principle is traced by him in his paper.

Mangala Mirasdar takes up the Jaina viewpoint of *pañca Astikāyas* and shows how *Ākāśa* is considered not as an element but some evolute giving space to other material objects.

Pratibha Pingale describes the *pañca Skandhas* as detailed in *Abhidharma Kośa* and other works.

S.D. Sharma discusses in his paper how in Astronomy the five elements were treated — their good and evil aspects and the methods of alleviating their evil effects and increasing the good effects.

From the papers that are presented here, one can see that the rudiments of later *Darśanas* were already there in the *Nāsadīya Sūkta*, the *Ambhas Sūkta* etc. The findings of Vedic seers are corroborated in some respects and controverted in others, with the development of modern science. The Upaniṣadic Philosophies still remain the bedrock of Indian thought. Their conclusions stress that it is not the *prāṇa, manas* etc., that animate the body, but a conscious principle running through the veins and arteries as the sap of a tree. This sap is universal but takes different shapes even as the bodies differ due to different wombs and seeds.

Another aspect of Vedic philosophy is that the *Brahman* expands and contracts in cycles and in this process the invisible makes itself visible through various forms. The infinite or all-pervading principle can neither increase nor decrease.

The third aspect is about the evolution of human beings. *Bṛhadāraṇyaka Upaniṣad* and other works talk of separate creations of man, animal and others in pairs of the male and female counterparts. This theory confirms that both the male and female aspects are not complete in themselves, but are complementary and supplementary to each other. The *Ardhanārīśvara* principle or Lakṣmī residing on the chest of Lord Viṣṇu are all born out of this understanding.

Finally I thank Dr. Kapila Vatsyayan for asking me to edit this volume and for the confidence that she reposed in me. I also extend my gratitude to Dr. Saroja Bhate for organising the seminar on "The Concept of Bhutas: Vedic, Buddhist and Jain Traditions" held at the Department of Sanskrit and Prakrit Languages, University of Poona in March 1992. Thanks are due to Dr. Sudha Gopalakrishnan for assistance in editing.

These seminars have enriched our understanding and the objective with which IGNCA started them, has been fulfilled to some extent. I hope and wish, that, readers of these Volumes will immensely benefit from these papers.

Sampat Narayanan

1

Pañcamahābhūtas
Origin and Myths in Vedic Literature

S.K. Lal

The relationship between man and the universe has been a most fascinating idea that attracted the mind of thinkers in almost every religion, philosophy, mythology, and ritual from primitive age to modern time. The seers of the *Vedas* have often wondered at various phenomena in the universe. They contemplated over the marvels of nature and the mysteries in the vast and variegated world that they lived in, and attempted to unravel the enigma of creation. They accepted not as final what they saw around them with their physical eyes. In this respect, Ṛṣi Kavaṣa remarks:

> नैतावदेना परो अन्यदस्त्युक्षा स द्यावापृथिवी बिभर्ति।
> *naitāvadenā paro anyadastyukṣā sa dyāvāpṛthivī bibharti* ।
> (*ṚV*, 10.31.8 ab)
>
> Not only here is this; more is beyond us. He is the bull, the Heaven's and Earth's supporter. — Tr. RTH Griffith (Gr.)

And therefore the *Ṛṣis* of the *Vedas* have not infrequently enquired into the mystery, the mechanism, the creation, and the establishment of the universe. Ṛṣi Dīrghatamas queries:

> वि यस्तस्तम्भ षळिमा रजांस्यजस्य रूपे किमपि स्विदेकम्।
> *vi yastastambha ṣalimā rajāṁsyajasya rupe kimapi svidekam* ।
> (*ṚV*, 1.164.6 cd)
>
> What is 'That One' who established and fixed world's six regions.
> — Tr. Gr.

Ṛṣi Atharvan enquires:

क्व प्रेप्सन् दीप्यत ऊर्ध्वो अग्निः क्व प्रेप्सन् पवेत मातरिश्वा।
kva prepsan dīpyata ūrdhvo agniḥ kva prepsan paveta mātariśvā।
(*AV*, 10.7, 4 ab)

Whither desiring to attain does Agni flame aloft? Whither desiring to attain blows Mātariśvan? — Tr. W.D. Whitney

Ṛṣi Viśvakarman questions:

किं स्विद्वनं क उ स वृक्ष आस यतो द्यावापृथिवी निष्टतक्षुः।[1]
kim svidvanaṁ ka u sa vṛkṣa āsa yato dyāvāpṛthivī niṣṭatakṣuḥ ।
(*ṚV*, 10.81.4 ab)

What was the tree, what wood in sooth produced it, from which they fashioned out the earth and heaven — Tr. Gr.

Such enquiries did stir the inner vision of the *Ṛṣis* which led them to deep thinking and contemplation. The *Ṛṣis* envisioned certain guesses, conjectures and conclusions, and put them forth for the sake of posterity. They presumed that the inferences resulting from their deep thinking, meditation, and contemplation were not only true to them in their age, but also to the generations to come in future:

देवानां नु वयं जाना प्र वोचाम विपन्यया।
उक्थेषु शस्यमानेषु यः पश्याद् उत्तरे युगे।।
devānāṁ nu vayaṁ jānā pra vocāma vipanyayā ।
ukthesu śasyamāneṣu yaḥ paśyāduttare yuge ।
(*ṚV*, 10.72.1)

Let us with tuneful skill proclaim these generations of the gods, that one may see them when these hymns are chanted in a **future age.** — Tr. Gr.

Thus, the Vedic seers have left for us a number of guesses, conjectures, speculations, and postulations regarding man, universe and its maker. Their opinions vary. Some time, the Creator of the universe was thought of as *Aja* (the primeval, everlasting, uncreated being);[2] some time, it is *Ekam* (the one) (*ṚV*, 10.81.3);[3] at other time, it is Indra who forces the earth and sky asunder (*ṚV*, 10.89.1), and brings out into existence that which was not yet existent (*ṚV*, 6. 24.5); or the omniscient *puruṣa* (*ṚV*, 10. 90); or Varuṇa who created air, and fire in the water (*ṚV*, 5.85.2-4). It could be, in the Ātharvaṇic phraseology, *Brahmāṇḍana* (*AV*, 4. 34, 35); or *Ucchiṣṭa* (*AV*, 11. 7), or *Ka* (*AV*, 10. 2); or *Prāṇa*

(*AV*, 11. 4); or *Skambha* (*AV*, 10.7,8); or *Virāja* (*AV*, 8. 9,10); or *Vena* (*AV*, 2.1); or *Kāla* (*AV*, 19. 53, 54); or *Brahmacārin* (*AV*, 11.5); or *Pṛthivī* (*AV*, 12.1); or *Rohita* (*AV*, 13.3); or *Madhu* (*AV*, 9.1).[4] It may be Prajāpati of the *Brāhmaṇas* (*ŚB*, 6.1.1.8); or *Puruṣa* or *Brahman* or *Ātman* of the *Upaniṣads* (*PraśnaUp*, 6.1; *BrUp*, 2.2.1; *TaittUp*, 2.1).

Once a primeval omnipotent Creator was assumed, speculations on the process of Creation must have begun. This may be regarded as the genesis of the concepts of the *Bhūtas*, the material causes or the gross (primary) elements of creation, and of a large number of myths woven around them. The creator must have needs to create material things.

It may be pointed out that the concept of the *bhūtas*, as it is understood in the *Upaniṣads* and in later philosophical texts, does not occur in the earliest *Veda*, the *Ṛgveda*. In the *Ṛgveda*, the term *bhūta* has been used mainly in the sense of 'past', often in the juxtaposition of 'future'.[5] Further, in almost all its occurrences, the word means sentient or insentient beings (*sthāvarajaṅgamātmakaṁ bhūtajātam*).

However, a few rudimentary ideas of the *bhūtas*, in the sense of gross elements, may be traced in the *Ṛgveda*. The hymn *ṚV*, 10.58 is an address to a dead man. It is said, the spirit that went away (after death) to the earth (vs. 3), to the billowing sea (vs. 5), to the beam of light (vs. 6), and to the waters and plants (vs. 7), may that spirit return.[6] In *ṚV*, 10.18.10, the spirit of a dead man is addressed to go and mingle with the earth. *ṚV*, 10.56.1 (where *Ṛṣi* Bṛhaduktha addresses his dead son Vājin) states, "Here is one light (terrestrial) for thee, another yonder (mid-air), enter the third (heaven) and be there with united (Tr. Gr.).[7] In *ṚV*, 10.16.3, (again a funeral hymn where a dead man has been addressed), it is mentioned, "May thy eye go to the sun, the mind to the spirit (*Ātman*), go you to the earth, or to the waters" (Tr. Gr.).

On the basis of the above references, it may be observed that the Vedic *Ṛṣis* did believe in some kind of union with different elements (*bhūtas*) after death, and that the different components of the gross (earthly) body united with the corresponding subtle elements, the *tanmātras* of the *Upaniṣads*. Further, it may be pointed out that the fine constituent members of the *bhūtas* occur in the *Ṛgveda* in the form of five deified natural objects. The words *pṛthivī, ap, agni, vāyu* and *ākāśa* (or *dyaus*) have been deified in the *Ṛgveda*. These divinities may be regarded as prototypal gross elements (*bhūtas*). A number of myths and legends have been woven around them to bring out their essential nature and characteristic features, that might have led the post-Vedic thinkers to conceive and transform them into the five *bhūtas* constituting the physical universe.

There is no fixed order in the enumeration of the five *bhūtas*. Sometimes, the order is *kham, vāyu, jyoti, āpaḥ* and *pṛthivī* (*MuṇḍUp*, 2.1.3); sometimes, it is *pṛthivī, ap, tejas, anila, kham* (*ŚvetUp*, 2.12; 6.2), and sometimes, it is *pṛthivī, vāyu, ākāśa, āpaḥ* and *jyoti* (*AitUp*, 3.3). Many a time synonyms are also used. In this paper we have put the order as : *āpaḥ, agni* (because they are found to be interlinked), *dyaus*, (*ākāśa*), *pṛthivī* (because they form a pair *dyāvāpṛthivī*), and *vāyu*.

Āpaḥ

Āpaḥ have been regarded as the first and the foremost element in the *Vedas*. Water (*ap*, singular) is the first creation. *ṚV*, 10.82.1 states that Viśvakarman first engendered the waters and then heaven and earth floating on the waters. Further, in the same *sūkta* (vs. 5), it is said that the waters were earlier than this earth and heaven, much before the *asuras* and the gods came into being. The waters received the primeval germ whence all the gods came into being. *AV*, 12.1.8 says that in the beginning, there was flood of waters. In the *Nāsadīyasūkta* (*RV*, 10.129), the water has been regarded as the first principle:

> तम आसीत्तमसा गूळ्हमग्रेऽप्रकेतं सलिलं सर्वमा इदम्।
> तुच्छ्येनाभ्वपिहितं यदासीत् तपसस्तन्महिनाजायतैकम्।।
> *tama āsīttamasā gūḷahmagre'praketaṁ salilaṁ sarvamā idam* ।
> *tucchyenābhvapihitaṁ yadāsīt tapasastanmahinājāyataikam* ।।
> (*ṚV*, 10.129.3)

> Darkness there was : at first concealed in darkness this all was indiscriminated chaos. All that existed then was void and formless; by the great power of warmth was born that unit.
> — Tr. Gr.

TS, 5.6.4.2 mentions that at first the universe was waters, the moving ocean. Prajāpati, becoming wind, rocked about on a lotus leaf[8] on the waters. On it he piled the fire; that became this earth, then he indeed formed support.[9] Regarding the waters as the first element, *ŚB*, 11.1.6.1-3 states through a myth:

> In the beginning this universe was water, nothing but a sea of water. The waters thought, "How can we be reproduced"? They toiled and performed austere penance.[10] When they were thus becoming heated, a golden egg was produced. In a year's time, a man, Prajāpati, was produced from that golden egg. He broke open the golden egg. There was no resting place (*pratiṣṭhā*) for him except the golden egg bearing him. It floated around for as long as a year. At the end of the year, he tried to speak. He uttered,

> *bhūḥ* this become this earth; *bhuvaḥ*, this become air (*antarikṣa*); and, *svaḥ*, this become the yonder sky (*dyaus*).

In the *Hiraṇyagarbha-sūkta* (*RV*, 10.121, vs. 7 and 8), it is stated that the mighty waters contained the universal germ producing *Agni*, thence sprang God's one spirit (*Ekaḥ*) into being. He surveyed the waters around him containing productive force (*dakṣam*); he is the one God among all gods (cf. also *TS*, 5.5.1.2).

Four whole hymns have been addressed to the waters (*ṚV*, 7.47; 49; 10.9; 30). The waters are regarded as the mistresses of the world (*ṚV*, 10.30.10). They are prayed to grant men procreative power (*ṚV*, 10. 9.3). The waters received that primeval germ wherein all the gods were gathered (*ṚV*, 10. 82.6). All creatures are born from the waters (*ṚV*, 1.23.16, 10.17.10; 32.2; 39.2). They are mostly motherless, and the producers of all that is fixed and all that moves (*ṚV*, 6. 501). They are the mothers of all beings (*ṚV*, 1.23.10; 6.50.7; 10.17.10). They are (as one unified divinity) the mother of the sun (*JB*, 3.114). They produce *Agni* (*ṚV*, 10.91.6; *AV*, 1.31.1). *Agni* entered into them (*ṚV*, 7.49.4). All objects, movable or immovable owe their existence to the waters (*GB*, 1.129). They are the wives of the gods (*JB*, 1.140). They are the maidens of Soma (*ṚV*, 10.30.5).

The *āpaḥ*, indeed, are all this world (*TĀ*, 10.22). *ChUp*, 7.10.1 says that it is the waters who pervade everything, big or small: the earth, the atmosphere, the heaven, the mountains, gods, men, animals, birds, grass, plants, dogs, worms, insects, ants. All these (worldly manifestations) are waters indeed.

Waters are the foundations (*pratiṣṭhā*) of all in the universe (*ŚB*, 12.5.2.14). They are a place of abode (*āyatana*)[11] for all the gods (*ŚB*, 14.3.2.13). *ŚB*, 8.2.3.5; 6 regards the waters as food.

ŚB, 6.1.1.8ff mentions that Prajāpati created the waters from *vāk*.[12] Waters pervaded everything here; because they pervaded (*āp*) everything here, therefore they are called waters (*āpaḥ*) (*AV*, 3.13.2). A hymn is compared with the flowing water (*ṚV*, 10.89.4). About the pervasiveness of the waters, *ŚB*, 11.1.6.16 gives the following legend:

> Parameṣṭhin,[13] son of Prajāpati, desired, "Would I were everything here". He became the waters, for, the waters are everything here. Prajāpati, the highest lord, is the waters (*ŚB*, 8.2.4.14).[14]

Agni (Tejas)

Agni has permeated the entire universe by his effulgence. He is in the earth, in the herbs, in the waters, in the stones, in men, kine, and horses. It is he who sends down heat (*AV*, 12.1.19) from the sky; the firmament belongs to him, and mortals on earth kindle him as an oblation-bearer (*AV*, 12.1.20). *Agni* is indeed the existence, for, it is because of *Agni* that everything exists (*bhū*) here (*ŚB*, 8.1.1.4.). *Agni* is our spring of life (*ṚV*, 1.31.10). He is described as thousand-eyed and hundred-headed monster (*ŚB*, 9.1.1.6); he was created as hundred-headed Rudra (*ŚB*, 9.2.3.32).

Agni has been described as a begetter *par-excellence*. He places the germ in all beings (*ṚV*, 3.2.10), and engenders life on the earth and offspring in women (*ṚV*, 10.183.3). He has created all that flies, walks, stands, or moves (*ṚV*, 10.88.4). He is the bull (*ṚV*, 1.58.5) abounding in procreative seed (*ṚV*, 4.5.3). He is the generator of the two worlds (heaven and earth : *ṚV*, 1.94.4; 7.5.7). He stretched them out (*ṚV*, 3.6.5; 7.5.4) like one does two skins (*ṚV*, 6.8.3); he kept asunder the two worlds (*ṚV*, 6.8.3).[15] But he is also the son of the heaven and earth (*ṚV*, 3.2.2; 25.1; 10.1.2; 2.7; 46.9). *ṚV*, 10.88.9 says that *Agni* heats the heaven and earth when an offering of fuel is made to him.

Agni is afterwards identified with the sun (*ṚV*, 3.2.14). He is born as the sun rising in the morning (*ṚV*, 10.88.6). *AB*, 8.28 remarks that the sun when setting enters into *Agni* and is produced from him; he unites with the light and rays of the sun (*ṚV*, 5.37.1; 7.2.2). He is the head and the summit of the sky (*ṚV*, 1.59.2; 6.7.1). He causes the sun to ascend the sky (*ṚV*, 10.156.4) who was lying hidden in the sea (*ṚV*, 10.72.7). *Agni*, kindled on the earth causes the sun to rise (*ṚV*, 5.6.4; *ŚB*, 2.3.1.5; *TS*, 4.7.13.3). The sun becomes visible when *Agni* is born (*ṚV*, 4.31.11). When men light *Agni* on the earth, the celestials light him in the heaven (*ṚV*, 6.2.3) where he shines (*ṚV*, 3.37.12).

Agni, in the form of the sun, is regarded as the soul, and, as such, he is compared with the *Puruṣa* (*ṚV*, 1.15.1; *ŚB*, 10.6.1.11). In the *MaitUp*, 6.35, he is regarded as the ruler and the preserver of the world. He is regarded as the *Brahman*, who has entered into all beings (*MaitUp*, 6.38). *Agni* is likened with a bird, he is a divine bird (*ṚV*, 1.164.52); he is the eagle of the sky (*ṚV*, 7.15.4); he has wings (*ṚV*, 1.58.5; 2.2.4). His abode is the highest in the heaven (*ṚV*, 8.11.7) whence he comes to the lower world (*ṚV*, 8.64.15). The third form of *Agni* is the highest (*ṚV*, 10.1.3). To the bright ocean, the sun has ascended (*ṚV*, 7.60.4). *Sūrya* has mounted up in the shining ocean (*ṚV*, 5.45.10).

The celestial form of *Agni* is manifest in *ṚV*, 7.39.5 where *Agni* is asked to bring *Agni*. In *AV*, 4. 39.9, it is stated that *Agni* moves having entered into the fire.

Agni is said to possess these forms, and much emphasis has been put on the tripartite form of *Agni*. Three forms of *Agni* — *Agni*, *Vāyu* (or Indra), and

Sūrya — have afterwards been mentioned in the *Ṛgveda* (*ṚV*, 1.164.44). He is regarded as the forehead of the sky, and as the earth's centre (*ṚV*, 1.59.2). *ṚV*, 10.56.1 says that there is one light here (for the dead man), another yonder, (and the dead man is asked to enter the third, the three fertilize the worlds with their genial moisture (*ṚV*, 7. 33.7), — the three are *Agni*, *Vāyu*, and *Sūrya*.

Heaven, air and earth are the triads regarded as the prototypes of the sun, wind, and fire (*ṚV*, 8.18.19). *Agni*, *Vāyu*, and *Āditya* are the hearts of the gods (*ŚB*, 9.1.1.23). They are the lights diffused all around (*ŚB*, 6.3.3.16). The sun, the lightning (in the mid-region), and the fire (*Agni* on the earth) have been regarded as three brothers (*ṚV*, 1.164.1). *ṚV*, 10.45.1 states that first *Agni* sprang to life from out of heaven (*dyaus*) as the sun, the second time from (us) mortals (in the form of sacrificial and domestic fire), and thirdly in the waters (in the mid-region) in the form of lightning. The tripartite nature of *Agni* has been explained through myths. In this connection, *ŚB*, 11.2.3.1; 3 gives the following myth:

> In the beginning, this universe was *Brahman* (neut.). *Brahman* created gods, and having created the gods, it made them ascend these worlds: *Agni* this (terrestrial) world, *Vāyu*, the atmosphere, and *Sūrya*, the sky. Then *Brahman* itself went up to the sphere beyond.[16] *ŚB*, 12.4.1.3 compares three sacrificial fires with three worlds: the *Gārhapatya* with earth, the *Dakṣiṇāgni* with atmosphere, and the *Āhavanīya* with heaven.

ŚB, 11.5.8.1-4 relates that: In the beginning Prajāpati alone was here. He desired, "May I exist, may I be generated". He practised austerity, he wearied himself. From him thus wearied and heated, three worlds were created, the earth, the air, and the sky. He heated these three worlds; from them thus heated, three lights issued forth: *Agni*, *Vāyu* (who blows here), and *Sūrya*. He heated these three lights; from them thus heated were produced three *Vedas* — the *Ṛgveda* from *Agni*, the *Yajurveda* from *Vāyu*, and the *Sāmaveda* from *Sūrya*. He heated these three *Vedas*, from them thus heated, three luminous essences were produced, namely, *bhūḥ* from the *Ṛgveda*, *bhuvaḥ* from the *Yajurveda*, and *svaḥ* from the *Sāmaveda*.[17]

The tripartite character of *Agni* has been carried on to the *Upaniṣads* also. *TaitUp*, 1.5.1-3 says that *bhūr* is this world, *bhuvaḥ*, the mid-air, and *svar*, the yonder world. *Mahas* is the sun, because through the sun all the worlds prosper (*mahīyante*).[18] *Mahas* is the fire, *bhuvaḥ*, the wind, *svar* the sun, *mahas* the *Brahman*, because through the *Brahman* all the *Vedas* prosper (*Tait Up*, 1.5.1-3).[19]

The Almighty primordial nature of *Agni* is found in the *ṚV*, 10.5.7, where *Agni* is regarded as both non-existent (*asat*), and existent (*sat*); that is, the first cause and the first effect.[20] *Agni* is the sap, *Agni* is the substance in this world (*ŚB*, 6.7.3.3). It is *Agni* who generated food (*ṚV*, 6.52.16). *ŚB*, 9.3.4.17 describes *Agni* as a universal sovereign. He is compared with the All-Creator Viśvakarman (*ŚB*, 9.2.2.6),[21] "who combines in his person the characters of a primeval divine sacrificer and of a creator".[22]

Agni is often compared with the *vedī*. The *vedī* is regarded as the navel of the earth (*ṚV*, 1.52.2), and thus, he is counted with the earth (*ŚB*, 6.2.1.29). Further, *Agni* has been identified with Prajāpti. *ŚB*, 6.1.1.1-5 deals with the birth of Prajāpati who is described as a combination of seven persons (*puruṣas*) into one person (*Puruṣa*: Prājāpati). And that *Puruṣa* is regarded as *Agni* (fire-altar) who is to be built. That Prajāpati desired, "May it multiply, may it be reproduced." By means of *Agni*, he (Prajāpati) entered into union with the earth. Thence an egg arose. He touched it and said, "May it grow". And the embryo which was inside was created as *Vāyu*. Likewise, by means of *Vāyu*, he entered into union with the mid-air (*antarikṣa*); thence an egg arose; from it, the yonder sun was created. By means of the sun, he entered into union with the sky (*dyu*); thence an egg arose; from it the moon was created, for the moon is the seed (*ŚB*, 6.1.2.1-4).

Almighty nature *Agni* has been brought forth in detail in the *Upaniṣads*. *Agni* permeates the entire universe. The universe has been compared with five great fires, Viz. (1) fire in the heaven, (2) fire in the clouds, (3) fire on the earth, (4) fire in man, and (5) fire in women. In this connection, *ChUp*, 5.4-9 says:

> The yonder world (heaven) is the fire; the sun is its fuel, the rays its smoke, the day its flame, the moon its coal, the stars its sparks; into this fire the gods offer an offering of faith, out of this sacrificial offering arises Soma. *Parjanya* (rain-cloud) is the sacrificial fire; the wind is its fuel, the clouds its smoke, the lightning its flame, the thunderbolt its coals, the hailstorms its sparks, into this fire the gods sacrifice king Soma. Out of this sacrificial offering arises the rain. The earth is a sacrificial fire; the year is its fuel, the ether is its smoke, the might its flame, the points of heaven its coals, the intermediate points (of direction) the sparks; into this fire the gods sacrifice the rain; out of this sacrificial offering arises the food. Indeed the man is the sacrificial fire; the speech its fuel, the breath is smoke, the tongue its flame, the eyes its coals, the ears, its sparks; into this fire, the gods sacrifice food; out of this offering arises the semen or sperm. Indeed the woman is the sacrificial fire; the lap or her

> sexual organ its fuel, when one appeals to her, it is the smoke, the vulva the flame, the insertion the coal, the sexual pleasure the sparks; into this fire the gods sacrifice the semen; out of this sacrificial offering, arises the foetus. Thus it occurs that during the fifth sacrificial offering the waters come to be called as *Puruṣa.* After the embryo, covered by the membrane, has lain in the interior for ten months or as long as it may be, he is born. After one is born, he lives so long as his life duration is. After he is dead, they carry him to his destination, the fire, from which he had come, out of which he had arisen.[23] *ŚB,* 12.5.2. It gives detailed rites for burning a dead body of a sacrificer. His dead body becomes the *vedī* and all implements of sacrifice are kept on him and then burnt. *ŚB,* 11.2.1.1 says that a man is born Three times; the three births are: biological, ritual and funerary.[24]

On the basis of the above, a few salient features of *Āpaḥ* and *Agni* may be put forth:

1. Both *Āpaḥ* and *Agni* are said to possess procreative powers. The waters are the mothers *par-excellence,* and the fire is the prolific generator and begetter.
2. Both of them are said to have pervaded the entire universe.
3. There is a close nexus between the fire and the water. *Agni* is said to have been born from the waters.
4. The tripartite nature of *Agni* has been connected with the three forms of waters, celestial, atmospheric and terrestrial.

FIRE AND WATER

Fire and water are regarded as the most important elements (*ṚV,* 1.161.9). *ṚV,* 10.51; 52; 53; and 124 relate a legend about *Agni* hiding in the waters (*ṚV,* 10.51.1) and in the plants (*śamī, aśvattha, ṚV,* 10.51.3) and being formed by the gods. In this respect, *ŚB,* 7.4.1.8 gives the following legend:

> *Agni* went away from the gods, and hid himself in the waters. The gods said to Prajāpati, "Go thou in search of him; to thee, his father, he will reveal himself". Prajāpati became a white horse, and went in search of *Agni.* He found him on a lotus leaf heaving forth from the waters (*ŚB,* 7.3.2.14).[25] Lotus means the waters and this earth is a leaf thereof, this earth is *Agni's* womb, for *Agni* (fire-altar) is this earth.

As dwelling in the waters, *Agni* resembled the acquatic bird *haṁsa* (*ṚV*, 1.56.9; 4.40.5; 10.124.9). He is regarded as the son of the waters (as lightning), as such he is known as *Apāṁ Napāt* (*ṚV*, 2.35; 10.30. 3; 4 etc.).[26] Another divinity, *Trita Āptya*, has been identified with *Agni*, as a god of lightning. He is regarded as the third or aerial form of fire (lightning), originally the middle member of the triad, *Agni*, *Vāyu*/Indra and *Sūrya*.[27] He is kindled in the waters (*ṚV*, 10.45.1; *AV*, 13.2.50). He is the bull who has grown in the lap of the waters (*ṚV*, 10.8.1).

Dyaus (*Ākāśa*)

The word *ākāśa* does not occur in the *Ṛgveda*. Its synonyms, *dyaus, nabhas, kham, antarikṣa*, etc. have been frequently used. Although all these words are generally understood as sky, space, mid-air, etc., one important point, regarding *antarikṣa* is that it is said to lie between the two worlds (*dyāvāpṛthivī*) (heaven and earth). However, the concepts of *dyaus* in the *Ṛgveda* is very similar to that of *ākāśa* in the *Upaniṣads*. In fact, *AV*, 10.7.3 mentions four worlds : *bhūmi* (earth), *antarikṣa*, (mid-air), *dyaus* (heaven or sky, and the fourth world is beyond the heaven (*uttaram divaḥ*).

In the *Ṛgveda*, the term *dyaus* designated the uppermost vault of the concrete sky.[28] The essential feature of *Dyaus* as a male divinity,[29] is his creative potentiality. He is regarded as a father (*ṚV*, 1.90.7; 164.33, 4.1.10). He is a great father (*ṚV*, 1.71.5; 159.2; 160.2 ; 185.1) rich in procreative seed (*suretāḥ*, *ṚV*, 4.17.4). Like a mighty bull (*ṚV*, 1.160.3; 5.36.5). He generated *Agni* (*ṚV*, 4. 72.1).

It may be pointed out that other than this feature of a begetter, *Dyaus* has nothing special in the *Ṛgveda*, until and unless he is combined with *Pṛthivī*. There is not a single whole hymn for *dyaus* in the *Ṛgveda*. In *ŚB*, 13.5.2.17, *ākāśa* is said to have been created first.

Pṛthivī

Besides other stray occurrences, *Pṛthivī* has been described in one short hymn in the *Ṛgveda* (5.84) and in a long and beautiful hymn in the *Atharvaveda* (12.1) In *ṚV*, 5.84.1, twofold nature of earth, as a divinity and as a gross element, is noticed. The mighty one makes mighty the earth with her might (*mahnā jinoṣi mahini*), and bears the hills and forests etc. She is a mother (*ṚV*, 10.18.10), an upholder of all (*ṚV*, 1.155.2). She protects all that is, and all that will be (*AV*, 12.1.1).

These are certain myths in the *Ṛgveda* and in the *Brāhmaṇas* regarding the birth of the earth. *ṚV*, 10.72.6 states that the gods stood in the deep abyss of waters closely clasping (*susanirabdhāḥ*) each other. Then from their feet, as if dancing, a cloud of dust arose which became earth. *ṚV,* 1.22.17 mentions that the earth has been formed from the dust raised by Viṣṇu when he measured the earth in three strides. *ŚB,* 6.1.1. 8-15 gives the following myth about the creation of the earth :

> Prajāpati desired, "May I be more than one, may I be reproduced". He toiled and practised *tapas.* Being worn out and exhausted with toil and austerity, he created first of all the *Brahman* (neut.) in the form of *trayīvidyā.* It became to him a foundation, and the foundation of everything else in the world. He then created the waters out of *Vāk.* Prajāpati further desired, "May I be reproduced from these waters". He entered the waters with the *trayīvidyā.*[30] Hence an egg arose. The embryo which was inside was created as *Agni.* Prajāpati further desired, "May I generate this (earth) from these waters". He compressed it (that is, the earth) when as yet in the form of the egg-shell (*kapāla*) and threw it into the waters; the whole (earth) dissolved itself all over the waters. All this universe appeared as one form only, namely, waters. He desired, "May it become more than one, may it reproduce itself". He tried and practised austerities; worn out with toil and austerity, he created foam. He thought that this indeed looked different, it was becoming more than one, I must toil indeed. Worn out with toil and austerity, he created (1) clay (*mṛda*), (2) mud (*suṣkāpa*), (3) saline soil (*ūṣa*), (4) sand (*sikatā*), (5) pebble (*śarkarā),* (6) rock (*aśmāna),* (7) ore (*ayaḥ*), (8) gold (*hiraṇya*), and (9) plants and trees. Therewith he clothed this earth.[31] This earth, then, was created as (consisting of) these same nine creations, "This earth has indeed become (*bhū*) a foundation", he thought; hence he became the earth (*bhūmi*). He spread it out (*prath)* and it became the broad one (*pṛthivī*).
>
> (Translation based on Eggeling's).

The creation of the earth out of the waters has given rise to a myth in the post-Vedic Purāṇic literature, which is known as the *Varāhāvatāra. ŚB,* 14.1.2.11 enjoins that in the preparation of the *Mahāvīrapātra,* the earth dug up by a boar should be used (*VS,* 37.5). Giving the *arthavāda* (explanation) for this act, the *Brāhmaṇa* says that a boar called Emuṣa lifted the earth up from the water, and became her (earth's) lord Prajāpati.[32] Further *TS,* 7.1.5.1 (= *PB,* 20.14-16) states that this world was in the beginning the water, the ocean. Prajāpati, becoming the wind, moved on it. He saw her (earth) and becoming a boar, he seized her, and becoming Viśvakarman, he wiped her. She extended, she became the earth, and hence the earth is called the earth (*pṛthivī*). Further, in *TS*, 1.10.8, it is said that the earth was uplifted by a black boar with a thousand arms.[33]

DYĀVĀPṚTHIVĪ (HEAVEN AND EARTH)

It is the combination of the two, *dyaus* and *pṛthivī* (as *dyāvāpṛthivī*),[34] which is most important in the mythology and in the cosmological speculations of the *Vedas*. *Dyaus* and *pṛthivī* form the universal parents. The one, *dyaus*, is a prolific bull; the other, earth, is a variegated cow (*ṚV*, 1.160.1). They are both rich in procretative seed (*ṚV*, 1.159.2; 6.70.1; 2). As a father and as a mother, they guard all beings (*ṚV*, 1.160.2).

As a father, *dyaus* is associated with *pṛthivī* (earth), who is regarded as a mother. In this respect Macdonell says: "*Dyāvāpṛthivī* appeared so indissolubly connected in nature that the myth of their conjugal union is found widely diffused among many primitive peoples.[35]

AB, 4.27.5; 6 describes the marriage of *Dyaus* and *Pṛthivī*:

> These two worlds (heaven and earth) were (once) joined. (Subsequently) they separated. (After their separation) there was neither rain, nor sun-shine. The five classes of beings (gods, men, etc.) then did not keep peace with one another. (Thereupon), the gods brought about a reconciliation of both these worlds. Both contracted a marriage with one another. In the form of the *Rathantara-Sāman*, this earth is wedded to the heaven, and in the form of the *Bṛhat-Sāman*, the heaven is wedded to the earth . . .
>
> — (Tr. M. Haug).

Words, such as, *pitarā* (dual),[36] *mātarā* (dual),[37] and *janitrī* (dual),[38] all meaning parents, have been used to designate their parenthood. *ṚV*, 1.191.6 says that *Dyaus* is men's father, and *Pṛthivī*, mother. They are regarded as prolific parents (*ṚV*, 1.59.2). They are addressed as father and mother (*ṚV*, 1.159.1-3; 160.2). They are primeval parents (*ṚV*, 7. 53.2; 10.58.2). They, have created and they sustain all creatures (*ṚV*, 1.159.2; 160.2; 185.1). No one knows who produced them, or which of the two first came into being (*ṚV*, 1.185.1).

The most striking delineation of these two divinities is their procreative potentiality and generative power. The mythology behind the universal parenthood of *Dyāvāpṛthivī* centres round each one's prolific procreative potency, and fecundity. *Dyaus* showers the procreative fluid in the form of rains which the earth absorbs in her womb, and fructifies herbs and plants to sustain all creatures. The fertility power of these two has been widely emphasized in the *Vedas*, and they have become a symbol of parenthood.[39] A very significant epithet, *retaḥsic*, has been used for them (*ŚB*, 8.2.3.5).[40]

Vāyu

Two words *vāyu* and *vāta*, have been used in the *Ṛgveda* for wind. However, a distinction has been maintained between the two. *Vāyu* is chiefly the divinity, and *vāta*, the element.[41] Both the words have been deified in the *Veda*. *Vāyu* has been celebrated in two, whole hymns (*ṚV*, 1.134; 4.48), and *vāta* too has two entire hymns to his credit (*ṚV*, 10.168;186).

The wind is the germ of the world and *Ātman* of all gods (*ṚV*, 10.168.4). *ŚB*, 13.3.8.6 says that *vāyu* is the transformer of seeds, for *vāyu* is the vital air, and vital air is the transformer of seeds. He is the breath of the gods (*ṚV*, 7.87.2; 10.92.13, *ŚB*, 9.3.1.5). He is immortal (*ṚV*, 10.186.3). He is the support of all beings (*ŚB*, 8.4.1.26). He exists in all three worlds (*ŚB*, 8.4.1.9). He is an abode of all beings (*ŚB*, 13.6.2.2). He is the breath of all (*ŚB*, 9.3.1.5). All beings pass over into the wind, and from out of the wind, they are again produced (*ŚB*, 11.5.3.11).

Vāyu is the 'combining force' in the universe. The yonder sun strings these worlds to himself on a thread; that thread is the same as the wind (*ŚB*, 8.7.3.10). *Vāyu* is said to have originated from the breath of the *Puruṣa* (*ṚV*, 10.90.11). Prajāpati is *Vāyu* (*ŚB*, 6.12.19; 2.2.11). *ŚB*, 6.1.2.1-2 mentions that Prajāpati by means of *Agni* entered into the union with the earth; hence an egg arose. The embryo which was inside was created as *Vāyu*. *ŚB*, 7.1.2.1 related a myth: Prajāpati having produced creatures relaxed. From him, when relaxed, the vital air went out. Now, the vital air which went out from within him is the wind that blows yonder. The gods heated him in the fire; and when the fire rose over him thus heated, that same vital air, which had gone out from within him, came back to him, and they put it into him. They raised him up; and, inasmuch as, they thus raised him upright, he is these worlds.

Vāyu is *Agni* (*ŚB*, 10.4.5.1). *Vāyu* is *prāṇa*. Like the spokes in the navel of a wheel everything is fixed fast in *Prāṇa*.[42] In *AV*, 11.4.15, breath is called the wind, he is Prajāpati (vs.12); breath is the lord of all, both what breathes and what does not (vs. 10).[43]

Significantly, *ŚB*, 8.1.1.7ff compares *vāyu* with Viśvakarman,[44] for it is he who makes everything here.

Vāyu has been associated with the waters. *ŚB*, 9.4.1.10 compares the wind with the *gandharva*; waters as his *apsarasas.* It says that as a *gandharva,* the wind went forth with the waters as the *apsarasas,* his mates. The waters are called *ūrjaḥ,* for the food is produced from the waters (*ibid*).

On the basis of the foregoing delineation of the five divinities, and the myths connected with them, one may draw a few conclusions which might have turned them into the five *bhūtas* in the post-Vedic Upaniṣadic and later philosophical speculations.

The foremost common feature of all the five is that they have been regarded as the all-pervasive and omnipresent elements. All this world has been pervaded by the waters. Waters are the foundations of the world. *Agni* is the very existence, and it is through *Agni* that everything exists. He permeates in every object that is seen in the universe. In this respect his tripartite character is very significant. As a terrestrial fire, he pervades the entire earth; as *vāyu,* he pervades the mid-region and causes rains, and as the sun, he pervades heaven. *Agni* is the five-fold sacrifice, from which the entire world emanates. *Dyaus* and *pṛthivī* are the universal parents. They are the *retaḥsic* (seed-shedders). *Vāyu* is a binding force in the universe.

The second most important characteristic of these divinities is that all of them are endowed with great creative potency. Waters received the primordial germ whence all the gods came into being. They are the mothers of all beings; they are the mothers of *sūrya* and *Agni.* They are the wives of gods and maidens of Soma. Likewise, *Pṛthivī* is the mother who upholds all beings. *Agni* has been described as a begetter *par-excellence.* He places the procreative germ in all beings. He is a bull abounding in seed. He generated the heaven and the earth. He is produced in the waters where he lives like a swan (*haṁsa*). *Dyaus* has been portrayed as a great progenitor and a universal father. He is a bull rich in seed (*suretāḥ*). *Vāyu* is the germ of the world and a transformer of seed. He is the breath of all.

These two common features of these five divinities, namely, all-pervasiveness and potent creative power may be regarded as conducive to regard them as individual members of the *Pañcabhūtas.* These five divinities may be regarded as having developed in two directions in the *Upaniṣads* : (1) as five gross elements (*pañcabhūtas*), and (2) as five subtle elements (*pañcatanmātras*), all the ten having their common source in the *Brahman,* or Prajāpati, or *Ātman.* It is this *Brahman,* or *Ātman* who endures inside (the human heart, *hṛdākāśa*)[45] and outside (the manifested universe that is). It is the *Brahman* who is microcosm, and it is the *Brahman* who (through the *pañcabhūtas*) becomes macrocosm.[46] *KaṭhUp,* 6.1 regards the *Brahman* as a three-footed entity, and compares it with a fig tree, the five elements, ether, water, etc., being its branches.[47] In this respect the *Īśopaniṣad* declares:

> योऽसावसौ पुरुषः सोऽहमस्मि।
> *yo'sāvasau puruṣaḥ so'hamasmi* ।
> (*ĪśaUp*, 16)

It is the *Brahman* from whom everything has emanated and it is the *Brahman* into which everything merges (*ŚvetUp*, 6.2; 3), and thus the *Brahmacakra* goes on revolving forever.

In mythological parlance, all the five elements are interlinked. Water and fire form one group, heaven (sky) and earth form a couple, and the wind is regarded as an all-pervasive binding force. And all of them are connected with Prajāpati who creates them by the power of *tapas*.

Notes

1. This line occurs also in *ṚV*, 10.31.7ab.
2. *ṚV*, 1.164.6; 8.41.10; 10.65.13; 82.6; *AV*, 13.1.6.
3. विश्वतश्चक्षुरुत विश्वतोमुखो विश्वतोबाहुरुत विश्वतस्पात्।
   सं बाहुभ्यां धमति सं पतत्रैर्द्यावाभूमी जनयन् देव एकः।।
   "He who hath eyes on all sides round about him, a mouth on all sides, arms and feet on all sides, he the *Sole God*, producing earth and heaven, wideth them, with his arms as wings, together". — Gr.
   Cf. also *ṚV*, 1.164.46; 10.129.3.
4. This *sūkta* is known as *madhusūkta* in *VaitŚS*, 16.12.
5. *Bhūtaṁ ca bhavyaṁ ca*, *ṚV*, 10.55.2; 58.12; 90.2; etc.
6. Four hymns, *ṚV*, 10.57-60, deal with the death of Subandhu. The legend is as follows: There was a king named Asamāti of the Ikṣvāku family. He had four *Purohitas*: Bandhu, Subandhu, Śrutabandhu, and Viprabandhu. One day the king dismissed the services of the four Bandhus, and appointed two new *Purohitas*, Ākuli and Kirāta, who were well-versed in sorcery (*māyāvinau*). The former priests, Bandhu and others, became displeased. They performed an *abhicāra* to harm the King. The two *māyāvins*, Ākuli and Kirāta, came to know of this, they performed a counter *abhicāra* and removed the *prāṇas* (life-forces) of Subandhu. The remaining three brothers recited these *sūktas* to bring back the *prāṇas* of Subandhu, which they succeded (*JB*, 3.168.70; *PB*, 12.12.5; *BrD*. 7.83-103; *Vedic Index*, s.v.).
7. इदं त एकं पर ऊ त एकं तृतीयेन ज्योतिषा सं विशस्व।
   ṚV, 10.56.1ab
8. For Prajāpati; waters, and lotus leaf, see *TB*, 1.1.3.5; *TĀ*, 1.23.1.
9. Cf. *ṚV*, 1.161.9; *ŚB*, 11.1.6; *TĀ*, 10.22; *BṛUp*, 5.5.1; *ManuS*, 1.8
10. *tā aśrāmyanstastāpo'tapyanta*. For the importance and role of *tapas* in Vedic mythology, vide Chauncey J. Blair, *Heat in the Rig Veda and Atharvaveda*, New Haven, 1961, p. 67 ff; 116ff; and David M. Knipe; *In the Image of Fire*, Delhi, 1975, p. 107ff.

11. For *Āyatana*, see J. Gonda, "Āyatana", *Adyar Library Bulletin*, 33 (1969), 1-79. In *ŚB*, 14.3.2.8, the sky is regarded as the abode of all gods.
12. About Prajāpati and *Vāk*, see A.B. Keith, *The Religion and Philosophy of the Veda and Upanishads*, rep. Delhi, 1976, 456f; S.K. Lal, *Female Divinities in Hindu Mythology and Ritual*, Poona, 1980, p. 158.

    TāṇḍBr, 6.5.10 narrates the following legend : The speech once passed away from the gods, she entered into the waters. The gods got her back after promising that no unclean substance would ever mix up with the waters. *JUB*, 1.16.1ff states that once the gods said to Heaven and Earth, "Unite, bring forth the *sāman*." But the Heaven did not like this earth. He said, "Verily, they do much on her (earth) of this kind or that; they spit on her; they go about on her; they sit on her. Cleanse her now, she is unclean." It was not before she was cleaned up that the heaven (*Dyaus*) united with her and the two generated the *sāman*. Echoes of pure environment.
13. *Agnī*, Indra, Soma and Parameṣṭhin were created out of Prajāpati (*ŚB*, 11.1.6.14).
14. *ŚB*, 7.1.1.13 believes that the ocean flows round this world on all sides.
15. In *ṚV*, 10.89.1, it is Indra who forces heaven and earth asunder. The myths of separation of the heaven and earth are widespread. Among the Polynesians and in the Maori myth of Bangi and Papa, it is their children who cause their separation. (*ERE*, Vol. V, 128a)
16. *AV*, 10.7.3 mentions four worlds : *bhūmi* (earth), *antarikṣa* (atmosphere, firmament, mid-region), *dyaus* (sky) and *uttaraṁ divaḥ* (beyond sky).
17. *AB*, 5.52 contains a very similar passage.
18. *Mahas* is regarded as the moon also because through the moon all the lights of the world prosper (*TaitUp*, 1.5.2).
19. For a detailed study of the concept of *mahas*, see J. A.B. Van Buitenen, "The Larger Ātman", In *History of Religion*, IV (1964), pp. 103-14; and Stella Kramrisch, "The Triple Structure of Creation in the Ṛgveda", In *History of Religion*, II (1962-63), p. 140ff.
20. Griffith, quoting Ludwig, says (on this *mantra* in his translation) that, "Here Agni is represented as Prajāpatī who as a yet undeveloped embryo is at the same time both male and female".
21. For the character and function of Viśvakarman refer to H.W. Wallis, *The Cosmology of the Ṛgveda*, London, 1887, p. 80f.
22. Wallis, *loc. cit.*
23. Translated by V.M. Bedekar and G.B. Palsule, *Sixty Upaniṣads of the Veda*, Delhi, 1980. *BṛUp*, 6.4.2-3 says that Prajāpati created woman with her loins as the sacrificial altar, and her vulva the central fire; knowledge of the sacrifice (== intercourse) wins the world for the knower.
24. Cf. also Wall is *op. cit.*, p. 133.
25. Reference is to the putting of a lotus leaf on the fire-altar. *TS*, 5.6.4.2 also has a similar idea. Waters were the world at first, the moving ocean; Prajāpati, becoming wind, rocked about on a lotus leaf; he could find no support; he saw the waters, on it he piled the fire, that became this earth; then he, indeed, found support.
26. For a detailed sketch of *Apāṁ napāt* see A.A. Macdonell, *Vedic Mythology*, rep. Delhi, 1981, p. 69ff.
27. *Ibid.*, p. 67ff.

28. *Ibid.*, p. 21.
29. In some of the passages of the *Ṛgveda* the word *dyaus* is feminine : *RV*, 3.25.3 (*devī amṛte*, 'immortal goddesses', heaven and earth); *RV*, 1.185.5 (*svasārā, yuvatī, jāmī*, two sisters, youthful ones, born together, heaven and earth); and in *ṚV*, 10.59.7, *dyaus* alone is mentioned as a shining goddess (*dyaur devī*). *ŚB*, 6.7.4.5 mentions udders of the sky. In the mythology of some other nations also, sky is a female. For instance, in the Egyptian mythology, Hathor is a Sky goddess (*ERE*, Vol. XI, 582b; *EB*, Vol. XI, s.v. p. 157).
30. *ŚB*, 10.4.2.21f says that all existing things are in the three *Vedas*.
31 In *ṚV*, 12.1.26, it is mentioned that the earth consists of *śilā* (rock), *aśmā* (stone), *pānsu* (dust), and *hiraṇya* (gold).
32. J. Muir, *Original Sanskrit Texts*, Vol. I, p. 53; Vol. IV, p. 27. In the Purāṇic mythology, it is Viṣṇu who in the form of a *varāha* rescued the earth, united with her, and a demon Naraka (also known as Bhauma) was born out of this union (vide Lal, *op. cit*, p. 5).
33. This episode of the earth lifted up by a boar provided a grand motive to the medieval poets and artists (Lal, *op. cit.*, p. 139).
34. Other words used for this pair are : *dyāvākṣamā, dyāvābhūmī, rodasī, jāmī, matī, mākī, urvī, varā, samīcine, dhiṣaṇe* and *camvā*.
35. *Op. cit.*, p. 126.

    Myths of Earth and Heaven as a divine pair are found among peoples of other nations also. For instance, among the African tribes and among the Yorubes, they are represented by the male and female organs of generation. Cf. also Polynesian myth of Rangi and Pépé and Greek mythology of Gaia and Ouranos (*ERE*, Vol. V, 128a; Vol. XI, 583a). In Egyptian mythology, Seb is a sky goddess, and Nut is an earth God (*ibid.*).
36. *ṚV*, 1.159.2; 3.3.11; 7.1; 10.11.6; 12.4; 65.8.
37. *ṚV*, 1.155.3; 159.3; 3.1.7; 5.7;7.1; 4.22.4; 10.17; 35.3; 59.8; 64.14; 120.7.
38. *ṚV*, 1.185.6; 3.31.12; 7.97.8; 10.110.9.
39. J. Gonda, *The Dual Deity in the Religion of the Veda*, Amsterdam, 1974, p. 95f.
40. Explaining as to why this epithet is used for the Heaven and Earth, *ŚB*, 7.4.2.22 states that the seed-shedders (*retaḥsic*) doubtless are these two worlds, for these two worlds do shed seed; this terrestrial world sheds seed upwards from here (in the form of smoke), it became rain in the yonder world, and that rain yonder world (sheds) from above: hence creatures are born within these two worlds; and therefore, these two worlds are seed-shedders.
41. Macdonell, *op. cit.*, p. 81. The distinction is not maintained always, and the one replaces the other to mean 'wind' in general.
42. *TB*, 3.12.8.1; *PraśnUp*, 2.5,6; *BṛUp*, 2.5.15; *MuṇḍUp*, 2.2.6.
43. The entire *sūkta AV*, 11.4 is an extollation of *Prāṇa*. Cf. also *BṛUp*, 1.3; 6.1; *KauśUp*, 2.14.
44. See fn. 21 for Viśvakarman, and *ṚV*, 10.81; 82.
45. For the concept of *hṛdākāśa*, vide *ChUp*, 8.1.1; 6.6; *KaṭhUp*, 6.1; 16; *MaitUp*, 6.21; 27; 7.11; *TaitUp*, 1.6.1-2.
46. Keith, *op.cit.*, p. 452.
47. Cf. *RV*, 1.164.22; 10.24.7.

2

पञ्चभूततत्त्वनिरूपणम्

श्रीदेवनाथ ताताचार्यः

हरिः ओम्, नमस्सदसे। नमस्सदसस्पतये। हरिः ओम्

तच्छंयोरावृणीमहे। गातुंयज्ञाय। गातुंयज्ञपतये। दैवीस्स्वस्तिरस्तुनः।
स्वस्तिर्मानुषेभ्यः। ऊर्ध्वं जिगातुभेषजम्। शन्नो अस्तु द्विपदे। शं चतुष्पदे।
ओम् शान्तिश्शान्तिश्शान्तिः

पुण्यतममिदं पुण्यपत्तनं, नाम्नैव विश्वविख्यातं विराजते। अत्र समवेतान् नानाशास्त्रपरिचयसंपन्नान् पण्डितप्रकाण्डान् प्रणम्य उपात्तविषये मदभिप्रायमाविष्करोमि। श्रुत्वा विद्वांसः प्रमाणम्।

(१) पृथिवी (२) आपः (३) तेजः (४) वायुः (५) आकाशः — इति पञ्चमहाभूतानि प्रपञ्चस्वरूपं निष्पादयन्ति। प्रपञ्चस्य उत्पत्तौ स्थितौ विनाशे (प्रलये) च इमानि पञ्च महाभूतानि प्रधानतरं भागं निर्वहन्ति। पञ्चभूतान्येव प्रपञ्चात्मना परिणमन्ति-ईश्वरसंकल्पविशेषेण, तेनैव च कारणेन यथोद्दिष्टकालं यावत् तिष्ठन्ति, तेनैव च कारणेन सूक्ष्मरूपतां प्रापिताः यथोत्पत्ति प्रलीयन्ते। अस्मिन् विषये भवगतः इच्छारूपः संकल्प एव प्रधानं कारणम्। स च, तत्तज्जीवात्मनां प्राचीनकर्मसु भोगप्रदानौपयिकतया परिणतेषु जायते। जातश्च कञ्चित्काल-मवस्थाय पुनरपैति। सर्वशक्तस्य भगवतः इदं सृष्टिस्थितिप्रलयं लीलारूपम्। अतएव च "लीला विभूतिः" इति परिदृश्यमानस्य प्रपञ्चस्य शास्त्रेषु व्यवहारः एवंविधप्रपञ्चबहिर्भूतोऽप्यन्यः प्रपञ्चभागो वर्तते। तत्र एवं विधः परिणामो न भवति। एकरूप एव सर्वदाप्ययं वर्तते। तस्य "नित्यविभूतिः" इति शास्त्रेषु व्यवहारः। तत्प्राप्तिरेव जीवात्मनां अपहतपाप्मनां मोक्षः "ब्रह्मानन्दानुभवः" इत्यादिशब्दैः शास्त्रेषु व्यपदिश्यते। इदं वेदेषु-उपनिषत्सु — तदनुसारिषु भगवद्गीता-विष्णुपुराणादिग्रंथेषु च प्रतिपाद्यते। इयं रामानुजीयानां "विशिष्टाद्वैतमतानुसारिणी प्रक्रिया। द्वैताद्वैतमतानुयायिनोऽपि इममेव विषयं ईषदन्यथाभावेन प्रतिपादयन्ति। तत्र अद्वैतं बौद्धमतच्छायानुसारि-अथापि न वेदबाह्यं — नापि नास्तिकमतम्।

पञ्चधासंभृतः कायो यदिपञ्चत्वमागतः।
कर्मभिः स्वशरीरोत्थैः तत्र का परिदेवना?॥

इति महर्षिः याज्ञवल्क्यस्य दिव्यसूक्तिः।

पञ्चानां भूतानां सृष्ट्युपयोगितया परिणामप्रकारः वेदेषु विस्तरेण प्रतिपाद्यते। तथा मूलप्रकृतेः पर्वक्रमेण तत्तदवस्थावाप्तिश्च। तमः-प्रकृतिः-महान्-अहंकारः-इतीमाः चतस्रः अवस्थाविशेषाः पञ्चभूतप्राक्कालीनाः वर्तन्ते। भूतानां अत्यन्तसूक्ष्मावस्था एताः। क्रमेण विकसितावस्थाप्राप्तौ "पञ्चभूत" पदेन निर्देशो जायते। यथा — कुसूले विद्यमानेषु बीजेषु अङ्कुराद्यवस्था नास्ति। जल-कर्दमादि संयोगे, पर्वक्रमेण अङ्कुरोत्पत्तिं पश्यामस्तेषु। तत्र बीजस्य अविकृतस्य स्थितिः "मूलप्रकृतिः" इति व्यपदेशार्हाभवति। पर्वक्रमेण तस्मिन् बीजे परिदृश्यमानाः विकासविशेषाः, महान्-अहङ्कार-इत्यादि पदैः व्यपदिश्यन्ते। विकासनिष्पत्तौ "अङ्कुर" पदेनव्यवहारः। एवमेव सूक्ष्म-स्थूल प्रपञ्चस्य परिस्थितिः। सर्वेषां कार्याणां सोपादानकारण एव लयस्य आनुभविकत्वात् यथा सृष्ट्येवं प्रलयोऽपि जायते नान्यथा।

भूमिरापोऽनलोवायुः खं मनोबुद्धिरेव च।
अहङ्कार इतीयं मे भिन्ना प्रकृतिरष्टधा।।
अपरेयं इतस्त्वन्यां प्रकृतिं विद्धि मे पराम्।
जीवभूतां महाबाहो यया संधार्यते जगत्।।

इति भगवद्गीता सूक्तिः अन्यान्यौपनिषदानि वाक्यानि च वस्तुतत्त्वमिदमुद्धोषयन्ति।

वेदबाह्याः बौद्धाः जैनाश्च इमां प्रक्रियां नाङ्गीकुर्वन्ति। आद्यानि चत्वारिमहाभूतान्येव तैरङ्गीक्रियन्ते। पञ्च-मस्य आकाशाख्यस्य भूतस्य न तन्मते अङ्गीकारो वर्तते, नतरां कालदिगात्मनाम्। कुतः ? शशशृङ्गवदसत्त्वादेव चतुर्णान्तु भूमि वार्यनलानिलरूपाणां प्रत्यक्षत्वान्नास्ति तेषु विसंवादावकाशः। "न हि दृष्टे अनुपपन्नं नाम"। पूर्वमीमांसाभाष्यकृत् शबरस्वामी एवमेव हि वदति —

अत्र चत्वारि भूतानि भूमिवार्यनलानिलाः।
चतुर्भ्यः खलु भूतेभ्यः चैतन्यमुपजायते।।

इत्यादयः तेषां व्यवहाराः।

एवं नास्तिकदर्शनेषु सदसद्भावविचारः आकाशादिष्वेव विपुलो दृश्यते। तत्रापि आकाशविषय एव विस्तृतः। तस्याभावे प्रसाधिते तुल्यन्यायतया तदतिरिक्तानां कालादीनामभावः अक्लेशेन साधितप्रायो भवेदि।

तत्र धर्मकीर्तिः अतिप्रौढ़ पण्डितः स्वीये "प्रमाणवार्तिक" ग्रंथे इमं विषयं प्रस्तौति। तदीयव्याख्याग्रंथेषु च ससंरंभं प्रपञ्चितो वर्ततेऽयं विषयः। किञ्चिदेवात्र प्रदर्श्यते —

नावस्थितेर्विघातोऽस्ति यदि भूतान्तरस्थितिः।
परस्पस्याभावेऽपि न विघातोऽस्त्यवस्थितेः।।१२८।।
महाभूतान्तराभावे महाभूतान्तरस्थितिः।
महाभूतान्तराभावमात्रमाकाशमुच्यताम्।।१२९।।

लोष्टस्य कथमाधारो नाकाशं पततः क्वचित्।
वायौ गतिमति व्योम्नः कथमाधारतागतिः ?।।१३०।।
वायोर्गत्यविबंधश्चेत् आकाशात् नेदमुत्तरम्।
गतेर्विबंधाभावो हि विबंधकविनाकृतः।।१३१।।

अथ

आकाशं व्यापिनित्यञ्च धार्यतेऽन्येन तत्कथम्?।
तेनानाधारता तस्य परं प्रति तु धारकम्।।१३२।।
व्यापित्वमात्मनोऽप्येतत् तदवस्थमरूपि च।
तस्यैवाधारभावः किं परं प्रति न कल्प्यते?।।१३३।।
यस्यात्मा नास्ति तादृक्षस्तस्याकाशेन का क्रिया?।
दिशोऽपि व्यापिता आकाशकृत्यं ताभिः प्रकल्प्यताम्।।१३४।।
परस्परव्यापितायामेकत्वं व्यापिनां न किम्?।
उपघातो यतस्तस्य तस्याभावेन तस्य सः।।१३५।।
आकाशान्नोपघातस्तु व्यक्तमाकाशचर्वणम्।
तस्मादभावो भूतानां चतुर्णां व्योम कथ्यते।।१३६।।
तदन्यत्र महाभूते व्यवहारोऽस्ति न प्रमा।

इति परार्थानुमानप्रकरणे "शब्दचिन्तायां" विलिखति सः। तत्कर्तृके "न्यायबिन्दु" नाम्न्यपि ग्रंथे अयं विषयः सम्यगेव निरूपितो विराजते।

अस्य प्रमाणवार्तिकग्रंथस्य अन्या अन्याः व्याख्याग्रंथा विलसन्ति। प्रज्ञाकरगुप्तनाम्ना महाविदुषा अस्य प्रमाणवार्तिकस्य "वार्तिकालंकारः" इति व्याख्या विरचिता विराजते।

आकाशास्तित्ववादिनां मतमनूद्य निपुणतरं दूषयत्ययं तत्पक्षं स्वव्याख्यायाम्। "कुड्यादिषु पुरतो वर्तमानेषु गतिमतां गमनं तैः व्याहन्यते। तदतिलंघ्य गन्तुं न खलु ते शक्नुवन्ति। असत्सुतुतेषु प्राणिनां अप्राणिनां वा यथासंभवं गमनं दृष्टम्। अतः आकाशमेवैकं अन्येषां पदार्थानां अवकाशं ददाति-गमनादिप्रतिघातश्च आकाशे न विद्यते। तस्मादप्रतिघातरूपेण लिङ्गेन आकाशस्य सत्तां साधयामः" इति हि ते वदन्ति।

तत्रायं पृच्छति — "किमिदमवकाशदानं नाम?" इति। तत्र तेषामुत्तरं — "अवस्थितेरव्याघातः" इति। तदुपरि अस्य प्रश्नः — अथ केयं स्थितिः? किं धार्यमाणता? अथ अविहन्यमानता? यदि धार्यता-तदसत्। नाकाशेन घटादयो धार्यन्ते, अपितु भुवा। अथ अनुपघातः? तदप्यसत्यं, यतः —

उपघातो यतस्तस्य तस्याभावेन तस्य सः।
आकाशान्नोपघातस्तु व्यक्तमाकाशचर्वणम्।। इति।

तस्मादभावो भूतानां चतुर्णां व्योम कथ्यते —पृथिव्यादि भूतचतुष्ट्याभाव एव आकाशशब्देन अस्तित्ववादिभि: व्यपदिश्यते, नातिरिक्तं पञ्चमं भूतं आकाशनामकमस्तीति साधयति। कुड्यादे: गति प्रतिबन्धकस्याभावे यथेच्छं गमनं भवति। तत्सत्त्वे तु न। अत: कुड्यादि: गमनस्य प्रतिबंधक:। तदभाव एव तत् कारणम्। प्रतिबंधकसंसर्गा-भावस्य कार्यसामान्यं प्रति कारणत्वस्य सर्वसंमतत्वात्। अतिरिक्तस्य आकाशाख्यस्य भूतस्य तत्कारणत्वकल्पना निराधारा। चक्षुष्मान् कश्चित् कुड्यादिना व्यवहितं, दूरस्थं, सूक्ष्मं च वस्तु न द्रष्टुं शक्नोति। व्यवधानापगमे सति सामीप्ये सति स्थूलत्वेऽपि वा सति पश्यत्येवायम्। तस्य तथाविधवस्तुदर्शने चक्षुरेव कारणमङ्गीक्रियते सर्वैरपि। नातिरिक्तं किञ्चित्। कुड्यादयस्तु दर्शनप्रतिबंधका:। तदभाव: प्रतिबंधकसंसर्गाभावविधया सर्वसाधारण्येन तत्र कारणीभावं प्रपद्यते, नातिरिक्तस्य कस्यापि तत्र कारणत्वकल्पना। अत: अवकाशदानाख्ययुक्त्या नाकाशस्य साधनं साध्यमिति।

एवं अवकाशप्रदत्वेन आकाशस्य प्रसाधने अनवस्थापि प्रदर्शिता तत्र। तद्यथा —

"ननु महाभूतान्तरस्य वाय्वादे: क्वावस्थानं? यदि नाकाशम्। नन्वाकाशस्यापि क्वावस्थानं ? यदि महाभूतान्तरं न भवेत्। इत्यनवस्था। अथाकाशमनाधारस्वभावं, आधारश्चान्यस्य इति चेत्; वायुरपि तर्हि अनाधारस्वभावोऽन्य-स्याधार इति अर्थान्तरपरिकल्पना न साध्वी। पूर्वोपदर्शितप्रमाणवार्तिकश्लोकयो: १३०-१३१ संख्यातयो: इत्थं विवरणं क्रियतेऽत्र।

"छिद्रमेवाकाशम्। अच्छिद्रकारकाभावे च तद्व्यवहार:।" इति आकाशास्तित्ववादिनां उक्तिमनूद्य दूषय-त्ययम्। "यदा वा अच्छिद्रकारिणोऽभाव: तदा आकाशं क्व गतवत्? नहि पार्श्वविदारणमुच्यते। व्योम्नस्तदभावे च तत्र चान्यत्र वा क्व गतमाकाशम्? विनष्टश्चेत्; साध्वी नित्यता। तत्रैवास्तु, इति चेत्; अच्छिद्रमाकाशमिति च व्याहतम्। तत्राप्यस्त्येव। अन्यथा तस्य पदार्थस्य स्थितिरेव न स्यात्" इति।

ईश्वरात्माकाशदिक्कालादीनां असत्त्वं अर्थक्रिया सामर्थ्यहीनतया तदुपोद्घाते निरूपितमस्ति। "अर्थक्रिया" इति पदस्य च विवरणं, "अर्थस्य-दाहपाकादे:, क्रिया-निष्पत्ति:, तस्या: स्थिति: अविचलनं अविसंवादनं व्यवस्था वा।"

"अर्थकरणमेव प्रयोगरूपेण केवलं सत्ताव्यापकं अभिज्ञायते।"

इति च तत्रत्यानि वाक्यानि भाव्यानि।

"यस्यार्थस्य संनिधानासंनिधानाभ्यां ज्ञानप्रतिभासभेद:, तत् स्वलक्षणम्" इति न्यायबिंदौ कथयन् धर्मकीर्ति: स्वलक्षणविरहेण आकाशाख्यस्य वस्तुनोऽसत्तां साधयति। शशशृङ्गमेवात्रोदाहरणम्। ज्ञानप्रतिभासभेद: यथा शशशृङ्गसत्त्वासत्त्वाभ्यां नोपजायत इति तुच्छत्वमेव तस्य सर्वाभ्युपगतम्, तत्राकाशे को वा भेद:? न हि आकाशस्य सत्त्वेनअसत्त्वेन वा ज्ञानप्रतिभासे कश्चित् भेद: अनुभूयते। अतस्तुच्छत्वमेवास्य इति प्रसाध्यतेऽत्र गुडस्य-लवणस्य-मरीचिकाया: वा सत्त्वेअसत्त्वे वा अथवा न्यूनाधिकभावे, रुचिभेदं अनुभवाम:। अयमेव ज्ञान प्रतिभासभेद: सार्वजनीन:। इदमेव च "स्वलक्षणं" इति च कथ्यते। एवंविधे स्वलक्षणे प्रसिद्धे सत्येव तद्विशिष्टस्य वस्तुन: सद्भाव: सर्वैरपि निर्विवाद: अङ्गीक्रियते। शशशृङ्गस्य आकाशस्य वा न ह्येवंविधं स्वलक्षणमस्ति। तस्मान्नास्त्येव तत्। इति तर्कं प्रदर्शयति धर्मकीर्ति:।

अर्थक्रियाकारित्वे सत्येव वस्तुसिद्धि: इति वाद: प्रामाणिक एव। तथैव स्वलक्षणसत्त्वञ्च वस्तुसत्ता स्थापकमित्यपि। आकाशादौ इदमुभयं नास्तीति यदुच्यते तत्रैव विसंवादो भवति वैदिकानाम्। आकाशादिषु

इदमुभयमपि विद्यत एव। तस्मात् तेऽपि प्रमाणसिद्धा एव भवन्ति। परन्तु पामरजनहृदयङ्गमतया आपातप्रतीतौ इदं निरूपयितुं न शक्यते। निपुणनिरूपणेन इदं शक्यमेव प्रदर्शयितुम्। "न हि यत् गिरिशृङ्गमारुह्य गृह्यते तदप्रत्यक्षम्" इति अभियुक्ता वदन्ति। सिद्धा अपि सोपपत्तिकमेव स्वपक्षं समर्थयितुं प्रयतन्ते। तथापि पामरजनसमूह-वशीकरणैकपरैः तैः बहवो युक्त्याभासाः बहुशः उपयुज्यन्ते। यथाहुः कुमारिलभट्टपादाः

> शाक्यादयश्च सर्वत्र कुर्वाणा धर्मदेशनम्।
> हेतुजालविनिर्मुक्तं न कदाचन कुर्वते।।

इति। तथा "उक्खित्तेलोऽम्मि उक्खेवे अत्थि कालणं, पदणे णत्थि कालणं, तस्मात् सव्वे भावा सकालणा उप्पज्झन्ति, अकालणा विणसन्दि" इति च।

बौद्धमते सर्वेषां पदार्थानां उत्पत्तौ प्रतिनियतं कारणमावश्यकम्। विनाशे तु न किञ्चित् कारणमस्ति। नाशः स्वाभाविकः। इमं सिद्धान्तं पामरजनान् बोधयितुं ते पूर्वोक्तं दृष्टान्तं प्रदर्शयन्ति।

भूमौ स्थितं लोष्टं हस्ते गृहीत्वा प्रदर्शयन्ति। अयं लोष्टः भूमौ विद्यमानः स्वयमेव आकाशे गच्छति वा? नहि नहि। हस्तेनादाय उत्क्षिप्तश्चेत् उपरि गच्छति। तस्मात् लोष्टस्य उपरिगमनं कारणसापेक्षम्। इत्थमेव सर्व-वस्तूनामुत्पत्तिः कारणसापेक्षा। उपरिक्षिप्तो लोष्टः किं तत्रैव तिष्ठति? नहि नहि। सत्वरं भूमौ पतति। तत्र किं कारणम्? न किमप्यस्ति। इत्थमेव सर्वेषां पदार्थानां किञ्चित्कारणमनपेक्ष्यैव स्वाभाविको विनाशो जायते इत्युपपादयन्ति ते। अत्र कियदौचित्यमस्तीति न निरूपणीयं विमर्शकानाम्। लोष्टस्य ऊर्ध्वगमनं पदार्थानामुत्पत्तेः नोपपन्नमुदाहरणम्। नापि तत्पतनं विनाशस्य। पामरजनाः इत्थं प्रलोभ्यन्ते तैः। आकाशविषयेऽप्ययमेव न्यायः तैराश्रितः।

तस्मादागमिकम्" (वैशेषिकसूत्रं २.१.१७)

इति सूत्रं प्रत्यक्षतोऽनधिगतेषु अनुमानसीमानमप्यतिलंघितेषु सूक्ष्मतरेषु आगमस्यैव प्रमाणत्वमभ्युपगच्छति कणादः। प्रत्यक्षमनुमानञ्चेति प्रमाणद्वयेनैव तृप्तः भगवान् कणादमहर्षिः सूक्ष्मतरेषु विषयेषु वेदं प्रमाणयति! किमुतास्मादृशाः वयं?। कणादमहर्षिः मतान्तरप्रतिक्षेपपूर्वकं आकाशाख्यं पञ्चमं भूतं शब्दाख्यगुणविशेषेण लिङ्गेन साधयति चतुर्भिस्सूत्रैः।

(१) कारणगुणपूर्वकः कार्यगुणो दृष्टः। (वैद. २.१.२४)

(२) कार्यान्तराप्रादुर्भावाच्च शब्दः स्पर्शवतामगुणः। (वैद. २.१.२५)

(३) परत्र समवायात् प्रत्यक्षत्वाच्च नात्मगुणो न मनोगुणः। (वैद. २.१.२६)

(४) परिशेषाल्लिङ्गमाकाशस्य। (वैद. २.१.२७)
इतीमान्येव तानि चत्वारि सूत्राणि।

एतेषु चतुर्थसूत्रं शब्दरूपात् लिङ्गात् आकाशाख्यस्य पञ्चमस्य भूतस्य सत्तां साधयति। "श्रोत्रग्रहणो योऽर्थः स शब्दः (वैद. २.२.२१) इति सूत्रेण शब्दाख्यो गुणः श्रोत्रेण गृह्यत इत्युक्तम्। तस्य शब्दस्य वीणावेण्वादिद्रव्यनिष्ठ-

त्वस्यानुपपत्त्या तदाधारतया आकाशाख्यं द्रव्यं सिद्ध्यतीति युक्त्या आकाशास्तित्वं साधयति। पूर्वाणि त्रीणि सूत्राणि शब्दस्य अन्यद्रव्यगुणत्वं युक्तिभिः निराकुर्वन्ति। वीणायां वाद्यमानायां सभामध्यासीनाः सर्वे वीणानादं श्रुत्वा सन्तुष्टमानसा भवन्ति। वीणायाः व्यवहिते देशे उपविष्टा अपि यथावस्थितं वीणानादं सम्यक् शृण्वन्ति। यदि वीणारूपे द्रव्य एव शब्दः स्यात्, व्यवहितैः न श्रूयेत। आकाशाधारत्वं तु शब्दस्य, वीणावादनप्रदेशे आकाशे उत्पादितः शब्दः स्वसजातीयान् अन्यान्यान् शब्दान् वीचीतरङ्गन्यायेन जनयन् श्रोत्रेऽपि शब्दान्तरमुत्पादयति — तदेव च श्रोत्रेण गृह्यते इत्युपपद्यते व्यवहितदेशस्थस्यापि शब्दप्रत्यक्षम्। अतः शब्दः आकाशसत्त्वे लिङ्गम्। "निष्क्रमणं प्रवेशनमित्याकाशस्य लिङ्गम्" इति (वैद. २.१.२९) सूत्रेण चलनात्मकक्रियायाः अवकाशदानमाकाशेनैव क्रियत इति सांख्यमतमत्रैव समनन्तरसूत्रेण खण्डितम्। बौद्धैरपि इदमवकाशदानरूपं लिङ्गं बहुधा खण्ड्यते। पृथिव्यादीनां गुणाः कारणगुणपूर्वका एव दृश्यन्ते। तन्तुरूपस्यैव पटे दर्शनात्। शब्दस्य वीणादि निष्ठत्वे वीणा-समवायि कारणीभूतेषु तदवयवेषु पूर्वतरं तस्य स्थितिः निरूपयितव्या। न च तथास्ति। अतः शब्दो न पृथिव्यादिद्रव्यगुणः। तदाधारतया अतिरिक्तमाकाशाख्यं पञ्चमं भूतं सिद्ध्यतीति कणादमहर्षेराशयः।

आवारकस्य गमनप्रतिबंधकस्य कुड्यादेरभाव एव आकाशशब्देन निर्दिश्यते, तदतिरिक्तं पञ्चमं भूतं नास्तीति वदतां बौद्धानां स्वमताभिनिवेश एव तत्र मूलम्। यो निबंधे तर्ककौशलञ्च। आकाशाख्यस्य पञ्चमस्य भूतस्य अङ्गीकारेण भगवतो बुद्धस्य सर्वलोकहिततमोपदेशानां ईषदपि हानिर्नोपजायते। अविकसितधिषणानां पामरजनानां प्रौढयुक्त्यनुसंधानं न सुलभम्। स एव मुख्योहेतुस्तेषां वादस्य। प्रतिबंधकस्य कुड्यादेरभावं सर्वे पामरजनाः अनायासेन वक्तुं शक्नुवन्ति। तावति तेऽपि विश्राम्यन्ति। अतिसूक्ष्मस्य आकाशाख्यस्य तत्त्वस्य सत्त्वं तर्ककौशलेन साधयितव्यम्। अत एव तेषामत्रन प्रवृत्तिः, न खलु पामरजनास्तत्र प्रभवः।

छान्दोग्योपनिषदि षष्ठप्रश्ने-द्वादशखण्डे श्वतकेतोरुद्दालकस्य च संवादः —

> "न्यग्रोधफलमत आहरेतीदं भगव इति भिन्द्धीति भिन्नं भगव इति किमत्र पश्यसीत्यण्व्य इवेमा धाना भगव इत्यासामङ्गैकां भिन्द्धीति भिन्ना भगव इति किमत्र पश्यसीति न किञ्चन भगव इति ।।1।। तं होवाच यं वै सोम्यैतमणिमानं न निभालयस एतस्य वै सोम्यैषोऽणिम्न एवं महान्न्यग्रोधस्तिष्ठति। श्रद्धत्स्व सोम्येति।।2।। स य एषोऽणिमैतदात्म्यमिदं सर्वं तत्सत्यं स आत्मा तत्त्वमसि श्वेतकेतो"

इति वाक्यानि विद्यन्ते। न्यग्रोधफलस्याभ्यन्तरे न किञ्चिद् इति वदन्तं श्वेतकेतुं शिष्यं आचार्यो बोधयति अतिमहान् न्यग्रोधवृक्षः अत्रैव वर्तते, श्रद्धत्स्व सोम्य इति। अत्रापि बौद्धाः श्वेतकेतोरेव शिष्यस्य पर्वणि विश्राम्येयुः। न तु तत् परमार्थः।

याज्ञवल्क्यस्मृतौ यतिधर्मप्रकरणे गर्भस्थः शिशुः पञ्चभ्योऽपि भूतेभ्यः तत्तदंशान् संगृह्य परिपूर्णो भवतीति वस्तुतत्त्वं विशदीक्रियते। अपां शैत्यमिव तेजसः उष्णत्वमिव च वस्तुतत्त्वमिदम्। नेदमपन्होतुं शक्यं केनापि। न वा कस्यचिन्मतस्य एतन्निषेधेन लाभो वा लोपो वा। पामरजनाः न समर्था एवंविधविषयमवगन्तुमित्येतावदेवात्र। "न ह्येषःस्थाणोरपराधो यदेनमन्धो न पश्यति"। पृथिव्यादिभूतचतुष्टयात् तत्तदंशानां गर्भस्थेन शिशुना संग्रहणात्पूर्वं भगवान् याज्ञवल्क्यो ब्रवीति —

"आकाशाल्लाघवं सौक्ष्म्यं शब्दं श्रोत्रं बलादिकम्" इति।

जातस्य शिशोः शरीरे इमे विषयाः वर्तन्त एव। तेषां संग्रहः आकाशादेव जायत इति महर्षिः ज्ञात्वैवोपदिशति।

वायोश्च स्पर्शनं चेष्टां व्यूहनं रौक्ष्यमेव च।
पित्तात्तु दर्शनं पक्तिं औष्ण्यं रूपं प्रकाशिताम्।
रसात्तुरसनं शैत्यं स्नेहं क्लेदं समार्दवम्।

इत्याद्यप्यनुपदमुपदिश्यत एवात्र। किमिदं सर्वं व्यामोहफलम्?

तथा व्याधिपीडितस्य वैद्यः नानाविधमूलिकादिनिर्मितं भेषजं दत्त्वा व्याधिं शमयति। भेषजसेवनकाले आहारनियमोऽपि व्याधिग्रस्थायोपदिश्यते। रस-वीर्य-विपाकादिकं तत्तद्वस्तुजातस्य वैद्य एव जानाति न व्याधिपीडितः। किं तत्रानास्था युज्यते? अर्थक्रियायत्तं वस्तुतत्त्वमिति वादो नात्र प्रसरं लभते। वस्तुतो विद्यमानाया अप्यर्थक्रियायाः स्थूलदृष्ट्या अपरिज्ञानात्। पश्चाज्जनिष्यमाणस्य स्वास्थ्यस्य तदभावस्य वा तदानीमज्ञानात् अनुमानैकसमधिगम्यत्वाच्च। अत्रापि बौद्धच्छात्रानुसारिणः विपरीतमेव वदेयुः। न त्वेतदुपपन्नम्।

गतिप्रतिबंधकस्य कुड्यादेरभाव एवाकाशः न तदतिरिक्तं वस्तु किञ्चित् इति वदन्तो बौद्धाः न खलु प्रतीतिस्वरूपं सम्यगवधारयन्ति। अभावज्ञाने नञ् पदप्रयोगः सर्वसाधारणः। घटो नास्तिपटोस्ति इति हि नञुपयोगेन वस्तुनोऽभावं जना व्यवहरन्ति। प्रतीतिर्नावरणाभावावलंबना, विधिरूपत्वात्। अतश्च इहावरणं नास्ति इत्यावरणाभावाश्रयतया इह-प्रत्ययालंबमस्मदभिमताकाशमेव।

इत्यादयः आकाशास्तित्ववादिनां सूक्तयोऽपि भाव्याः।

(श्रीमन्निगमान्तमहादेशिकविरचितं न्यायसिद्धाञ्जनम्) इह खगः पतति इति बुद्धौ पक्षिपतनाधारतया किञ्चिद्वस्तु नूनं दृश्यत एव। किन्तदन्यदाकाशत् ?

सद्रूपेणैव भानात् न भवति वरणाभावमात्रं विहायः
संसर्गाभावमात्रं न च भवति यतो नास्ति संसर्गि बोधः।
अत्यन्ताभाव नाशावजननिरपि वा सत्सु तेष्वेव न स्युः
तादात्म्याभावसिद्धिः कथमपि च भवेत्? तं तमर्थं विहाय।।

तत्त्वमुक्ताकलापग्रंथे श्रीमन्निगमान्तमहादेशिकश्लोकः।

अन्यच्चात्रावधेयम्। आकाशः शब्दः इति पदयोः अर्थः कः ? यं कञ्चिदर्थमवलंब्य वादिनो विवदन्ते। सर्वेऽपि यथार्थवादिन एव। शब्दो द्रव्यमिति मीमांसकाः। सः गुण एवेति तार्किकाः। स नित्य इति मीमांसकाः। अनित्य एवायमिति तार्किकाः। पूर्वमीमांसायां प्रथमाध्याये प्रथमपादे षष्ठमधिकरणं शब्दनित्यत्वाधिकरणं इत्येव व्यवह्रियते। अद्यत्वे सर्वसाधारणे यन्त्रमूलके शब्दप्रचारे निदानभूताः बहवो विषयाः अत्र सूत्रेषु भाष्ये च परिदृश्यन्ते। कण्ठताल्वादि-शब्दोच्चारणकारणीभूताः अवयवाः किं शब्दमुत्पादयन्ति? उत विद्यमानमेव शब्दमभिव्यञ्जन्ति? इति विचार्य निर्णीयतेऽत्र कण्ठताल्वाद्यभिघातेन वायवीयाः अवयवाः प्रणुद्यन्ते। ते नैरन्तर्येण स्तिमिततया विद्यमानानि वाय्वन्तराणि प्रतिबाधन्ते। तेन सत एव शब्दतत्त्वस्याभिव्यक्तिर्जायते न शब्द उत्पाद्यते तैः। अत्र

शाबरभाष्यं — "अभिघातेन हि प्रेरिता वायवः स्तिमितानि वाय्वन्तराणि प्रतिबाधमानाः सर्वतोदिक्कान् संयोग-विभागानुत्पादयन्ति, यावद्वेगमभिप्रतिष्ठन्ते। ते च वायोरप्रत्यक्षत्वात् संयोगविभागा नोपलभ्यन्ते। अनुपरतेष्वेव तेषु शब्द उपलभ्यते, नोपरतेषु। अतो न दोषः। अत एवानुवातं दूरादुपलभ्यते शब्दः" इति। "आकाशदेशश्च शब्दः" इति च। इदं तत्त्वनिरूपणं नानादरमर्हति। युगपत् उत्पन्नयोः द्वयोः पदार्थयोः एकतरस्य पूर्वं अन्यस्य पश्चाच्च उपलंभः अनुभवे वर्तते। ते वस्तुनी के? इति प्रश्नः महाभारते यक्षप्रश्ने दृश्यते। "विद्युत् गर्जितञ्च" इति तस्योत्तरं युधिष्ठिरेण दत्तम्। शब्दः आकाशे प्रयाति तेजोऽपि। तयोः तेजसः वेगवत्तरत्वं तात्त्विकं अत्र प्रतिपाद्यते। "शब्द" शब्देन अत्र किं निर्दिश्यते ? चलनवान् पदार्थः नित्यः विभुः शब्दः द्रव्यमेव, न गुणः इति मीमांसकमतम्। तदभिव्यञ्जकानां ध्वनीनामेवात्र शब्दशब्देन निर्देशः क्रियते। वाय्वभिघातवशात् ध्वनेः सर्वतो-दिक्कं प्रसरणं जायते, तेन च शब्दस्याभिव्यक्तिर्भवति। एतादृशं ध्वनिमेव शब्दशब्देन निर्दिशन्तो मीमांसकेतरमतस्थाः शब्दस्यानित्यत्वं वदन्ति।

अन्तर्धानं स्मृतिस्सौक्ष्म्यं दृष्टिः श्रोत्रज्ञता तथा।
निजं शरीरमुत्सृज्य परकायप्रवेशनम्।।
अर्थानां छन्दतस्सृष्टिर्योगसिद्धेश्च लक्षणम्।
सिद्धे योगे त्यजन्देहममृतत्वाय कल्पते।।

इति वदन् योगीश्वरो याज्ञवल्क्यमहर्षिः गहनान् अनेकान् विषयान् विवृणोति। साधारणजनानां कुड्यादिभिः उपरोधे सञ्चारः प्रतिबध्यते। योगिनस्तु अप्रतिहतगतयो विराजन्ते। "सौक्ष्म्यं" इति तत्त्वं अत्र कारणतया प्रदर्श्यते। तथा दवीयसामपि वस्तूनां दर्शनं शब्दानां श्रवणञ्च योगिनां सुकरम्। तथा परकायप्रवेशश्च। एवमादिकं न सहसा निराकर्तुं शक्यम्। वेदेषु, "पृथिव्यै स्वाहा अग्नये स्वाहावायवे स्वाहा अद्भ्यस्स्वाहा, वनस्पतिभ्यस्स्वाहा, इत्यादि वाक्यैः जडपदार्थानां देवतात्वं प्रतिपाद्यते। नेदं मुग्धभाषितं न वा विप्रलंभकवचः। अत्र किञ्चिदौचित्यं संभावितमेव। तदन्वेष्टव्यम्। एकं उदाहरणं दर्श्यते।

सोमयागाङ्गं अग्नीषोमीयपशुयागः। तत्र पशुर्बध्यते। तदर्थं वृक्षस्य शाखा एका छिद्यते। तत्र स्वधितेर्वृक्षस्य बिभ्यतः प्रथमेन शकलेन (वृक्षस्य) तेजः परापततियः प्रथमशशकलः परापतेत् तमाहरेत् स तेजसमेवैनमाहरति" इति श्रूयते। स्वधितिः इति छेदनसाधनस्य कुठारादेः नाम। तस्मात् शब्दात् पञ्चम्येकवचनान्तं पदं स्वधितेः इत्येतत्। त्रासार्थानां इति पञ्चमी। वृक्षः स्वधितेः बिभेति। कुतः? "मामयं छेत्स्यति" इति। अत्र वृक्षस्य भयं विस्पष्टं श्रूयते। तत् सूक्ष्मेक्षिकया ज्ञात्वा वेदो वदति। स्थूलदृष्ट्या नेदं ज्ञातुं शक्यम्। किमिदं न परमार्थः? अद्यतनाः वैज्ञानिकाः निपुणतरमिदं निरूपयन्ति। तथा "अग्ने! गर्भो अपां असि" "अग्निं या गर्भंदधिरे" इत्यादि वेदवाक्यानि अप्सु अन्तः गर्भभूतः अग्निः वसति-इति कथयन्ति। आपातप्रतीतौ इदमनुपपन्नमिव। ज्ञानचक्षुषा तु सम्यगेव निरीक्ष्यते। अपां नपात् इति अग्निर्व्यपदिश्यते। नपात् - पुत्रः, पौत्रः, प्रपौत्रः, इत्यर्थः। प्रथमे-द्वितीये-तृतीये वा पर्वणि अद्भ्यः वैद्युताग्नेरुत्पत्तिं वैज्ञानिका निरूपयन्त्येव। अतः वेदो सर्वमेवानुपपन्नमति वादो न साधीयान्। परोक्षेषु येषु सहसा निषेधो न खलु सुशकः। 'अव्यतिरेकस्तु अर्थानुपलब्धे" इति भगवान् जैमिनिः इममेवार्थं कथयति।

शब्दोच्चारणकाले शरीरान्तर्भागे यादृशो व्यापारः प्रवर्तते, सिक्षाकाराः निरूपयन्तिः —

आत्माबुद्ध्या समेत्यार्थान्मनोयुंक्ते विवक्षया।

मनः कायाग्निमाहन्ति स प्रेरयति मारुतम्।।

इत्यादिना। एवं विधानि शिक्षाकारवचनानि वस्तुतत्त्वप्रतिपादकान्येव। वैज्ञानिकाः निपुणाः इदं सर्वं सम्यक् निरूपयितुं प्रभवन्त्येव। न तु पामरजनाः। तावता किमिदं सर्वं मिथ्यैव?। अतः आकाशाख्यस्य पञ्चमस्य भूतस्य ततोऽपि पूर्वतनानां अहंकारमहदादीनां तत्त्वं अप्रकंप्यमेव। साधारणजनदुर्विज्ञेयत्वमात्रेण एषामपलापो न युज्यते। नहि सर्वस्सर्वं जानाति।

English Translation of
"Pañcabhūtatattvanirūpaṇam"

The best of holy cities — this city of Pune, is well-known in the world. Offering my prostrations to the learned people well-versed in various *śāstras* and assembled here, I would like to express my thoughts before them for their consideration on the chosen subject.

Pṛthivī, āpaḥ, tejaḥ, vāyuḥ and *ākāśaḥ* are five *mahābhūtas* that constitute this universe. In the creation, continuation and destruction of this universe — the above five *mahābhūtas* play a major role. These five *bhūtas* transform themselves into *prapañca* by the desire of *Īśvara* and by that very same desire of God they continue to exist up to a particular period; by the very same *saṅkalpa* of God these *bhūtas* disappear. In this process the main cause is the desire of God. To give them the experience destined for them, according to the various deeds (*karmas*) of all the *jivātmās* (souls), God creates this universe.

Thus created, it stands for some time and again disappears. This process of creation, existence and dissolution is described in the *śāstras* as the sport of Lord God. That is why this universe is called *Līlā Vibhūti.*

Apart from this universe, there is another part, which is not transformed like this universe. There is no change of any kind here. And this part is called *Nitya Vibhūti* and stands all the time without any change. To attain this place is what is called *mokṣa* or *Brahmānanda anubhava* attainable by only those who have overvcome their *puṇya* and *pāpa.* This fact is vouchsafed in the *Vedas, Upaniṣads, Bhagavad-Gītā, Viṣṇu Purāṇa* etc. This is the philosophical position of *viśiṣṭādvaita* of Bhagavān Rāmānuja. The followers of *dvaita* and *advaita* systems also explain this very same philosophy with little variations here and there. Though the *advaita* borders on the philosophy of Buddhism it is not *vedabāḥya,* out of Vedic-fold, nor is it *nāstika.*

Says Maharṣi Yājñavalkya —

> This body made up of these five *mahābhūtas* due to *karma*, when disintegrated into the five *bhūtas*, where is the need for sorrow?.

How the *mahābhūtas* become instrumental in the formulation of this universe is described in detail in the *Vedas*. *Mūla Prakṛti* in its subtle state is called *tamas*; it transforms itself into *mahat, ahaṅkāra* etc. There are three states of *Mūla Prakṛti* called *tamas, akṣara* and *avyakta* all of which are very subtle. Even the other transformations following these four states, namely *mahat, ahaṅkāra* and *tanmātras* are also subtle and when they attain the state of *vikāsa* they get the name *bhūtas*. As the seeds kept in a storage do not sprout, but when combined with water and mud, gradually sprout, in the same manner the non-transformed state of the seeds represents *Mūla Prakṛti*, because, when it attains *vikāsa* it represents the sprout. This is how the universe takes shape. All the created things dissolve into their origin, the cause, and this can be seen in our daily experience.

Those who follow the tenets of the Buddhism or Jainism do not accept this process. They accept only the four visible *mahābhūtas*. They do not accept *ākāśa* which is not experienced by any sense-perception. Nor do they accept the principles like *kāla* (Time), *dik* (Direction) and *ātmā* (Soul), because all these things are not experienced by the sense-perceptions, whereas in the case of other four *bhūtas* namely *bhūmi, jala, vāyu* and *agni*, there is no dispute, as experience cannot be denied. Thus, in the *nāstika* system of philosophy the only disputable point is about *ākāśa*.

If the non-existence of *ākāśa* is established by arguments and syllogism, on the same analogy the other unseen *tattvas* like *kāla* (Time) etc. can also be denied.

Dharmakīrti a well-known and erudite Buddhist scholar, in his work called *Pramāṇa Vārtika* discussed this aspect. It has also been dealt with in an exhaustive manner in the commentaries on that work. Let us consider some of those points :

1. There can be no destruction of an existence but only a transformation is possible.
2. When there is an absence of obstructing agent, then also that existence cannot be affected.
3. If there is absence of one *mahābhūta*, it means there is existence of another *bhūta* in its place.

4. Thus the absence of the other four *mahābhūtas* is to be construed as *ākāśa* and nothing else.
5. How come *ākāśa* does not support a piece of stone thrown in the space?
6. *Vāyu* which is moving all the time is not supported by *ākāśa*. Why is it so?
7. If the reply is that *ākāśa* does not obstruct the movement of the Air, this is not the answer. Since the non-obstruction of the Air's movement is due to the absence of the obstructing agency.
8. Those who accept *ākāśa* say that it is all-pervasive and eternal. How is it that such a matter is not being supported by another? It comes to this that *ākāśa* does not need a support, but it is its own support that supports all the other things.
9. In that case we may ask, "why accept *ākāśa* alone as having no other support? Why not accept this in the case of others too"?
10. Direction (*dik*) is also all-pervading. Then why not accept this quality of *ākāśa* in direction itself?
11. There are several principles which are all-prevading, like *ātmā, kāla, vāyu, dik* etc. If these are all-pervading, how is it that all these do not become one?
12. The likely answer to this question is that there is no obstructing agency and thus they all have their own existence in all places. Simply saying that there is no obstruction from *ākāśa* amounts to building castles in the air. Thus, we may conclude that the absence of the four *mahābhūtas* is *ākāśa*. Other than this, accepting a matter separately and calling it *ākāśa* is not real.

The above arguments of Dharmakīrti are again discussed in detail in his other work called *Nyāya Bindu*. There are several annotations for *Pramāṇa Vārtika*, among which is the one called *vārtikālaṅkāra* by Prajñākara Gupta. In this *vyākhyā* the author recounts the arguments of those who accept *ākāśa* and gives counter-arguments very effectively.

When there is a wall in front, then the movement of objects is obstructed. These objects are not in a position to overcome the obstruction and go forward. But if there are no such obstructions then both living and non-living things move ahead. This is seen in experience. Therefore, the acceptance of *ākāśa* is supported by the reason of non-obstruction. All objects remain in the space provided by *ākāśa* and *ākāśa* does not obstruct their movements.

This argument is countered below. What is meant by the phrase 'providing spaces'? The answer is "unobstruction of existence". What is this existence? Is it being supported by something else or is it a non-hindrance? If it is meant as getting support from another source, then it is wrong. Because things like pots etc., are not supported by *ākāśa* but by the earth. If the answer is non-hindrance, that is also wrong, because it is due to the absence of an obstructing agency. Therefore, the statement that *ākāśa* does not obstruct the existence of other things is null and void. Therefore, *ākāśa* means the absence of the other four *mahābhūtas* such as *pṛthivī*, and there is no fifth matter called *ākāśa.*

The absence of obstructing agencies like walls makes movement possible, if there is an obstruction then it becomes impossible. Thus the wall is an obstructing agent of movement. This is called *pratibandhaka.* The absence of *pratibandhaka* is a general cause for all created things. This is accepted by all the philosophers. Therefore, construing an element as *ākāśa* and positing it as the giver of space has no basis. A person with eyes cannot see a thing which is obstructed by a wall or if the object is at a long distance, or if it is very small in size. If the obstruction is removed, if the distance is decreased or if the size of the object is big enough, one can see it. In the perception of this object the cause is only the eye and nothing else. The wall and other things are obstructing agencies for perception. Therefore, the absence of the obstructing agency becomes a cause for all creations. No other cause may be construed in this regard. Therefore, acceptance of the fifth *bhūta, ākāśa* on the basis of the argument that it provides space for all other things is untenable.

If *ākāśa* is providing space then where do the other *mahābhūtas* like *vāyu* stand, and where does *ākāśa* itself exist? If there is no need for a sixth *mahābhūta* and *ākāśa* is capable of providing space both for itself and for other *bhūtas,* then *vāyu* also can be construed as of that quality.

For the question, "What is *ākāśa*" the answer given by Prajñākara Gupta is this :

> *Ākāśa* means an opening or hole and this is made possible by the absence of some matter occupying space. If it is the absence of a matter which occupies space, then, where was *ākāśa*? One cannot say that it tore away through the sides. In both cases of existence and non-existence of *ākāśa,* where the *ākāśa* did go cannot be answered. If it is said that *ākāśa* was destroyed, then well done of its eternality! if it is said that all the time *ākāśa* itself was there, then absence of space and existence of *ākāśa* cannot

> go hand in hand. The existence and non-existence of a thing cannot exist simultaneoulsy.

Īśvara, ātmā, ākāśa, dik, kāla etc., are not existing things, because they do not create or contribute in the creation of another thing visible, that is, absence of *artha kriyā*. This is another reasoning. Earth causes burning, cooking etc., there is *artha kriyā. Kriyā* means coming into existence of a new object. Non-happenings of these movements or non-agreement of same is called the absence of *artha kriyā*. Wherever there is existence, one can see the coming into being of another object or transformation.

With the existing of a particular thing or its absence, if some knowledge is obtained by its absence, then that is called *svalakṣaṇa*. That is how Dharmakīrti defines *svalakṣaṇa* in his *Nyāya Bindu* and by the absence of this so-called *svalakṣaṇa* he establishes the absence of *ākāśa*. There he cites the example of the horns of a hare: whether the hare's horns exist or not, there is no change in the knowledge. This is called *tuccha*. Non-existence, in the same manner, such as, whether *ākāśa* exists or not, indicates that no change occurs in the perception. Therefore, *ākāśa* does not exist. We experience differences in taste when there is more sugar or less, or salt or chillies in our food. This is what is called difference in perception. Known to all and sundry, this is also called *svalakṣaṇa*. If such definitions of *svalakṣaṇa* are known, only then the existence of an object can be accepted by all and without any controversy. In the case of the horns of a hare or *ākāśa* there is no such *svalakṣaṇa* and, therefore, there is no *ākāśa*.

The existence of a thing can be accepted only when there is *artha kriyā* and this is a correct proposition. Likewise, the existence of *svalakṣaṇa* also confirms the existence of a thing. *Ākāśa* does not possess either of the above two qualities as stated by the Buddhist. Only here the *vaidikas* differ. They say that both qualities do exist in *ākāśa*. Therefore, *ākāśa* is to be accepted as real and existing. But the difference is in the perception of laymen and thinkers. It cannot be convincingly proved to exist to the experience of laymen. Whereas for an analytical thinker, it can be proved. A thing that is obtained after climbing the hill cannot be called invisible before climbing. Both sides give all the possible reasonings, but the Buddhists use many false illustrations and syllogisms to attract the laymen.

Kumārila Bhaṭṭa says this — the followers of Buddha all the time preach *dharma* but never without reasoning. According to the philosophy of the Bauddhas, all the things in their creation need definite causes but in their destruction they do not need any cause, because destruction is natural; not the creation. To teach this tenet to ordinary people they always use several examples. For example:

> Taking a pebble from the ground they say that the pebble does not go up in the space by itself. If thrown up by us, up it goes. Therefore, the pebble's going up is dependent on some causes. In the same manner, the creations of all things depend on causes. But, once thrown up, the pebble does not stand in the space itself; it immediately comes down. What is the cause for this? There is nothing visible. Likewise, all created things without another agency, get destroyed naturally and by themselves.

In the example cited above, one can analyse how much reasoning is involved in it. Citing the example of a pebble's going up caused by an agency does not properly fit in for proving that all created things need an agency for their coming into being. Gullible people are led to believe anything by this sort of exposition. In the case of *ākāśa* also these logicians have adopted a similar method. The *Vaiśe. Sūtra* — (2-1-71) tells us that in those cases where knowledge cannot be gained through *pratyakṣa* or *anumāna* such subtle matters are to be known only by the authority of the *Vedas*: Ṛṣi Kaṇāda, who was content with only two *pramāṇas* — *pratyakṣa* and *anumāna*, takes recourse to *Vedas* in respect of all subtle matters as a source of knowledge. If that is the case with him, then what to say of people like us. This Ṛṣi Kaṇāda, after dislodging all the arguments of the opponents, establishes the existence of the fifth *bhūta*, that is *ākāśaḥ*, with the *hetu, śabda guṇa* in a long drawn discourse.

The quality which is grasped by the ears is called *śabda*. This *śabda* cannot be inherent in *vīṇā* or in bamboo. Therefore, there must be a substratum for this *śabda* and the substratum is what is called *ākāśa*. By several resonings, he has discarded the other matters as the *āśraya* (substratum) for the quality *śabda*. If sound resides in the *vīṇā* itself, then people sitting at a distance cannot hear this sound, because *vīṇā* does not travel from its place. Whereas if it is accepted that sound through the medium of *vīṇā* was generated in *ākāśa*, which in turn generated a series of sound waves till it reached the ear-drum of the people sitting in various directions, it is quite logical. Therefore, in the existence of *ākāśa, śabda* is the deciding factor. Getting out and entering in are other factors to prove that *ākāśa* is the cause for space.

Movement needs space and this is given by *ākāśa*. This is how the *Sāṁkhyas* argue. Ṛṣi Kaṇāda has effectively countered their arguments on this point. Even Bauddhas reject this argument "giving space" as the deciding factor for proving the existence of *ākāśa*. Wherever there is a quality in a thing created, it is seen that quality comes into being from the corresponding causes already existing, namely the colour of the cloth is derived from the colour of the thread used for weaving the cloth. In the same manner if *śabda* is a *guṇa* inherent in *vīṇā* then that *guṇa* should be shown to exist in the causal elements of the *vīṇā* or its parts. It cannot be proved in this way. Therefore, *śabda* is not a *guṇa* of *pṛthivī* etc., but it must have its own substratum which is the fifth *mahābhūta* the *ākāśa*.

There was another argument by the Bauddhas — the absence of an obstructing agency, and that was called *ākāśa* and not a separate *bhūta*. Here, we can only say that Bauddhas are simply guided by their fanaticism and not by reasoning. Ordinary people can understand the absence of an obstruction like the wall. Simply with that much reasoning, they stop contented but accept or reject a substance like *ākāśa* which is very subtle and beyond the sense-perception; it is not sufficient. It needs sharp intellect and argumentative power but the ordinary people are not endowed with this quality and Bauddhas exploited this situation to their advantage.

In the sixth chapter of the *Chāndogya Upaniṣad* there is a dialogue between Śvetaketu and Uddālaka : "Bring the fruit of the *pīpal* tree. Here, it is. Breaking the seeds, what you see? Very small seeds. Break one of these small seeds. Again it is broken. What you see in it? I do not see anything. Dear son, that which you are not able to see in this small space, from that very space this great *peepal* tree standing before you has arisen. Therefore, have belief that this *ātmā* also is so subtle that it cannot be seen or experienced but all the created things are having their *ātmā* as their soul and this is the truth, and you are that".

When Śvetaketu says that he is not able to see anything within that small seed when broken up and from that very same thing Uddālaka says that the great *pīpal* tree has arisen, he wants his son to believe that. Bauddhas also would like their *śiṣyas*/followers to stop arguing and believe their statements. But that is not the end of it.

In the *Yājñavalkya Smṛti, Yati Dharma Prakaraṇa,* the formation of a child within the womb is described, where it is said that the child gets parts of all the five *bhūtas* and gets its body formed. By accepting or rejecting this theory nobody is going to gain anything or lose anything. It is just the state of affairs, as it exists. Because the blind man is not able to see it and gets dashed against it, it is not the fault of the post (pillar) that it exists there.

From the *bhūta ākāśa* the child gets the quality of *lightness, subtleness, śabda, guṇa, śrotra indriya* and *bala*. Once the body of the child is formed all these qualities exist in its body. This has been explained by Maharṣi Yājñavalkya and he goes on explaining the formation of the other qualities, too, in the body from the other *bhūtas*. Is it just to mislead the people?

A patient suffering from a disease gets medicine from the Doctor as per his diagnosis; the Doctor prescribes certain restrictions in regard to the intake of food etc. The transformation of different kinds of food within the body and how they are to be tackled are known to the Doctor and not to the patient. Does that mean that the patient should disbelieve the Doctor.

Artha kriyā goes to prove the existence of a thing; this was one of the reasonings but even though *artha kriyā* might be there in a body, it may be invisible. It does not mean that it is not there. This can be seen in the case of the patient. After consuming the medicine he becomes hale and hearty. These are things which are ascertained by proper reasoning. An obstructing object like a wall or its absence as *ākāśa* as propounded by the Bauddhas does not stand to reasoning. When you negate a thing, the use of a negative word is common. This negative word does not denote the absence of a covering agent. In that case people should say, "there is no covering agent here". In this sentence they will use the word **here** as the basis for the experience. And that difference is the proof for the existence of *ākāśa.* That is the *ākāśa* intended by us and is denoted by the word **here.** "Here the Bird flies". In this sentence the *ādhāra* for the Bird to fly is *ākāśa.* It is a positive denotation and cannot be explained by the use of a negative word.

Let us consider another point. What are the meanings of these two words *ākāśa* and *śabda*? People dispute about this but they do accept that these two words have come to denote something. They are matters according to the *Mīmāṁsakas.* It is only a quality and not a matter according to *Naiyāyikas.* It is eternal according to the *Mīmāṁsakas* but it is **momentary** according to the *tārkikas.* In the first Chapter, first *Pada,* Sixth *Adhikaraṇa* of the *Pūrvamīmāṁsā* the quality of eternality of *śabda* is established. The qualities of sound, how they are transmitted and how they are received are all well-known to modern science today. All these are discussed in this chapter. It is further discussed there, whether the parts of the body like the **gullet, palate** etc., produce the sound or just help in making it audible. In this argument it was established that Air, which is still, at one point gets disturbed by the movement of the parts of the body, gets dislodged, and goes on generating waves travelling in all Directions. Because Air is not visible, we are not able to see their conjoint or disjoint functions.

In the *Yakṣa Praśna* of *Mahābhārata* there is a question — of the two things born simultaneously one is experienced first and the other later. Which are these two? The answer is lightning and the roaring of the clouds; from this one can understand that *śabda* is a matter which travels according to the *Mīmāṁsā*; it is eternal, all-pervading and a matter. We use the word *śabda* for those *dhvani* which make the *śabda* known by our ears. *Dhvani* gets transmitted in all directions because of the impact of *vāyu.* And thus, *śabda* is experienced by us. Therefore, subtleness is one cause for our not being able to prove or disprove a thing. Therefore, we cannot simply deny the existence of a thing by its mere non-experience. Therefore, in things known not directly, we cannot deny anything just like that. Therefore, *ākāśa* the fifth *bhūta* and its two prior evolutes like *ahaṅkāra* and *mahat* are **Indisputable.** Non-visibility by ordinary people is not sufficient to deny their existence.

3

Bhūtas in Vedic Rituals and Literature

T. N. Dharmadhikari

According to the Vedic tradition, there are five elements (*bhūtas*) — *pṛthivī, āpaḥ, tejas, vāyu* and *ākāśa.* The *bhūtas* are inextricably linked to the Vedic concept of cosmology and ritual.

The *Aitareya Up.* (3.3)[1] gives a list of five *bhūtas* while *Taittirīya Up.* (2.1)[2] relates the order of their creation. The *Praśna Up.* (2.2; 4.8),[3] *Chāndogya Up.* (1.1.2)[4] etc. also enumerate them. *Sāṅkhyas*[5] accord sanction to them.

Formation and frame of Vedic sacrifice were conceived by the master-minds, the *ṛṣis,* the seers, when they constantly observed and meditated upon the ever rotating disciplined cycles of the universe, which they understood as cosmos and not chaos. The ancient Vedic ritualistic texts rightly state that the sacrifice is a prototype[6] or dramatisation of the game of universe, the creation of Prajāpati, and that the sacrifice is a royal[7] road leading to *ṛta,* the cosmic law.

The five *bhūtas* are cosmic elements. If the cosmic prototypes are thought to be manipulated through sacrifice, the *bhūtas* must be found playing an important role in the frame and sacrifice.

Deep investigations into Vedic sacrifice reveals that the entire sacrificial procedure is scheduled round the *Loka,* i.e., space-encompassing *bhūtas* and round the *Kāla,* i.e., Time.

We are concerned here, with the *bhūtas. Loka* or its collateral dialectic form *u-loka*[8] (*ṚV,* I.936, II. 30.6, III. 2.9. etc.) (which may be an abridged form of *uru-loka)* originally may mean — 'the wide open space'.

Further the three or seven worlds — i.e., *vyāhṛtis* viz. *bhūḥ, bhuvaḥ, svaḥ, mahaḥ, janaḥ, tapaḥ* and *satyam,* covered by the wide space, are secondarily known as *Lokas.*

Pṛthivī

Bhūḥ represents the global planet, as well as the basic element — *pṛthivī* — earth. *Bhūḥ* or *pṛthivī* is seen in its physical, deified and metaphysical forms in Vedic rituals.

Mait. S., I.8.5[9] enjoins to recite three *vyāhṛtis* viz., *bhūḥ, bhuvaḥ, svaḥ* before each offering in sacrifice, because, according to this *Saṁhitā,* these three *vyāhṛtis* are raised to the position of *Brahman,* the eternal Truth.

In *Ādhāna* rite (depositing fires), the materials viz., gravel, saline soil, the soil from mole-hill and ant-hill, the earth dug up by a boar (with his snout) are placed on the *vedī*-ground. These materials are called *pārthiva-saṁbhāras.*

In this context, the *Taittirīya Br.* (I.1.3) narrates a myth of the birth of *Pṛthivī*[10] as follows: in the beginning this water was indeed a surge (*śarīram*). Prajāpati, practising penance (for further creation) became weary. Incidentally he saw a lotus-leaf floating on the surge. He thought — must there be some substratum wherein the stalk of lotus, stands firm. He assumed a form of a boar and dived deep. He reached the earth below. He rammed into it and emerged. He spread it on the lotus leaf. Since it was spread it (*aprathayat*), it became known as *Pṛthivī.*

Thus, in placing the earth dug by a boar, on the *Vedī*-ground, the *Adhvaryu* as if places the earth brought out by Prajāpati. In that he verily dramatises the role of Prajāpati.

This myth summarily reminds us of the myth of *varāha*-incarnation appearing in *Purāṇas.*

For the performance of sacrifices, *Pṛthivī* is the very substratum, for it forms an altar for sacrifice. According to *TS,* the sacrifice is the navel of the world and the *vedī* — the altar[11] ground is the furthest end of *Pṛthivī.* Since the sacrifice is performed on it, the *vedī* — the earth — is called *devakṣetra.*[12]

In Agniciti, a *svayam-ātṛṇṇā* — i.e., a self-perforated pebble is placed on the altar being piled. *TS,* 5.2.8 identifies this pebble with *Pṛthivī.*[13] The formula for placing this pebble (*TS,* 4.2.9) reveals that it is being placed by Prajāpati[14] and that it is Aditi — all sustaining, a sustainer of all the world.

Prajāpati[15] once desired to pile the fire-altar. Pṛthivī said to him, "you shall not pile the fire-altar on me; you shall burn me excessively; and I getting burned, will shake you apart, you will fall into a sorrowful state". Prajāpati replied — "I shall so pile as it will not burn you exececessively". He touched the earth, made it a brick and set it down to prevent exececessive burning. This implies the role of the cosmic *Pṛthivī* in the ritual of *Agni.*

In placing the *Retaḥsic iṣṭakās,*[16] *TS*, 5.5.4 narrates a myth conveying that the *Pṛthivī* and *dyuḥ* are born of the seed of fire. Thus the *virāj* brick represents the earth and the *svarāj,* the sky.

Thus *Pṛthivī* and sky of cosmos are represented by the two bricks in the *Agni*-rite.

Iḍā is one of the important rites in *iṣṭi* and *paśu* sacrifices, wherein *Iḍā* is identified with *Pṛthivī.*

Āgnidh priest partakes of a portion from *Iḍā,* addressing it with the term 'mother earth'[17] (*VS*, II.10; *TBr.*, 3.7.6, *Kāt, ŚS*, 3.4.1).

Iḍā, i.e., *pṛthivī* is sometimes personified as a *Pṛśni*;[18] or *devahū*[19] (heavenly cow).

In the famous *Pṛthivī*[20] *sūkta* of *Atharva Veda,* (12.1.1-63), *Pṛthivī* is frequently referred to as mother.

According to the *Nyāya*-system of Philosophy, the *Pṛthivī* element is endowed with a specific characteristic, viz. *gandha* — smell. The *gandha*[21] of *Pṛthivī* is referred to in this *sūkta* (vide *AV*, 12.1.23-25).

Kauśika Sūtra employs this *sūkta* in many rituals — e.g.[22] *Āgrahāyaṇī* (24.24),[23] protection of town or city (38.12-16), pacifying[24] earth-quakes (98.1) etc. (Cf. also *Vaitāna ŚS*, 12.6, *Śāntikalpa,* 17.5, 18.8).

Iḍā, i.e., *Pṛthivī* is associated with *dyauḥ*— the sky. In *Āgrayaṇa-iṣṭi,*[25] the cake baked on one potsherd, or clarified butter (*ājya*) is offered to *dyāvāpṛthivī* jointly (*ŚBr.*, 2.4.3, *Kāt ŚS*, 4.6.5,7). According to *ŚBr, eka-kapāla,* i.e., one pot-sherd represents *Pṛthivī.*

In *Vaiśvadeva parvan*[26] of *Cāturmāsya* sacrifice also, a cake oblation is offered to *dyāvāpṛthivī* jointly. Oblations are offered to *dyāvāpṛthivī* in certain *kāmyeṣṭis* and *kāmya paśu* sacrifices.[27]

It is regarded by the *śrutis,* that the *dyāvāpṛthivī*[28] the earth and sky were close together — not separated in the beginning of creation. The oblations jointly offered to them may mark this mile-stone in the concept of the process of creation.

Śrutis further state that, while separating;[29] the earth and sky said to each other, due to execessive love and affection — (Sāyaṇa, *TBr*, 1.1.3 — *snehātiśayāt* that they should share together what is worthy of sacrifice. What of sky worthy of sacrifice was placed in this earth that became — *ūṣa* — the saline soil. What of this earth was worthy of sacrifice, was placed in the sky. That became the black spot on the moon. When the *adhvaryu* places the *ūṣa* in the *vedī* — he should also think of yonder black on the moon. By that he places on the *vedī*, what is worthy of both, i.e., of earth and of sky. In this connection it may be noted that the clay of ant-hill deposited on the *vedī*, is actually the *pṛthivī* element. It is identified with the earth by *ŚBr.*[30]

It may also be noted that in Vedic rituals, *dyauḥ* and *pṛthivī* are constantly mentioned in the forms of father and mother.[31] The joint oblation to *dyāvāpṛthivī* and their character of being united may have further formed a base for the concept of *Ardhanārīśvara* form of *Īśvara*.

Pṛthivī is found identified with *citrā*[32] sacrifice performed by one who desires cattle. It is also identified with the *Hotṛ*, priest,[33] with *Vāmabhṛt*[34] brick placed on the *Uttaravedī* in *Agniciti*; with *Vāravantīya Sāman*,[35] with *nidhana*,[36] the last part of *sāman*, with *svayam-ātṛṇṇā*[37] pebble, with *prātaḥ-savana*,[38] with *dakṣiṇa-havirdhāna*,[39] with *rathantara*,[40] *chandas*, with the first[41] layer of *Agniciti*, with *prāyaṇīyā iṣṭi*[42] and finally also with *prajāpati*.[43] These identifications, though sometimes formed *arthavāda*, indicate how *Pṛthivī* commanded high respect from ritualists.

Pṛthivī is more significantly identified with goddess Aditi.[44]

A *caru* (oblation of cooked rice) is offered to Aditi for one who is about to engage in war.[45] Aditi is this very earth. The *yājyā* and *puronuvākyā*[46] verses, for this *caru* offering to Aditi, are very significant. Aditi, i.e., *pṛthivī* is, in these verses regarded as the mother of those who follow the holy cosmic law, since she is a protector of holy order. Aditi the *pṛthivī* is regarded as a divine-ship, full of good oars, giving good protection — the ship that leakes not, hence dependable to convey across.

T. Br. enjoins to offer *caru* to Aditi[47] and *Punarvasū* in the context of *Nakṣatreṣṭi*. In the *yājyānuvākyā* verses related to this oblation, the Aditi,[48] *Pṛthivī* is called a nourishing (mother) of beings and giving firm foundation to them. Bhaṭṭa Bhāskara here derives the word Aditi from √*aya* 'to go'.[49]

The *Pṛthivī* is once called *Sarpa-rājñī*,[50] the queen of moving objects. Bhaṭṭa Bhāskara while commenting on *TS*, 7.3.1.3. derives this word from √*sṛp*,[51] to move, and states that 'the *Pṛthivī* is a queen amongst those who have assumed movement (*sarpasya gatimataḥ*).

Further *sarpa-rājñī* is a technical name of certain verses (*TS*, 1.5.3) *bhūmir bhūmnā* . . . etc.) utilised for depositing the fire in the mound of *gārhapatya*, in *Agnyādhāna* rite (*Āp ŚS*, 5.27.9-11). In this context, it will be interesting to note that the *gārhapatya* is often identified with *bhūḥ*, i.e., *Pṛthivī*. *Śatapatha Br.* further states that the mound[52] of the *gārhapatya* fire-place is circular, because this *pṛthivī* is also circular.

Praśna Up.[53] refers to the deity presiding over *Pṛthivī*. The deity is responsible to pull down the *apāna* in a *puruṣa*. Śaṅkarācārya while commenting on this passage explains that the *Pṛthivī* favours a man by pulling down the *apāna* in his body. Otherwise he may either have faltered/become unsteady/hesitant in his movement or gone up in space. This may hint at the gravitational force of *Pṛthivī*.

The Vedic texts specifically hold the view that *Pṛthivī*[54] is a source of vegetation and food. Peace/happiness (*śāntiḥ*) is brought on earth due to vegetation and food.[55] If the god *Mahādeva* kills the cattle, it is due to polluted vegetation[56] (*Tāṇḍ Br.*, 6.9.9).

With these discussions, one may safely conclude that, *Pṛthivī*, besides its global shape, was known to Vedic ritualists and seers in the form of 'element' also. They deified it and visualised it in its essential form of *Brahman* also.

Āpaḥ

According to *śrutis*, 'water' appears to be the first essential cosmic principle. *Ṛgveda*[57] states that 'all this was water in the beginning, not distinguished from darkness which wrapped it'. *TBr.*[58] corroborated this view, saying — 'in the beginning water was indeed a surge'.

Next to breath, water is an animating cosmic element, a primordial liquid, vivifying organism. After air, it is the first need of a living creature, a basic factor for existence. *ŚBr.*[59] therefore states 'as long as there is water in vital airs, so long man speaks with speech'. *TS*[60] also prays water for obtaining long life and lusture.

According to *TĀ*[61] (7.3.2), *Agni* is an antecedent form and sun the later. Water is a compound and lightning is the joining element. *Mait S*[62] further divides water in three places — in sky, earth and mid-region.

The Vedic seers possessed a deep awareness of the medicinal characteristics of waters.

ṚV[63] sheds sufficient light on medicinal quality of waters. The hymn considers water as the reservoir of all curative medicines and of nectar. It invokes waters which the cows drink and declares the intention to offer oblations to deities presiding over the flowing waters. *VS*[64] describes the medicinal use of waters in clear terms, saying — "O water, which we have drunk, become refreshing in our belly. May you be pleasant to us by driving away diseases and pains — O divine immortal waters". The verses are utilised for touching one's navel after drinking liquid in a sacrificial procedure.

This hydro-therapy finds its climax in *Atharva veda*. *AV*[65] hymns (6.23; 24 & 57) are exclusively devoted to medicinal use of waters.

AV prays waters to obtain cure from *kṣetrīya,* i.e., incurable diseases.

AV describes the various sources of waters and addresses them as *ayakṣaṁ-karaṇīḥ,* i.e., dispeller of diseases and as — *bhiṣagbhyo bhiṣaktarāḥ* — more healing than any other healer.

None of the recipes except raw water[68] can quench the thirst. In this sense only, Yāska in his *Nirukta* referred to water as containing all tastes.

Like *Agni* and *Vāyu, Āpaḥ* (waters) also serve as a purifying agent. *KS.*[69] declared in clear terms, that waters are purifiers. In the rituals of *Iṣṭi, Prokṣaṇī*[70] waters are utilised for purification.

Aṅgirasas,[71] leaving for heaven, placed in the waters, the *dīkṣā* and *tapas.* The sacrificer therefore takes bath in waters at *tīrtha* (ford). This is related by *TS,* 6.1.1. The formula for sprinkling on the sacrificer and for his bath (*TS*, 1.2.1)[72] are prayers to waters for purifications.

After a bath at consecration, the sacrificer is required to sip the water. He thereby becomes pure within.[73]

TS, 5.6.1. collects thirteen[74] formulae, all addressed to waters, in connection with the *kumbheṣṭhakās* in *Agni*-rite. One of the formulae compares the blissful savour of water with the mother's[75] milk. The related Brāhmaṇa (*TS,* 5.6.2), while commenting on the formulae, declare that,[76] the waters are ambrosia, therefore they sprinkle with water, him, who has fainted — (Cf. Bhaṭṭa Bhāskara here, — *avatāntam mūrchitam).*

In the *Tānūnaptra* offerings (in Soma sacrifice) the *ghee* and ladle come near the Soma, placed on *Āsandī,* near *Āhavanīya* fire place. Soma becomes afraid of them, for gods once made the *ghee* a weapon and ladle arms and had struck him. The *Ṛtviks* sprinkle the frightened *soma* with waters and make him swell. *Mait S*[77] here remarks that — 'all sprinkle him with water who has fainted'.

For preparation of *ukhā* pot (of clay), one has to dig the earth. In digging he acts harshly on earth. He therefore pours water on the pit and says[78] — 'the waters are for appeasing' — verily with waters be appeased, thus he calms her pains.

In a similar context *Mait S*[79] states that 'the waters are tranquilizer for the disturbed'.

Waters cause the plants to grow. *TS* states[80] — 'where there are waters, the plants take root (and where plants take root, cattle find support through them)'.

If the drops of milk fall down on earth, while milking a cow, one should pour water over the drops — for, as *Mait S*[81] states — waters avert pain, they are restoration/cure, they are medicine. Wherever the waters fall on earth, the excellent plants grow abundantly.

Impressed by the unique characteristics of water, Sāyaṇa, commenting on *RV*, [82] I.161.9 states — 'there exists no better element[83] other than water which is more benificent to the living beings. Hence waters are supreme'.

In the context of placing *Nakṣatreṣṭakās* in *Agniciti*, *TS*[84] and *Mait S* prescribe — 'waters are the deities, which preside over *Pūrvāṣāḍhā* constellation; and *Viśvedevāḥ* over *Uttarāṣāḍhā*'. *Mait S*[85] further states that waters themselves are *Viśvedevāḥ*.

Varuṇa[86] is also regarded to be a deity presiding over waters, and is associated with the *śatabhiṣak*[87] constellation. Here the name *śatabhiṣak* is self-explanatory.

Indra,[88] desired to be sturdy and steady. He offered a *puroḍāśa* to (i) Varuṇa, (ii) the constellation *śatabhiṣaj*, and (iii) *bhiṣaj*. He became sturdy and steady. Thus Varuṇa, with the divinity and waters, is related to medicine and cures; even in ritualistic performances.

Every Soma-sacrifice concludes with *Avabhṛtha iṣṭi*, in which a cake is offered to Varuṇa. All the offerings in this *iṣṭi* are offered in waters, because according to *TS*,[89] Varuṇa dwells in waters. In this *iṣṭi* the sacrificer beholds the waters and murmurs a verse, meaning — "O Varuṇa, the ruler, you possess hundreds[90] or thousands of medicines." According to *ŚBr*, the *Avabhṛtha* bath is a whirlpool[91] in the waters and that indeed is either Varuṇa's son or brother. That whirlpool in water is praised in the *Avabhṛtha*, with the verses prominently addressed to waters.[92]

In a Soma-sacrifice *Vasatīvarī* waters are drawn from a flowing stream and not from a stagnant pool. *TS* says that the stagnant waters are seized by Varuṇa.[93] The flowing waters are therefore pure, the stagnant impure. Thus what is covered is also seized by Varuṇa.

A dreadful drop is also caused by the wrath of Varuṇa. A[94] sacrifice is offered to him for atonement.

Thus the two aspects of Varuṇa — the cosmic ruler[95] and a deity presiding over waters are interrelated with each other, due to their medicinal and curing qualities. The wrath of Varuṇa also works through (impure) waters.

Tejas

Out of five *bhūtas Tejas* may be regarded as a dominating *bhūta. Tejas,* the broader aspect of *Agni* is always seen rising from its physical, i.e., material state to divine height and from the divine height to the metaphysical **light**, which is its essential characteristic.

All the *Gṛhya Saṁskāras,* from conception to cremation, and all the *śrauta* rites beginning from *Agnyādhāna* to *Antyeṣṭi* are performed in constant association with *Agni,* which is never missed.

In the rite of *Agnyādhāna,* the Fire is churned out, from the lower and upper enkindling logs called *araṇīs,* representing Urvaśī and Purūravas, the female and male forms. According to Vedic tradition, the seer Atharvan was held responsible for inventing the engendering of fire by the device of churning. All further sacrifices are performed with libations offered on this fire.

TS prescribes a cake (*puroḍāśa*) baked on twelve potsherds to be offered to Vaiśvānara.[96] Yāska states that the *Agni* in mid-region and that in heaven is named as Vaiśvānara, and *Agni* on the earth is Vaiśvānara, which is born of the upper two fires.[97] The fire of lightning, i.e., *vaidyuta* and the *Agni* of *Āditya,* the sun, are the fires of mid-region and heaven — respectively. These *Agnis* appear to be physical, but are deified, since the libation is offered to a deity Vaiśvānara *Agni,* born of upper two *Agnis,* who are also divine. According to Yāska, there are only three divinities. viz, (i) *Agni* — whose sphere is earth, (ii) *Vāyu* or Indra, whose sphere is mid-region, and (iii) *Sūrya* — whose sphere is heaven. It means that *Vāyu* or Indra is regarded by him, as a form creating *Agni* in mid-region. Yāska therefore repeatedly warns that one should not think that there is only one fire which is on the earth. There are fires in upper two regions[98] also.

In the *Kārīriṣṭi,* performed for rains; a cake is offered to *Agni, Maruts* and *Sūrya;* (the deities of three regions) because, as *TS* states — *Agni* thence causes the rains to arise, the *Maruts* lead it out when produced, when yonder Sun moves low with his rays, then it rains.[99]

This view is corroborated by *TĀ* which describes that — *Agni*[100] (on earth) is a former form, *Āditya* — the Sun is a latter form; water in mid-region is a compound and the lightning is the uniting force.

In the mid-region, *Agni* assumes the speed of wind. This is described in *ṚV.*[101]

While commenting on this verse, Sāyaṇa explains that this fire is *Vaidyuta*. He further states, only *Agni* knows how to expel waters from the clouds.[102] The three sacrificial fires viz. *Dakṣina, Gārhapatya* and *Āhavanīya*, therefore represent the three regions.[103]

In daily Agnihotra, therefore, a libation is offered to *Agni* in the evening and to *Sūrya* in the morning.[104] Occasionally in *Parjanyeṣṭi*, it is offered to the deity of mid-region.

ṚV, X 88.6 states[105] — the head of all, i.e., Sun becomes *Agni* during night, then at the rising, *Agni* is born as a Sun.

TBr. also concurs with this view when it states that *Agni*[106] enters in sun in the morning and the sun into *Agni* in the evening. Thus the *Agni* on earth and the sun in the third region are identified with each other.

In Vedic ritual tradition, *Agniciti* is an important rite, which is generally augmented to Soma-sacrifices, wherein *Agni* is identified with Rudra, having two aspects, viz. benevolent and malevolent.[107]

Prayāja and *Anūyāja* oblations in *iṣṭi*, are offered to different forms of *Agni*. In *Paśu* sacrifice, the *Yājyā* verses, termed as *Āprīs*, are utilised in praise of the various forms of *Agni*. Thus *Agni* is deified in various forms.[108]

Now, while leaving his residence on journey, the sacrificer — the *yajamāna* requests *Agni* to exchange their names, until he returns, with the words[109] — 'the name that first, O all knower (*Agni*), my father and mother bestowed upon me aforetime — do thou bear it, until I return. O *Agni*, may I bear thy name. My name and thine — O *Jātavedas*, which like men changing garments, we bear, let us exchange'.

Sacrificer's this prayer brings about his heart-felt feelings towards *Agni*. To him, *Agni* is not only a physical element but something beyond that, with whom he can communicate and establish with him, some sort of personal relations, nay identify his soul with *Agni*.

The Sacrificer wishing to pile an altar, first symbolically deposits his sacrificial fire in his own person with the words — 'In me I first take *Agni* — the immortal *Agni*, who has entered into mortals, within the hearts, may we enclose him in our *Ātman*. May he not abandon us and go afar'.[110]

After having thus deposited *Agni* in himself the sacrificer proceeds for piling the *Agniciti*. *ŚBr.* here remarks 'being[111] about to construct fire altar, he takes *Agni*, in his own self. . . . when he constructs *Agniciti* after taking *Agni* into his ownself, he causes *Agni* to be born from *Agni*, the immortal from immortal'.

ŚBr., X.1.4.14 puts a question — what is done here in constructing an *Agniciti*, whereby the sacrificer wins over the re-birth? The answer is — well, he who builds an altar, becomes *Agni* . . . . *Agni* indeed is immortal, etc.[112]

Even with two *Agnihotra* offerings, to the two *Jyotis* — viz. *Agni* and *Sūrya*, the sacrificer is said to be relieved of cycles of births. This is promised by *ŚBr*, 2.3.3.9 — which says — 'This is the release from death in the *Agnihotra* and verily he who knows that release from death in the *Agnihotra* is freed from death.[113]

ṚV[114] therefore rightly states that this flame is immortal in mortals.

Agni is therefore concerned here in the form of the Vedāntic immortal *Ātman*. That is why *Agni* at places is referred to as *Prajāpati*[115] or *Brahman*.

Śāṅkhāyana Br. states — 'the *Puruṣa*, made known in *Āditya* is *Indra*. He is *Prajāpati*. He is *Brahman*.[116]

The epithets of *Agni* like *Jātavedas* — meaning all knower, or *kavikratuḥ* — having the intuition of a prophet — also aim at praising *Agni* in its Divine or Omniscient form.

Sun is the presiding deity of *svaḥ*; the yonder world, the Vedic heaven. In fact, the *sūrya* is the *ātmā* of moving and stable world.[117] It is an inexhaustible source of energy. According to *ṚV*, the sun is a perpetual flame.[118]

While commenting on the formula[119] of *TS*, I.6.6, both the commentators viz., Bhaṭṭa Bhāskara[120] and Sāyaṇa[121] unanimously describe the inner *Puruṣa* in *sūrya* as an entrance to salvation.

Ṛgveda aims to point out that *Agni* is indicative of immortality — when it enjoins — 'Make[122] the altar ready, set the *Agni* in blaze, let we two (i.e., the sacrificer and wife) perform a sacrifice, which is indicative of immortality'.

The altar here appears to be an inner one where Divine force is to be kept ablaze. It is there the sacrifice of awakening of the consciousness to immortality is performed.

Agni in Vedic tradition is not only a material physical element. It transcends its physical character. Even its physical state appears to be controlled by its metaphysical essential.

Vāyu[123]

Air or wind plays an important role in the environment. Accordingly, the Vedic *Ṛṣis* recognised air as a vital cosmic constituent and included it in five elements.[124] *Vāyu* is referred to as a deity presiding over the mid-region.[125]

The concept of Vedic sacrifice is supposed to be an outcome of cosmological reflections of *Ṛṣis.* It is maintained that *Adhvaryu* sets the sacrifice in motion with *Vāta* and finally he bestows it again in *Vāta.*[126]

The *Vāta*-offerings are enjoined at least in *Pravargya,*[127] *Agniciti*[128] and *Kārīrī iṣṭi.*[129]

In *Pravargya Vāyu* is referred to as the soul of sacrifice.[130] In the formulae for *vāta*-offerings in *Agniciti, vāta* is addressed as *Śaṁbhu*[131] and *Mayobhū,* i.e., bringing welfare and happiness.

The formulae and *Brāhmaṇa* for *Vāta*-offerings in *kārīrī* and placing *vāyavyā* brick in *Agniciti* reveal the rain bringing character of *vāyu.*[132]

Incidentaly it may be pointed out that Durgācārya on *Nirukta,* X.1 divided *Vāta* in four categories of which the last brings the rains.[133]

Thus the role of wind in bringing rains was observed by Vedic *Ṛṣis.* It is not at all necessary to dilate on the point of necessity of rains for the livelihood of all living organisms on earth.

That the pure, unpolluted air is a source of health, happiness and consequently of long life, was also observed by the Vedic *Ṛṣis.* Two small *Ṛgvedic sūktas;* X. 188[134] and X. 137,[135] may be regarded important from this point of view.

In *ṚV,* X.186, *Vāta* is referred to as causing welfare and happiness. The *Ṛṣi* is also emotional to this element that he addresses *Vāta* as his father, brother and friend. *Vāta* is a store-house of ambrosia for him. He prays for it and requests it to blow with its medicinal qualities.

ṚV, X.137 divides the wind into two categories, the one bringing vigour and the other blowing away the evil. Since *vāta* is the Universal medicine, he prays the wind to blow with its medicinal qualities.

Further *TS* and *Maitt S* positively state that whatever smells ill, is spread out in a windy place, for *Vāyu* is its purifier.[136] This is seen in the context of drawing *aindravāyava-graha* of Soma. The myth[137] is as follows :

> The gods wished to slay Soma. They could not kill him, because *Vāyu* the breath had pervaded the Soma from within. The gods directed *vāyu* to leave Soma and take to the resort of the gods. *Vāyu* did so. The gods then killed Soma. The Soma so killed became foul. The gods were disgusted due to the foul smell. *Vāyu* then said — I shall make him palatable and delicious. *Vāyu* entered Soma from within. He thus made Soma delicious. Hence they spread the fermentation Soma in a windy place .... Sāyaṇa commenting on this passage is more explicit.

On account of this purifying nature, *Vāyu*, i.e., wind appears to be identified with *Yajña*—the sacrifice. This is the view of *Ch. Up.*[138] The wind acquires this quality of purifying the ill-smelled things through its ever-moving and constantly active character.[139]

Any material over which the wind does not blow belongs to Varuṇa.[140] Varuṇa is a deity which covers and consequently does not allow fresh air to enter.

A knot of bag containing paddy for *Puroḍāśa* is therefore loosened with a formula[141] — *Uru-vātāya* (*TS*, 1.1.4) — 'be widely open to wind'. *TBr.* further states — 'one who enters a covered or enclosed place, enters darkness'.[142] This suggests that the wind purifies the material which has become foul due to storage.

Thus according to vedic *Ṛṣis*, Air inherits the intrinsic quality of neutralising pollution.

Prāṇa the breath may be regarded as one of the vital forms of air.

[143]Once, the breath and sense-organs, disputed about their superiority. They went to *Brahma* who said — one of you is the most excellent, after whose departure the body is thought to be worse off. *Vāk, Cakṣuḥ, Śrotram* and even *Manas* departed from the body by turn. Still the body persisted. Then as the breath was about to depart, even as a mighty horse of Sindu land, might pull up the pegs to which his feet are tied, even so did it pull out those organs together. They said, "Venerable Sir, do not you go out. We shall not be able to live without you". They confirmed that their firm basis lies in *Prāṇa*,[144] i.e., vital Air.

This allegorical discourse appears in *Bṛ. Up.*, 6.17.13 and also in *Ch. Up.*, 5.1.1.15.

Bṛ. Up., 3.7.2[145] corroborates this view when it states that — By air, as by thread, this world, the other world, and all beings are held together. . . therefore, when a person dies, his limbs are loosened. For they were held together by air before his death.

Thus the Vedic *Ṛṣis* were so fully aware of the medicinal qualities and the intrinsic essentiality of this environmental element, that they eulogized it to the extent that it forms an integral part of Prajāpati.[146]

They also prayed that the wind[147] should blow sweet for one who wishes to offer sacrifice.

Ākāśa

While delineating *pṛthivī*, I have already portrayed few characteristics of *dyauḥ*

— i.e., sky. The word *loka* (as stated earlier) originally means the space and secondarily the worlds. The word *Ākāśa* denotes space.

In *Agnciti* the *lokaṁpr̥ṇā* the space-filler-bricks — are placed on the fire altar — with the formula[148] 'fill the space, fill the holes' etc.

[149]The *cātvāla,* i. e., a pit, dug in earth, towards the north-east of the *vedī,* in sacrifices is identified with *Ākāśa* by *JU,* 1.5.5.

Sadasya is regarded as a seventeenth *R̥tvij* in the Soma-sacrifices and is related to *Ākāśa* by *Ṣaḍviṁśa Br.*

Thus *Ākāśa,* according to *Ṣaḍ Br.* is placed in the midst of *bhūtas.* Therefore, they give a seat to *sadasya* in the midst of *sadas-paṇḍāl.*[150]

A sacrificer in all the three pressings of Soma-sacrifice seeks permission of the priests for partaking Soma from *camasas.*

While seeking permission from *Sadasya*-priest he identifies him with *Ākāśa* in the morning pressing, with the *Ākāśa* in eye in the midday pressing and with *Ākāśa* in the body, in the third pressing.[151]

Sacrificer, while requesting the priests to accord sanction to the sacrificial ground (*devayajñam*), identifies *sadasya* with *Ākāśa.*[152]

When the sacrificer offers (*dakṣiṇā*) to *Sadasya,* he should say — 'O *sadasya,* I offer myself (*ātmānam*) to you'. Verily *Ākāśa* is *ātmā,* he therefore gives *Ākāśa* to *Sadasya.* As long as *Ākāśa* does not decrease, his gifts also do not wane. This is stated by *Jbr.*[153]

Thus the identification of *sadasya* and the gift, with *Ākāśa* points out the unwaning characteristic of widely spread *Ākāśa.*

In the context of *Vaiśvānara-vidyā,* as propounded in *ŚBr,* Mahāśāla Jābāla identifies *Vaiśvānara*[154] with *Ākāśa* which is plenteous. Sāyaṇa, commenting on this passage states — *bahutvam ākāśasya, sarvagatatvāt.* Thus plenteousness, the special characteristic of *Ākāśa,* has been noted here by *ŚBr.*

Further *JBr.* identifies *Ākāśa* with *puruṣa*[155] and finally *Puruṣa* with *Prajāpati.*

It is well-known that *khaṁ,* i.e., *Ākāśa,* according to the *Upaniṣads,* at a particular stage of *upāsanā,* is identified with *Brahman.*[156]

Thus, all the *bhūtas* in ritual tradition are not regarded only as material or physical elements, they really transcend their physical character. They are deified and raised to the status of *Prajāpati* or *Brahman.*

This is corroborated by the *Upaniṣads* when they state that all the *bhūtas* are controlled by their metaphysical essential character.

Kena Up.[157] describes that *vāyu* could not blow and *Agni* could not burn, even a blade of grass, when the immortal element withdrew from them. Thus the *bhūtas* according to this *Upaniṣad* are activated only because the immortal element pervades them. It means that matter, the *Prakṛti,* can work only if an essential element has entered into it.

Yājñavalkya[158] in his *Bṛhadāraṇyaka Up.* has further elaborated this point, when he states that the *Ātman* dwells in the elements, is within them, whom the elements do not know, whose body is elements, who controls them from within. He is the inner controller, the immortal.

This may explain why electrons, protons and neutrons in atoms of the so-called physical elements move and rotate, and thereby show the characteristic of the sentient.

Notes

1. इमानि च पञ्च महाभूतानि पृथिवी वायुः आकाश आपो ज्योतींषि (*Ait. Up.* 3.3)।
2. तस्माद्वा एतस्मादात्मनः आकाशः संभूतः आकाशाद् वायुः। वायोरग्निः। अग्नेरापः। अद्भ्यः पृथिवी (*Tait. Up.*, 2.1)।
3. आकाशो ह वा एष देवो वायुरग्निरापः पृथिवी . . .। पृथिवी च पृथिवीमात्रा च। आपश्चापोमात्रा च। तेजश्च तेजोमात्रा च। वायुश्च वायुमात्रा च। आकाशश्चाकाशमात्रा च (*Pr. Up.*, 2.2; also 4.8.)।
4. एषां भूतानां पृथिवी रसः। पृथिव्या आपो रसः (*Ch. Up.*, 1.1.2)।
5. मूलप्रकृतिरविकृतिर्महदाद्याः प्रकृति-विकृतयः सप्त। षोडशकस्तु विकारः न प्रकृतिर्न विकृतिः पुरुषः (*Sāṅkā-3*)।
6 मनुर्वा अग्रे यज्ञेनेजे तदनुकृत्य इमाः प्रजाः यजन्ते; (*S. Br.*,1.5.1.7)।

   एष वै प्रत्यक्षं यज्ञः यत्प्रजापतिः (*Ś.Br.*, 4.3.4.3)।

   अथैतमात्मनः प्रतिमामसृजत यद् यज्ञं तस्मादाहुः प्रजापतिर्यज्ञ इति आत्मनो ह्येतं प्रतिमामसृजत (*S. Br.*, 1.1.8.3)।
7. एष वा ऋतस्य पन्थाः यद् यज्ञः (*Mait. S.*, 4.8.2)। यो वै यज्ञियो मेध्यः स ऋतस्य पन्थाः (*KS.*)। Also यज्ञो वा ऋतस्य योनिः (*Ś.Br.*, 1.3.4.16)।
8. उ यज्ञाय चक्रथुरु लोकम् (*Ṛ͏V.* I.93.6)।अस्मिन् भयस्थे कृणुतमु लोकम् (II.30.6)। उ लोकमु द्वे उप जामिमीयतुः (III.2.9.)।
9. भूर्भुवः स्वः इति पुरस्ताद् होतोः वदेत्। एतद्वै ब्रह्म एतत् सत्यम् एतदृतं न वा एतस्मादृते यज्ञोऽस्ति तस्मादेवं वदितव्यम्।
10. आपो वा इदमग्रे सलिलमासीत् . . . etc. (*T.Br.*, 1.1.3)। या अर्णवेऽधि सलिलमग्र आसीत्। Cf., (*AV.*, 12.1.8) यावद्वै वराहस्य चषालं तावतीयमग्र आसीत् etc. (Also *Mait S.* 1.6.3)।
11. वेदिमाहुः परमन्तं पृथिव्याः यज्ञमाहुः भुवनस्य नाभिम् (*TS*, 7.4.18)। यस्यां वेदिं परिगृह्णन्ति भूम्यां . . . etc. (Cf. *AV.*, 12. 1.13)। एतावती वा इयं पृथिवी यावती वेदिः (Cf. also *Mait S*, 3.8.6)। सर्वा वा इयं पृथिवी वेदिः (*MaitS.*, 3.8.3)। पृथिवा वेदिः (*TS*, 2.6.5)।

12. वेदिमति दीक्षते . . . यदिमां व्यकल्पयन् . . . अथो देवक्षेत्रमेव प्रावस्यति . . . (*Mait S.*, 3.6.1.)।

13. इयं वै स्वयमातृण्णा इमामेवोपधत्ते (*TS*, 5.2.8.)।

14. प्रजापतिस्त्वा सादयतु पृथिव्याः पृष्ठे व्यचस्वतीं प्रयस्वतीं प्रथोऽसि पृथिव्यसि भूरसि भूमिरसि अदितिरसि विश्वधाया विश्वस्य भुवनस्य धर्त्री पृथिवीं यच्छ पृथिवीं दृंह etc. (*TS*, 4.2.9.)।

15. प्रजापतिरग्निमचिकीषत तं पृथिव्यब्रवीत् न मय्यग्निं चेष्यसेऽति मा धक्ष्यति सा त्वाऽतिदह्यमाना विधविष्ये स पापीयान् भविष्यसीति सोऽब्रवीत् तथा वा अहं करिष्यामि यथा त्वा नातिधक्ष्यतीति स इमामभ्यमृशत् प्रजापतिस्त्वा सादयतु तया देवतयाऽङ्गिरस्वद् ध्रुव सीदेतीमामेवेष्टकां कृत्वोपाधत्तानतिदाहाय . . . (*TS*, 5.5.2.)।

16. आपो वरुणस्य पत्नय आसन् ता अग्निभ्यध्यायत् ताः समभवत् तस्य रेतः पराऽपतत् तदियमभवद् यद् द्वितीयं परापतत् तदसावभवदियं वै विराऽसौ स्वराड् यद् विराजावुपदधातीमे एवोपधत्ते . . . (*TS*, 5.4.4.)।

17. उपहूता पृथिवी माता। उप मां माता पृथिवी ह्वयताम् (*Kāt ŚS*, 3.4.17; *VS*, 2.10, *T Br.*, 3.7.6.)।

18. देवा वै पृश्निमदुह्रन्। तस्या एते स्तना (स्थालयः) आसन्। इयं वै पृश्निः . . . यजमान इमां दुहे (*T Br*, 1.4.1.; *S Br*, 1.8.3.15)। इयं वै वशा पृश्निः, इयं वै वशा पृश्निः . . . तेनेयं वशा पृश्निः Also Cf. (*Ś Br.*, 5.1.3.3)।

19. इडा देवहूः . . . पृथिवी मातर्मा मा हिंसीः . . . (*TS*, 3.3.2.)।

20. सा नो भूमिर्विसृजतां माता पुत्राय मे पयः (*AV*, 12.1.10)। माता भूमिः पुत्रो अहं पृथिव्याः (*AV*, 12.1.12.)।

21. यस्ते गन्धः पृथिवी संबभूव . . . तेन मां सुरभिं कृणु etc. (*AV*, 12.1.23-26.)।

22. सत्यं बृहदित्याग्रहायण्याम् (*Kauśika Sūtra*, 24.24.)।

23. ग्रामपत्तनादि रक्षार्थमनेनानुवाकेन चतुरः पुरोडाशान् अश्मोत्तरान् कृत्वा . . . etc. (Sāyaṇa on *AV*, 12-1) । intro. भौमस्य दृतिकर्मणि। पुरोडाशान् अश्मोत्तरान् etc. (*Kauśika Sūtra*, 38.12.)।

24. यत्रैतद् भूमिचलो भवति तज्जुहुयात् (*Kauśika Sūtra*, 98.1.)।

25. एतं द्यावापृथिव्यमेककपालं पुरोडाशं तस्माद् द्यावापृथिव्य एककपालः पुरोडाशो भवति तस्येयमेव कपालम् एकेव हीयं तस्मात् एककपालः (*Ś. Br.*, 2.3.5.8)। द्यावापृथिवीय एककपालः आत्यस्य वा यजेत् (*Kāt. ŚS*, 4.6.5.7)।

26. द्यावापृथिव्यमेककपालम् (*TS.*, 1.8.2.)। अथ द्यावापृथिव्य एककपालः पुरोडाशो भवति (*Ś.Br.*, 2.5.1.17), (Cf. *Mait S*, 1.10.1.)।

27. स यदा संग्रामं जयेत् . . . द्यावापृथिवीयं द्विकपालम् (*Mait S*, 2.1.3)। द्यावापृथिव्यामालभेत कृषमाणः प्रतिष्ठाकामः (*TS*. 3.4.2)। द्यावापृथिव्यां धेनुमालभेत ज्योगपरुद्धः (*TS*, 2.1.4. etc.)।

28. द्यावापृथिवी सहास्ताम् . . ., (*T.Br.*, 1.1.3) Also, (*TS*, 5.2.3.)।

29. ते वियती (i.e., while separating) अब्रूताम्। अस्त्वेव नौ सह यज्ञियमिति। यदमुष्या यज्ञियमासीत् तदस्यामदधात्। त ऊषा अभवन् यदस्या यज्ञियमासीत् तदमुष्यामदधात्। तददश्चन्द्रमसि कृष्णम्। ऊषान्निवपन्नदो ध्यायेत्। द्यावापृथिव्योरेव यज्ञियेऽग्निमाधत्ते (*T.Br.*, 1.13)।

30. इयं वै वल्मीकवपा (*Ś. Br.*, 6.3.3.5)।

31. द्यौ पितः पृथिवी मातरध्रुक् अग्ने भ्रातर्वसवो मृडता नः . . . etc. (*Mait S*, 4.14.11; *T.Br.*, 2.8.6)। द्यौः पिता पृथिवी माता प्रजापतिर्बन्धुः . . . etc. (*T.Br.*, 3.7.5.)।

32. इयं वै चित्रा यद्वा अस्यां विश्वं भूतमधि प्रजायते तेनेयं चित्रा (*TS*, 2.4.6.)।

33. इयं वै होता असौ अध्वर्युः (*TS*, 3.2.9.)।

34. सेयं वामभृत्। प्राणा वै वामं यद्धि किंच प्राणीयं तत्सर्वं बिभर्ति तेनेयं वामभृत् (*Ś. Br.*, 7.4.2.35)।

35. इयं वै वारवन्तीयम् इयं प्रतिष्ठा (*J Br.*, 3.155)।

36. द्यौर्हिंकार: आदित्य: प्रस्ताव: अन्तरिक्षमुद्गीथ: अग्नि: प्रतिहार: पृथिवी निधनम् (*Ch. Up.*, 2.2.2)।

37. इयं वै स्वयमातृण्णा इमामेवोपधत्ते (*TS*, 5.2.8.)।

38. अयं वै लोक: प्रात:सवनम् (*Ś.Br.* 12.8.2.8)।

39. अयं वै लोको दक्षिणं हविर्धानम् (*Śāṅkhāyana, Br.*, 9.4.)।

40. इयं वाव रथन्तरम् असौ बृहत् (*TS.*, 3.1.7)।अयं वै लोको रथन्तरं छन्द: (*Ś Br.* 8.5.2.5.; Cf. *Ait Br.* 8.2.)।

41. इयं वाव प्रथमा चिति: (*TS*, 5.6.10.2 Also *Mait S.*, 3.3.3)।

42. अयम् एव लोक: प्रायणीय: असौ उदयनीय: (*T Br.*, 3.372)।

43. इयं वै प्रजापति: (*Mait.S.*, 3.1.3 Also *TS*, 5.1.2)।

44. आविन्ना देव्यदितिर्विश्वरूपीत्याह। इयं वै देव्यदितिर्विश्वरूपी (*T Br.*, 1.7.6.)। उदस्थाद्देव्यदितिरिति। इयं वै देव्यदिति: etc. (*T Br*, 1.4.3.)।

45. आदित्यं चरुं निर्वपेत् संग्राममुपप्रयास्यन् इयं वा अदिति: . . . (*TS*, 2.2.6.)।

46. अदितिर्न उरुष्यतु . . .। महीमूषु मातरं सुव्रतानाम् ऋतस्य पत्नीम् . . .। सुत्रामाणं पृथिवीं द्याम् . . .। इमां सु नावमारुहम् etc. (*TS*, 1.5.11)।

47. सैतमदित्यै चरुं निरवपत् . . . अदित्यै स्वाहा पुनर्वसुभ्यां स्वाहा . . . etc. (*T.Br.*, 3.1.4.)।

48. विश्वस्य भर्त्री जगत: प्रतिष्ठा . . . (*T.Br.*, 3.1.1.)।

49. अयनशीला वा अदिति: देवी पृथिवी (Bhaṭṭa Bhāskara on *T.Br.*, 3.1.1)।

50. सर्पराज्ञिया ऋग्भि: स्तुवन्ति . . . इयं वै सर्पतो राज्ञी यद्वा अस्यां किं चार्चन्ति यदानृचुस्तेनेयं सर्पराज्ञी . . . (*TS*, 3.1)।

51. इयं पृथिवी सर्पतो गतिमत: सर्पस्य राज्ञी स्वामिनी . . . (Bhaṭṭa Bhāskāra on *TS*, 7.3.1)। इयमेव भूमि: सर्पत: संचारं कुर्वत: सर्वस्य प्राणिनो राज्ञी (vide also Sāyaṇa)।

52. अयं वै लोको गार्हपत्य: (*Ś Br.*, 7.1.1.6)। अयं वै लोको गार्हपत्य: परिमण्डल उ वा अयं लोक: (*Ś Br.*, 7.1.1.37)।

53. पृथिव्यां या देवता सैषा पुरुषस्यापानमवष्टभ्य . . . (*Praśna Up.*, 3.12)। पृथिव्यामभिमानिनी या देवता प्रसिद्धा सैषा पुरुषस्यापानम् अपानवृत्तिम् अवष्टभ्य आकृष्य वशीकृत्य अध एवापकर्षणेन अनुग्रहं कुर्वती वर्तत इत्यर्थ:। अन्यथा हि शरीरं गुरुत्वात् पतेत् सावकाशे वोद्गच्छेत् (*Śāṅkara bhāṣya*)।

54. पृथिव्या ओषधय: ओषधीभ्योऽन्नम् (*TĀ*, 8.1.1)।

55. पृथिवी शान्ति: सौषधीभि: शान्ति: (*Mait S*, 4.9.27)।

56. विषेण वै तां समामोषधयो अक्ता भवन्ति यां समां महादेव: पशून् हन्ति। यच्छा३ राजन्नोषधीभ्य इत्याह ओषधीरेवास्मै स्वदयति। उभय्योऽस्मै स्वदिता: पच्यन्तेऽकृष्टपच्याश्च कृष्टपच्याश्च (*Tāṇḍya Br.*, 6.9.9)।

57. तम आसीत् तमसा गूळ्हमग्रेऽप्रकेतं सलिलं सर्वमा: इदम् . . . (*ṚV*, 10.129.3)।

58. आपो वा इदमग्रे सलिलमासीत् (*T Br.*, 1.1.3)।

59. यावद्वै प्राणेष्वापो भवन्ति तावद्वाचा वदति . . . (*Ś Br.*, 5.3.5.16)।

60. आप उन्दन्तु जीवसे दीर्घायुत्वाय वर्चसे (*TS*, 1.2.1.1.)।

61. अग्निः पूर्वरूपम् आदित्य उत्तररूपम् आपः संधिः वैद्युत संधानम् (*TĀ*, 7.3.2)।

62. त्रयीर्वा आपो दिव्याः पार्थिवाः समुद्रियाः (*Mait S.*, 3.6.3.)। या दिव्या आपः पयसा संबभूवुः। या अन्तरिक्ष उत पार्थिवीर्याः etc. (Cf. *T.Br.*, 3.1.2)।

63. अप्स्वन्तरमृतमप्सु भेषजम् . . .। अप्सु मे सोमोऽब्रवीदन्तर्विश्वानि भेषजा। अग्निं च विश्वशंभुवम् आपश्च विश्वभेषजीः। अपो देवीरूपह्वये यत्र गावः पिबन्ति नः। सिन्धुभ्यः कर्त्वं हविः . . . etc. (*ṚV.*, 1.23.16-21)।

64. श्वात्राः पीता भवत यूयमापो अस्माकमन्तरुदरे सुशेवाः। ता अस्मभ्यम् अयक्ष्मा अनमीवा अनागसः स्वदन्तु देवीरमृता ऋतावृधः (*VS*, 4.12)।

65. सस्रुषीस्तदपसो . . . शं नो भवन्त्वप ओषधीः शिवाः (*AV*, 6.23.1-3)। हिमवतः प्रस्रवन्ति . . . . आपो ह मह्यं तद् देवीर्ददन् हृद्योतभेषजम्। . . . दत्त नस्तस्य भेषजं . . . etc. (*AV*, 6.24.1-3.)। इदमिद वा उ भेषजम् . . . विश्वं नो अस्तु भेषजं सर्वं नो अस्तु भेषजम् etc. (*AV*, 6.57.1-3)।

66. आप इद् वा उ भेषजीरापो अमीवचातनीः। आपो विश्वस्य भेषजीः . . .। तास्त्वा मुञ्चन्तु क्षेत्रियात् . . . etc. (*AV*, 3.7.5-7)।

67. ता अपः शिवा अपोऽयक्ष्मंकरणीरपः। यथैव तृप्यते मयस्तास्त आ दत्त भेषजीः . . .; (*AV*, 19.2.5)। भिषग्भ्यो भिषक्तरा आपः . . . (*AV*, 19.2.3.)।

68. सर्वेरसा अनुप्राप्ता पानीयम् (*Nirukta*, I.16)।

69. आपो वै पवित्रम् (*KS*, 8.8)।

70. आपः प्रोक्षण्यः (Cf. *Ait. Br.*, 5.8)।

71. अङ्गिरसः सुवर्गं लोकं यन्तोऽप्सु दीक्षातपसी प्रावेशयन्नप्सु स्नाति साक्षादेव दीक्षा तपसी अवरुन्धे तीर्थे स्नाति तीर्थे हि ते तां प्रावेशयन् (*TS*, 6.1.1)।

72. आपो अस्मान् मातरः शुन्धन्तु घृतेन नो घृतप्वः पुनन्तु। विश्वमस्मत्प्रवहन्तु रिप्रमुदिदाभ्य शुचिरापूत एमि . . . etc. (*TS*, 1.2.1)।

73. अपोऽश्नाति अन्तरत एव मेध्यो भवति (*TS*, 6. 1.1.)।

74. हिरण्यवर्णाः शुचयः पावकाः . . . etc. (*TS*, 5.6.1. beginning from)।

75. यो वः शिवतमो रसः तस्य भाजयतेह नः। उशतीरिव मातरः। . . . etc. (*TS.*, 5.6.1.)

76. अमृतं वा आपः (*TS*, 5.6.2.)। तस्माद‌द्भिरवतान्तमभिषिञ्चन्ति। Cf. also अद्भिः तान्तमभिषिञ्चन्ति (*KS*, 2.5.6)।

77. सर्वे ऋत्विज आप्याययन्ति सर्वे तान्तं भिषज्यन्ति (*Mait, S.*, 3.8.2)।

78. क्रूरमिव वा एतत् करोति यत् खनति अप उपसृजति आपो वै शान्ताः शान्ताभिरेवास्यै शुचं शमयति (*TS*, 5.1.5)।

79. आपो वा अशान्तस्य शमयित्रिकाः (*Mait, S.*, 3.1.6)।

80. यत्र वा आप उपगच्छन्ति तदोषधयः प्रतितिष्ठन्ति। ओषधीः प्रतितिष्ठन्तीः पशवोऽनुप्रतितिष्ठन्ति . . etc. (*TS*, 5.1.3)। अद्भ्यो वा अन्नं जायते (Cf Also *TĀ.*, 1.2.4.4)। आपो वा ओषधयः (*Mait S*, 2.5.4)।

81. यत्र स्कन्देत् तदपो निनयेत् आपो वै शान्तिरापो निष्कृतिः आपो भेषजा यत्र वा एता अस्या उपयन्ति तत् प्रशस्ततरा ओषधयो जायन्ते बंहीयसीः . . . (*Mait S.*, 1.8.3)।

82. आपो भूयिष्ठा इत्येको अब्रवीत् अग्निः भूयिष्ठः इत्यन्यो अब्रवीत् (*ṚV*, 1.161.9)।

83. एकः त्रयाणामन्यतमः आपो भूयिष्ठाः इति अब्रवीत् नहि उदकात् प्रशस्तं लोकोपकारकं तत्त्वान्तरम् असि (Sāyaṇa)।

84. अषाढा नक्षत्रमापो देवताऽषाढा नक्षत्रं विश्वे देवा देवता; (*TS*, 4.4.10 *Mait.S.* 2.13.20)। यासामषाढा अनुयन्ति कामम् . . . (Cf. *T.Br.*, 3.1.2)।

85. आपः खलु वै विश्वे देवाः (*Mait S*, 4.5.1; 4.5.3)।

86. वारुणीः आपः (*Mait. S*, 4.3.10, 4. 4.2)। यासां राजा वरुणः (2.13.1)। एता वा प्रत्यक्षं वारुणीः यदापः (2.5.6)। आपो वै वरुणः (4.8.5)।

87. क्षत्रस्य राजा वरुणोऽधिराजः नक्षत्राणां शतभिषक् वसिष्ठः। . . . तन्नो नक्षत्रं शतभिषग्जुषाणम्। दीर्घमायुः प्रतिरद्भेषजानि etc. (*T.Br.*, 3.1.2)।

88. इन्द्रो वा अकामयत दृढोऽशिथिलः स्यामिति। स एतं वरुणाय शतभिषजे भेषजेभ्यः . . . etc. (*T.Br.*, 3.1.5)।

89. अपोऽवभृथमवैति अप्सु वै वरुणः (*TS*, 6.3.3)।

90. शतं ते राजन् भिषजः सहस्रं . . . etc. (*TS*, 1.4.45)।

91. यो ह वा अयमपावर्तः स हावभृथः स हैव वरुणस्य पुत्रो वा भ्राता वा तमेवैतत् स्तौति . . .(*Ś. Br.*, 12.9.2.3)।

92. यदापो अघ्न्या . . . सुमित्रिया न आप ओषधयः सन्तु . . . etc. (*VS*, 20.18-19)।

93. वहन्तीनां गृह्णाति या एव मेध्या यज्ञिया सदेवा आपस्तासामेव गृह्णाति . . . न स्थावराणां गृह्णीयात् वरुणगृहीता वै स्थावरा . . . etc. (*TS*, 6.4.2, Cf. *Ś. Br.*, 4.4.5.10.)।

94. यो वरुणगृहीतः स्यात्। स एतं वारुणं कृष्णम् एकशितिपादमालभेत (*TS*, 2.1.2.1)।

95. निषसाद धृतव्रतो वरुणः पस्त्यास्वा। साम्राज्याय सुक्रतुः (*MS*, 2.6. 12)।

96. अग्नये वैश्वानराय द्वादशकपाल (*TS*, 7.5.14)। आग्नेयमष्टाकपालं निर्वपेत् वैश्वानरं द्वादशकपालम् अग्निमुद्वासयिष्यन् (*TS.*, 2.2.5)। वैश्वानरं द्वादशकपालं निर्वपेत् अमावास्यां वा पौर्णमासीं वाऽतिपाद्य . . . etc. (*TS.*, 2.2.5)।

97. तत् को वैश्वानरः ? मध्यम इति आचार्याः। . . . अयमेव अग्निः वैश्वानरः इति शाकपूणिः। विश्वानरौ एते उत्तरे ज्योतिषी। वैश्वानरः अयम्। यत् ताभ्यां जायते। कथं नु अयमेताभ्यां जायते इति। यत्र वैद्युतः शरणम् अभिहन्ति यावदनुपात्तो भवति . . . अथ आदित्यात्। उदीचि प्रथम समावृत्ते आदित्ये कंसं वा मणिं वा परिमृज्य प्रतिस्वरे यत्र शुष्कगोमयम् असंस्पर्शन् धारयति तत् प्रदीप्यते। स अयमेव संपद्यते . . . etc. (*Nirukta*, VII.22-23)।

98. स न मन्येत अयमेव अग्निरिति। अपि एते उत्तरे ज्योतिषी अग्नी उच्येते . . . जातवेदसौ उच्येते विश्वानरौ . . . etc. (*Nir.*, 7.16-20)।

99. अग्नये धामच्छदे पुरोडाशमष्टाकपालं निर्वपेत् मारुतं सप्तकपालं सौर्यमेककपालम् अग्निर्वा इतो वृष्टिमुदीरयति मरुतः सृष्टां नयन्ति यदा खलु वा असावादित्यो न्यङ् रश्मिभिः पर्यावर्ततेऽथ वर्षति धामच्छदिव खलु वै भूत्वा वर्षति एता वै देवताः वृष्ट्या ईशते . . . (*TS*, 2.4.10)।

100. अग्निः पूर्वरूपम् आदित्य उत्तररूपम् आपः सन्धिः वैद्युतः सन्धानम्। इत्यधि ज्यौतिषम् (*TĀ*, 7.3.2 Vide Note 63)।

101. हिरण्यकेशो रजसो विसारे अहिः धुनिः वात इव ध्रजीयान् . . . etc. (*ṚV*, 1.79.1; *TS*, 3.1.11.4)।

102. मेघादुदकस्य निःसारणम् अग्निरेव जानाति (Sāyaṇa on *ṚV*, 1.7.92)।

103. सह वा अग्नेस्तन्वः इयमोदनपचनः अन्तरिक्षं गार्हपत्यः द्यौराहवनीयः (*KS*, 8.8)।

104. अग्निर्ज्योतिर्ज्योतिरग्निः स्वाहा इति सायम्। अग्निहोत्रं जुहोति सूर्यो ज्योतिर्ज्योतिः सूर्यः स्वाहेति प्रातः (*Ap ŚS*, 6.10.8)। तस्मादग्नये सायं हूयते सूर्याय प्रातः (*T Br.*, 2.1.2)।

105. मूर्धा भुवो भवति नक्तमग्निः ततः सूर्यो जायते प्रातरुद्यन् (*ṚV*, 10.88.6)।

106. अग्निं वावादित्यः सायं प्रविशति। उद्यन्तं वावादित्यमग्निरनुसमारोहति . . . (*T Br.*, 2.1.2)।

107. रुद्रो वा एष यदग्निः (*TS*, 4.4.3.1)। रुद्रो वा एष यदग्निस्तस्यै द्वे तनुवौ घोराऽन्या शिवाऽन्या . . . (*TS*; 5.7.3)।

108. (a) Prayājā deities in Iṣṭi — Samidhaḥ, Tanūrapāt, Iḍaḥ, Barhiḥ and Svāhā.

(b) Anuyāja deities in Iṣṭi — Devo barhiḥ, Nārāśaṁsaḥ, Agniḥ Sviṣṭakṛt.

(c) Prayāja deities in Paśu — Samidhaḥ Tanūnapāt or Nārāśaṃsa, Īḍāna, Barhiḥ, Deviḥ dvāraḥ, Uṣāsānaktā, Devyau hotārau, Tisro Devīḥ, Tvaṣṭṛ, Vanaspati and Svāhākāra. All are different forms of Agni.

109. मम नाम प्रथमं जातवेदः पिता माता च दधतुर्यदग्रे। तत्त्वं बिभृहि पुनरा मदैतोः तवाहं नाम बिभराण्यग्ने।। मम नाम तव च जातवेदो वाससी इव विवसानौ ये चरावः। आयुषे त्वं जीवसे वयं यथायथं वि परि दधावहै पुनस्ते (*TS*, 1.5.10)।

110. मयि गृह्णाम्यग्ने अग्निं . . .। यो नो अग्निः पितरो . . . मा सो अस्मां अवहाय परा गात् (*TS*, 5.7.9)।

111. आत्मन्नग्निं गृह्णीते चेष्यन्। आत्मनो वा एतमधिजनयति यादृशाद्ध जायते तादृङ्ङेव भवति . . . यदात्मन्नग्निं गृहीत्वा चिनोति तदग्नेरेवाध्यग्निं जनयत्यमृतादमृतम् . . . etc. (*Ś. Br.*, 7.4.1.1)।

112. किं तदग्नौ क्रियते येन यजमानः पुनर्मृत्युमपजयतीत्यग्निर्वा एष देवता भवति योऽग्निं चिनुतेऽमृतमु वा अग्निः (*ŚBr.*, 10.1.4.14)।

113. तदेतं मृत्युमतिमुच्यते सैषाग्निहोत्रे मृत्योरतिमुक्तिः अति ह वै पुनर्मृत्युं मुच्यते . . . etc. (*ŚBr.*, 2.3.3.9)।

114. इदं ज्योतिः अमृतं मर्त्येषु (*ṚV*, 6.9.4)।

115. अग्निर्वै प्रजापतिः (*Mait. S.*, 3.4.6)।

116. यमेतमादित्ये पुरुषं वेद्यन्ते स इन्द्रः स प्रजापतिः तद् ब्रह्म। तदत्रैव यजमानः सर्वासां देवतानां सलोकतां सायुज्यमाप्नोति (*Śāṅ, Br.*, 8.3)।

117. सूर्य आत्मा जगतस्तस्थुषश्च (*ṚV*, 1.115.1)।

118. यत्र ज्योतिः अजस्रं यस्मिन् लोके स्वर्हितम्। तस्मिन् मां धेहि पवमान अमृते लोके अक्षित . . . (*ṚV*, 9.113.7)।

119. अगन्म सुवः सुवः अगन्म (*TS*, 1.6.6)।

120. सुवः सुष्ठु अरणीयम् आदित्यान्तरपुरुषं मुक्तिस्थानम् (Bhaṭṭa Bhāskara on *TS*, 1.6.6)।

121. सुवः शब्देन मोक्षद्वारभूत आदित्यलोकः।—ततो मोक्षद्वारमादित्यलोकं गम्यास्म (Sāyaṇa on *TS*, 1.6.6)।

122. अरं कृण्वन्तु वेदिं समग्निमिन्धतां पुरः। यत्रामृतस्य चेतनं यज्ञं ते तनवावहै (*ṚV*, I.70.4)।

123. I have incorporated here the gist of my paper viz. 'Approach of Vedic Seers towards Air' — read at a seminar on environmenal awareness reflected in Sanskrit literature — *CASS*, Pune, 1991.

124. इमानि पञ्च महाभूतानि पृथिवी वायुः आकाश आप ज्योतींषि (*Ait. Up.*, 3.3.)।

125. वायुर्वा अन्तरिक्षस्याध्यक्षः (*Mait S*, 4.1.1)। अथातो मध्यस्थाना: देवताः तासां वायुः प्रथमगामी (*KS.* 30.10) etc.।

126. वाताद्यज्ञः प्रयुज्यताम् (*T.Br.*, 3.7.4)। वाते धाः (*T.S*, 1.1.3)। स त्वा अध्वर्युः स्यात् यो यतो यज्ञं प्रयुङ्क्ते तदेनं प्रतिष्ठापयति। वाताद्वा अध्वर्युर्यज्ञं प्रयुङ्क्ते यत एव प्रयुङ्क्ते तदेनं प्रतिष्ठापयति (*T.Br.*, 3.3.9)। वातात् यज्ञः प्रयुज्यताम् इत्येतरस्य अच्छिद्रकाण्डगतस्य मन्त्रस्य प्रथमं जपितत्वात्। अतः समाप्तावपि देवा गातुविदः इत्येष वायुविषयो मन्त्रो युक्तः (Sāyaṇa on *TS*, 1.1.3.)।

127. पञ्च वातनामानि व्याचष्टे समुद्राय त्वा वाताय स्वाहेति . . . (*ĀpŚ S*, XV.10.8; Cf. *TĀ*, 4.9;)। उद्धत्य वातनामान्याह (*TĀ*, 5.7.)।

128. समुद्रोऽसि नभस्वान् (*TS*, 4.7.12)। वातनामानि जुहोति (*TS*, 5.4.9)।

129. पुरोवातो वर्षञ्जिन्व (*TS*, 2.4.7)। वातनामनि जुहोति। वायुर्वै वृष्ट्या ईशे (*TS*, 2.4.9)।

130. शिरो बा एतद् यज्ञस्य यत् प्रवर्ग्यः। आत्मा वायुः (*TĀ*, 5.7.)।

131. शंभूर्मयोभूरभि मा वाहि (*TS*, 4.7.12.)।

132. मारुतमसि मरुतामोजः। अपां धारां भिन्द्धि . . . पुरो वातो वर्षन् जिन्वरावृत् स्वाहा . . . etc. (*TS*, 2.4.7)। वातनामानि जुहोति वायुर्वै वृष्ट्या ईशे . . . स एवास्मै पर्जन्यं वर्षयति (*TS*, 2.4.9.)। Cf. also यां दिशं वायुरेति तां दिशं वृष्टिरन्वेति (*Ś.Br.*, 8.2.3.5)। वायुः वृष्टिं वहति (*KS*, 19.5.)।

133. वान्ति पर्णशुषो वाताः ततः पर्णमुचो परे। ततः पर्णरुहो वाताः ततो देवः प्रवर्षति (Durga on *Nirukta*, X.1)।

134. वात आ वातु भेषजं शंभु मयोभु नो हृदे। प्र ण आयूंषि तारिषत्। उत वात पितासि नः उत भ्रातोत नः सखा। स नो जीवातवे कृधि। यददो वात ते गृहेऽमृतस्य निधिर्हितः। ततो नो देहि जीवसे (*ṚV*, X.186.1-3)।

135. द्वाविमौ वातौ वातः आ सिन्धोरा परावतः। दक्षं ते अन्य आ वातु परान्यो वातु यद् रपः। आ वात वाहि भेषजं नि वात वाहि यद् रपः। त्वं हि विश्वभेषजो देवानां दूत ईयसे (*ṚV*, X.137.2-3)।

136. यत् पूयति तत् प्रवाते विषजन्ति वायुर्हि तस्य पवयिता (*TS*, 6.4.7)। लोके द्रवाधिक्यात् पूतिगन्धोपेतं भवति। तत् शोषयितुं प्रकृष्टे वायौ विषजन्ति प्रसार्य स्थापयन्ति। अतः तादृशस्य वस्तुतः वायुः शोधयिता (Sāyaṇa on *TS*, 6.4.7)। देवा वै सोममजिघांसन् (*Mait.S*, 4.5.8)।

137. तं नाशक्नुवन् हन्तुं वायुर्ह्यस्मिन्नन्तरा आसीत् प्राणः। तं देवा अपाशासुः उप ना आवर्तस्वेति . . . ततो वै देवाः सोममघ्नन् स हतोऽपूयत तस्माद्देवा उदबीभत्सन्त स वायुरब्रवीत् अहं व एतं सोमं स्वदयिष्यामि . . . तं वायुर्मध्यतो व्यवाट् तमस्वदयत् . . . तस्मादु शुक्तं प्रवाते विषजन्ति।

138. एष वै यज्ञो योऽयं पवते एष ह यन्निदं सर्वं पुनाति (*Ch. Up.*, 4.16.1.)।

139. एष ह यन् गच्छन् चलन् सर्वं जगत् पुनाति पावयति शोधयति। न हि अचलतः शुद्धिरस्ति। दोषनिरसनं चलतो दृष्टं न स्थिरस्य (Śaṅkarācārya on above)।

140. यत् वै किं च वातो नाभिवाति तत्सर्वं वरुणदेवत्यम् (*T. Br.*, 3.2.4.)।

141. उरु वातायेति परीणाहमपच्छाद्य (*Āp ŚS*, 1.17.9)। वायुप्रवेशार्थं विस्तीर्णं भव (Sāyaṇa on *TS.*, 1.1.4.)।

142. तमसीव वा एषोऽन्तश्चरति यः परीणहि (*T. Br.*, 3.2.4.)।

143. ते ह प्राणा अहं श्रेयसे विवदमाना ब्रह्म जग्मुः। तद्धोचुः को नो वसिष्ठ इति। तद्धोवाच यस्मिन् व उत्क्रान्ते इदं शरीरं पापीयो मन्यते स वो वसिष्ठ इति . . . अथ ह प्राण उत्क्रमिष्यन् यथा महासुहयः सैन्धवः पड्वीशशङ्कून् संवृहेत् एवं ह इमान् प्राणान् संववर्ह। ते होचुः मा भगव उत्क्रमीः। न वै शक्ष्यामः त्वदृते जीवितुमिति (*Br. Up.*, 6.1.7-13, Cf. also *Ch Up.*, 5.1.1-15.)।

144. वायुर्वै गौतम तत्सूत्रम्। वायुना वै गौतम सूत्रेणायं च लोकः परश्च लोकः सर्वाणि च भूतानि सदृब्धानि भवन्ति . . .। तस्माद्वै गौतम पुरुषं प्रेतमाहुः व्यस्रंसिषतास्याङ्गानीति (*Br. Up.*, 3.7.2)। Cf. also वायुर्वाव संवर्गः etc.

(*Ch.Up.* 4.2.1-3.)।

145. अर्धं ह प्रजापतेर्वायुः अर्धं प्रजापतिः (*Ś Br*, 6.2.2.11.)।

146. मधु वाता ऋतायते . . . (*Ṛ̣V*, 1. 90.6.)।

147. लोकं पृण छिद्रं पृण (*TS*, 4.2.4.)।

148. तत् यत् चात्वालं खातं तत् संप्रति स दिव आकाशः (*JU*, I. 5. 5)।

149. अथैष आकाशो मध्यतो भूतानां सन्नः तस्मात् मध्ये सदस्यम् आसयन्ति (*Ṣaḍ Br*, 2.4.5)।

150. आकाशो मे सदस्यः (*Ṣaḍ Br*, 2.5.6)। योयमन्तश्चक्षुष्याकाशः स मे सदस्यः (2.6.3.)। योऽयमन्तःपुरुष आकाशः स मे सदस्यः (2.7.3)।

151. आकाशो मे सदस्यः स मे देवयजनं ददातु (*Ṣaḍ Br*, 3.3.9)।

152. सदस्याय ददत् ब्रूयात् सदस्य आत्मानं ते ददानि . . . स यत् आत्मानं ददाति आकाशो वा आत्मा . . . .। तद् यावद् आकाशो न क्षीयते तावत् अस्य तद् दत्तं तिष्ठति (*J Br*, 2.54)।

153. कं वैश्वानरं वेत्थ आकाशमेव राजान्निति होवाच . . . एष वै बहुला वैश्वानर एतं हि वै बहुलं वैश्वानरं वेत्थ . . . (*Ś Br*, 10.6.1.1.6)।

154. पुरुषो वै प्रजापतिः स यो ह पुरुषो य एवायमन्तरिक्ष आकाश एष एव स पुरुषः (*J Br*. 2.56)।

155. प्राणो ब्रह्म कं ब्रह्म खं ब्रह्मेति। यद् वाव कं तदेव खं यदेव खं तदेव कमिति . . .(*Ch Up*. 4.10.4-5)।

156. ब्रह्म ह देवेभ्यो विजिग्ये . . . etc. (*Kena Up*. 3.1-12)।

157. यः पृथिव्यां तिष्ठन् पृथिव्या अन्तरो यं पृथिवी न वेद यस्य पृथिवी शरीरं यः पृथिवीमन्तरो यमयति . . . etc. (*Br Up*. 3.7.3 onwards)।

4

Water Element
in Vedic Cosmogony

Usha R. Bhise

Speculations about the origin of the Universe have occupied considerable space in the primitive religions. Cosmogony may be defined as "attempts at finding out the common origin of the diverse phenomena of nature, in nature itself". Such speculations started — not from unknown principle — but from the tangible and knowable concrete.

Turning to the Vedic literature, we find that no single uniform cosmogonic theory had been formulated. The oldest monument of Indian literature, viz. the *Ṛgveda* has various theories which are not mutually exclusive. Probing through Vedic literature, one comes across a process in the evolution of ideas. The various theories of cosmogony fall into three categories :

1. The most primitive ones begin with material principles like water, earth, fire, ether etc.
2. Next come the abstract principles like chaos, time, night, desire, non-being etc. (However, *asat* only meant primordial non-differentiation).
3. In the latest stage of development we come across divine principles like Prajāpati, *Brahman,* Viśvakarman etc.

A few more features of Vedic cosmogony may deserve mention here. According to *Ṛgveda,* Creation is not a single definite act as it is ever-proceeding. Creation out of nothingness is practically unknown. Further, it does not have teleological significance. The Creator was not moved by any idea of executing a deliberate plan. Considering the theories of the first category mentioned above, one finds that only the material cause of the Universe is stated. They are silent about deities being the efficient cause. Out of the Five Great Elements, *pṛthivī* and *ap* are the most tangible elements, *tejas* gets the next place. Even there, two concrete forms of it viz. the Sun and the fire get the privilege of being frequently mentioned in cosmogonical deliberations.

In the early Vedic cosmogony, the *ap-tattva* receives a good deal of attention. This was prompted, probably, by the historical background of the period. Frequent floods in the Indus Valley have influenced the thought-process of Vedic Āryans when they stated that water was the primordial substance out of which the Universe came into being (*ambhaḥ kimāsīd gahanaṁ gabhīram — ṚV,* 10.129.1).

The Indus Valley appears to be a target of frequent floods. So also its extention viz. Lothal, Rangpur-Koth in Saurashtra. The accumulation of flood-debris at various sites is an evidence for the inundation of Mohen-jo-daro. The 12 meter-high hill of silt at Budh Takkar is the result of a great flood of long duration, almost a deluge, which must have turned the lower Indus Valley into a vast lake. The Carbon-14 dates for the two great floods at Lothal are 2015 ± 115 BC and 1900 ± 115 BC. The flood debris of the latest level of HR mound at Mohen-jo-daro is assigned to 2000 BC. The flood in *circa* 1900 BC assumed such fierce proportion and was so prolonged and devastating that all the Harappan settlements in Saurāṣṭra, Kutch and S. Gujarat were wiped out.

Speaking about creation from primal matter, we find that *ap-tattva* plays a prominent role. To the Ṛgvedic thinker, affected severely by frequent floods, water appeared to be the earliest element. In his thought-process what was prior temporally, must have worked like the cause of the Universe. No question is asked about the origin of waters. Even Viśvakarman was preceded by them. In the *Brāhmaṇas* water is described as co-eval with Prajāpati. The *Śat. Br.* (XI.1.6) states that it is preceded Prajāpati. It was reasonable to Vedic people who saw land growing out of accumulations of river-torn silt that water was the primary element and source of all that existed.

A striking feature of Vedic Cosmology is the distinction made between *āp* and *salila,* i.e., 'waters' and 'creative waters' respectively. The following pair of quotations will drive home this point :

> समुद्रज्येष्ठाः सलिलस्य मध्यात् पुनाना यन्त्यनिविशमानाः।
> *samudrajyeṣṭhāḥ salilasya madhyāt punānā yantyaniviśamānāḥ* ।
> *ṚV,* 7.49.1

> The divine waters, *āpaḥ* having ocean as their chief lord, go forth purifying (themselves, others) without encamping, from the middle of *salila.*

आपो ह वा इदमग्रे सलिलमेवास।
āpo ha vā idamagre salilamevāsa ।
Śat. Br., XI.1.6.

Before creation (*agre*) the waters (*āpaḥ*) were *salila.*

The same text proceeds to say *tā'kāmayanta* "Entertaining a desire (to create)" they practised *tapas,* as a result of which *hiraṇyaya aṇḍa,* was born. From it *puruṣa* was produced and thereafter, Prajāpati was created.

It also states — VI.1.1.8 *saḥ* (*prajaptiḥ*) *apo'sṛjata.* Thus *āp* came at a late stage in the hierarchy of Creation. It was ordinary water created along with other diversities of the world, whereas, *salila,* preceded Prajāpati who gets fifth place in the creative process as could be seen from the above passage.

The distinction between *āp* and *salila* lies in the fact that *salila* contains something in it which was beyond the ken of ordinary knowledge and which, later, was going to manifest itself as the world. This fact has been made clear by the Nāsadīya hymn of the *Ṛgveda* (10.129):

1. अम्भः किमासीद् गहनं गभीरम्
   ambhaḥ kimāsīd gahanaṁ gabhīram

   Was it water, deep and fathomless (i.e., beyond the limits of knowledge).

2. तुच्छ्येन अभ्वपिहितं यदासीत्
   tucchyena abhvapihitaṁ yadāsīt

   The emergent principle lay concealed by the worthless (water).

ābhu is that which is about to come into existence, the implication being that it has the energy necessary for coming into being. The same idea has been presented by the *Bāṣkalamantropaniṣat* (V.14) as

(सरसः परस्य) सरिरस्य मध्ये एति इव।
(*sarasaḥ parasya*) *sarirasya madhye eti iva* ।

That which moves about, as it were, in the *sarira,* which is beyond the lake of the mid-regions.

Here the lake of mid-regions is the place of origin of rain showers, and thus, represents ordinary waters. *Sarira* exists beyond that. It contains something which is described as *eti iva* which is a sure reference to the principle which is capable of moving, i.e., endowed with energy that is necessary for movement. The words *salila/sarira* are derived from *sṛ* 'to move'. The energy itself is called *tapas* 'heat' or *kāma* 'desire'. The ability to know all this is possessed by *kavis* 'men of vision', through a process of knowledge which is not usual but may be described as intuitive (*hṛdi pratīṣyā kavayo manīṣā*)

The following statements strengthen the proposition set up in the earlier paragraph:

1. यद्देवा अदः सलिले सुसंरब्धा अतिष्ठत।
   yaddevā adaḥ salile susaṁrabdhā atiṣṭhata ।
   ṚV, 10.72.6

   When the gods were firmly established in this *salila.*

The hymn in which this occurs is a cosmogonical hymn which describes the genesis of gods and mortals from Aditi. The concept of Aditi stands for infinity, eternity, immensity, unbondage. She is all that is born and all that will be born (*ṚV,* 1.89.10). In the present quotation *salila* stands for the womb of mother Aditi. The *AV* equates her with primal waters.

2. सलिले एको द्रष्टाऽद्वैतो भवति।
   salile eko draṣṭā'dvaito bhavati ।
   Bṛ. Up., 4.3.32

   There is one seer (i.e., a sentient principle) who is without a second in the *salila.*

3. स एवाग्निः सलिले संनिविष्टः।
   sa evāgniḥ salile saṁniviṣṭaḥ
   Śvet. Up., 6.15

   Saḥ is the swan, *Brahman* who resides in *salila* as *Agni. Agni* may be equated to *tapas* 'heat'.

4. Verily this world was *salila.* There, Prajāpati was born alone on a lotus-leaf. In his mind desire (*kāma*) arose.
   Nṛ. Pūrva. Up., 1.1

5. पृश्निः सलिलमेव च।
   pṛśniḥ salilameva ca
   Cūlikā Up., 13

The idea of the presence of energy/heat in primal waters, later gave rise to the conception of *vaḍavānala* being present in waters. *Apām Napāt,* according to Oldenberg, was originally a water-dragon. He, later on, got identified with *Agni* because of latter's relation to the cloud-water in the form of lightning. The presence of lightning in the water-laden cloud gave rise to the concept of fire being a child who resides in the watery womb of cloud before its birth.

Thus, *salila* is the primordial substance containing the emergent world together with the energy necessary for emerging activity. However, the idea of water being the carrier of important entities continues to hold good even though there is no clear evidence that they are primal waters. To quote

स एष अप्सु प्रतिष्ठितः।
sa eṣa apsu pratiṣṭhitaḥ ।
Br. Up., 1.2.1

अप्सु पुरुषः एतं ब्रह्मोपासे।
apsu puruṣaḥ etaṁ brahmopāse ।
Bṛh. Up., 2.1.8

अप्सु अमृतमयः पुरुषः।
apsu amṛtamayaḥ puruṣaḥ ।
Bṛh. Up., 2.5.2

The word *āp* is sought to be explained as:

आपोऽऽप्यायनात्।
āpo' pyāyanāt ।
Mait. Up., 6.7.

Even at the stage of *āp*, energy in some form or the other is said to reside in it. *Tejas* in particular is intimately linked with water in this way. (*Kauś. Up.*, 4.2)

The Upaniṣadic philosophy which is quite advanced in its speculations regards only one entity as real and that is *Brahman/Ātman*. The *Kauś Up.* (4.10) presents an interesting dialogue between Bālāki and King Ajātaśatru. Therein Bālāki tries to establish that the *Puruṣa*, i.e., the sentient principle underlying various entities like the Sun, the Moon etc. is *Brahman*. Ajātaśatru refutes, one after the other, the statements of Bālāki which take the form like *ya evaiṣa āditye puruṣastamevāhamupāse iti* । Ajātaśatru denies all such statements made about moon, lightning, thunder, sky, wind, fire, water, mirror, echo, sound, shadow, bodily *puruṣa, prājña ātman, puruṣa* in the right eye and the one in the left eye. After silencing Bālāki, Ajātaśatru takes him to a sleeping royal personage and, there, addresses him as "O *prāṇa* clad in waters". But he does not wake up, since he, the *jīvātmā* was different from *prāṇa*. The lesson which Ajātaśatru tries to teach is that *prāṇa* is clad in waters but is not the ultimate reality.

The idea of water being the clothing of *prāṇa* is also found in the *Chā. Up.* (5.2.2) in the famous dialogue between the sense-organs and vital breath. It is also called the body of *prāṇa.* (*Bṛ. Up.*, 1.5.13: *prāṇasya āpaḥ śarīram*)

There is an interesting piece of conversation between King Satyayajña and Buḍila, the son of Aśvatarāśva. Herein (*Chā. Up.*, 5.16.1) the king asks Buḍila as to the *Ātman* which is meditated upon by him. He replies that it is *āpaḥ*. Thereupon, the King remarks that this *ātman* is known as Rayi Ātmā Vaiśvānara. Hence, Buḍila is wealthy and strong. This remark is important for two reasons. The first one is that it implies the identity between *āpaḥ* and Vaiśvānara "the fire which resides in all the human beings". The idea of water getting transformed into Vaiśvānara lies at the basis of the identity. The second reason why it is important is the relation between *rayi* 'wealth' and waters, *rayi* is, in fact, the outcome of the *upāsanā* of *āp*. This is a case of the object of *upāsanā* being identified with its fruit. For the sake of *upāsanā*, waters are also found to be identified with *Brahman* (*Chā. Up.*, 7.10.1).

Upaniṣadic philosophers were aware of "matter being indestructible". The so-called disappearance of matter was only its transformation into something else. Thus, the drying up of water meant its transformation into *vāyu*, (*yad āpa ucchuṣyati vāyumeva apiyanti*— *Chā. Up.*, 4.3.2).

Water gets transformed into *puruṣa* 'human being' through five successive stages. This truth has been expressed through the metaphor of a sacrifice : *pañcamyām āhutāv āpaḥ puruṣavacaso bhavanti* (*Chā. Up.*, 5.3.3). Sacrifice was a salient feature of the Vedic culture; hence, the cosmic activity itself was viewed as a great sacrifice. The five oblations (*āhuti*) offered into five fires may be stated in a tabular form as:

Fire (Agni)	*Oblation (āhuti)*	*Product/Fruit*
Dyuloka	*Śraddhā*	King Soma
Parjanya	Soma	*Varṣā* (showers)
Pṛthivī	*Vārṣa*	*Anna*
Puruṣa	*Anna*	*Retaḥ*
Yoṣā	*Retaḥ*	*Garbha*

Herein, the product of the earlier *āhuti* becomes the *āhuti* of the next stage. After the fifth oblation waters get the designation of *puruṣa.*

The transformation of water which is drunk by a person is threefold. (*Chā. Up.*, 6.5.2) The gross part of water is turned into wine, the medium part into blood and the subtle part into *prāṇa.* The subtle part (*aṇiman*) of water rises up and becomes *prāṇa* (*Chā. Up.*, 6.6.3). In support of the transformation of water into *prāṇa,* it is said that if a person does not eat for a fortnight but drinks water to his heart's content, his *prāṇa* does not get cut off (*vicchinna*) (*Chā. Up.*, 6.7.1). The moon is the brilliant form of water (*Bṛ. Up.*, 1.5.13). The *śara* 'scum', of water formed itself into the earth. (*Bṛ. Up.*, 1.2.2).

Resorting to the metaphor of a tree (*Chā. Up.*, 6.8.3,4,6) it is said that *sat* 'existence' is the root of which *tejas* is the sprout (*śuṅga*). *Tejas* in its turn becomes the root of which *āp* (water) is the sprout, *āp* in its turn becomes the root of which *anna* is the sprout. *Taitt. Up.*, 3.8.1. identified *Agni* with *āp.*

This very fact is presented in a slightly different mode in which *sat, tejas* and *āp* are conceived as sentient beings capable of thinking and entertaining desires (*Chā. Up.*, 6.2.3). The *sat* thought that it should be manifold: it created *tejas.* Then, *tejas* thought that it should be manifold; it created water. Then water thought that it should be manifold; it created food. *Taitt. Up.*, 2.1.1 states that water was produced from fire and the earth was produced from water. Yet another passgae in *Chā. Up.* (6.4.1) states that *tejas, āp* and *anna* are but three forms of *Agni* having three colours red, white and black respectively.

Keeping in view the principle of transformation the waters are called *oṣadhis* and *vanaspatis.* (*Taitt. Up.*, 1.3.2)

Once *āpaḥ* are conceived to be sentient beings who can think, entertain desires and resolve (i.e., have *saṅkalpa*) (*Chā. Up.*, 7.4.2), it is only a step forward to regard them as *devatās. Āp* is deified as early as the most ancient strata of the *Ṛgveda* (7.49). They are invoked as purifiers (*punānāḥ* V.1; *śucayah,* V.2.3; *pāvakāḥ* V.3) with a request to favour the poet-seer. The favour consists of purifying the supplicant both physically and metaphorically by getting rid of the sin. Since they purify themselves as well as others Varuṇa, the moral governor, is said to reside in them,(1.25.10). Agni Vaiśvānara is also said to have entered them. As a corollary to the rivers in general and Sarasvati in particular they are regarded as holy and divine.

Water thus plays a prominent role in Vedic cosmogony. The genesis of the Universe takes place in the primeval water. Once the chaotic condition existing before the genesis is overcome through creative process, the emergent one *abhu* emerges into an orderly cosmos. Thereafter, water-element *ap-tattva* appears as one of the products of creative process. It has a role to play in the further development of the Universe through its transformations.

5

Gist of Cosmological Ideas in Vedas

Srinivas Madabhushi

Cosmology is an important aspect of ancient Indian thinking and wisdom. *Vedas,* the towering monuments of human race contain some important ideas on cosmology. Before attempting to examine the cosmological insights revealed in the *Vedas,* let us examine some of the modern scientific theories on the origin of the universe.

The modern views of cosmogony are summarised by Richard J. Ordway (1971) in his book *Earth Science.* Kuiper's '*protoplanet* hypothesis' in a way is a modification of the 'nebular hypothesis' of Kant and Laplace. The latter presupposes a great cloud of slowly rotating hot gaseous material as the starting point of the universe. As this cloud cooled, it shrank and rotated more rapidly. The cloud got gradually compressed at polar regions into a lens-shaped disc which gradually left off masses of gases which cooled down first to a liquid state and then to solid state, giving rise to planets. If this hypothesis were to be valid, the gases should disperse instead of collecting into planets; the sun should be rapidly spinning and all satellites should be revolving in the west-to-east direction. This and a number of other theories like the 'binary star hypothesis' unsuccessfully attempted to explain cosmogony. According to Kuiper's '*proto-planet* hypothesis', the solar system originated from a hot gaseous cloud or nebula, perhaps one-tenth as massive as the sun, that surrounds a large dark central mass that would subsequently form into a star. As the nebula contracted, and flattened, it becomes unstable, and divided into a number of separate clouds of 'protoplanets'. Solid particles accumulated into a central core in each protoplanet and became surrounded by a very large gaseous envelope. The composition of the nebula was chiefly hydrogen, with some helium, and 1 to 2 per cent of heavier elements. The protoplanets were of different sizes, but all were far larger and more massive than the present planets. The satellites were also formed in a similar manner, but they were relatively closer. The rotation of the protosatellites was slowed down by tidal friction until they rotated and revolved at the same rate and in the same direction. Thus they remained spherical and did not subdivide further. The original nebula rotated in a counter-clockwise direction. The tidal attraction of the sun on the protoplanets stretched them into elongated shapes and kept their long axes always pointed towards the sun. This made the direction of rotation the same as the direction of revolution, with periods of rotation and revolution once equal.

By this time the central mass had contracted enough to become a star. As the sun's temperature rose, its radiations and ejected particles ionized the gases around it. These gases interacted with the sun's rotation and transferred most of its angular momentum to the particles in the nebula; they moved faster as a result of the transfer. This solar wind of raditions and ejected particles gradually swept off into space the remaining portion of the nebula and most of the lighter gases of the protoplanets. A comet's tail is directed away from the sun for the same reason. Only a small fraction of the original nebula remains as the masses of the present planets.

Thus the most modern theory on cosmology assumes the pre-existence of a rotating, hot gaseous nebula, but is silent on how this came into being, and which motivated such rotation. With this background let us examine the cosmological ideas and cosmogony in *Vedas.*

Ṛg Veda

The Hymn of Creation (X.129) explains the origin of the world as the evolution of existent from non-existent. Water came into being first; from it was evolved intelligence by heat.

> नासदासीन्नो सदासीत्तदानीं।
> *nāsadāsīnno sadāsīttadānīṁ* ।
>
> There was not the non-existent nor the existent then.
>
> तम आसीत्तमसा गूळ्हमग्रे ऽप्रकेतं सलिलं सर्वमा इदम्।
> *tama āsīttamasā gūlhamagre 'praketaṁ salilaṁ sarvamā idam* ।
>
> Darkness was in the beginning hidden by darkness. This all was water.

The *Aitareya Upaniṣad* states:

> आत्मा वा इदमेक एवाग्र आसीत्। नान्यत् किंचन मिषत्।
> *ātmā vā idameka evāgra āsīt* । *nānyat kiṅcana miṣat* ।
> (I. 1.1)

In the beginning this was but the absolute self alone. There was nothing else whatsoever.

स इमाँल्लोकानसृजत। अम्भोमरीचिर्मरमापो . . . .
sa imāṁrallokānasrjata । *ambhomarīcirmaramāpo* . . . .
(I. 1.2)

He created these worlds, viz., *ambhas; marīci; mara* and *āpaḥ*.

Yajurveda

ŚUKLA YAJURVEDA

Śatapatha Brāhmaṇa

प्रजापतिर्वा इदमग्र आसीत्। . . . तस्मात्पुरुषात्तप्तदापो जायन्ते। . . . .
अपां तप्तानां फेनो जायन्ते। . . . .

prajāpatirvā idamagra āsīt । . . . *tasmātpuruṣāttaptadāpo jāyante* ।. . . . *apāṁ taptānāṁ pheno jāyante* । (V1.1.3)

In the beginning there was only the Creator. From him the 'water' was formed; from the water heated, the 'foam' was formed.

The *Bṛhadāraṇyakopaniṣad* says:

नैवेह किञ्चनाग्र आसीत्। मृत्युनैवेदमावृतमासीत्।
तन्मनोऽकुरुत सोऽर्चन्नचरत। तस्यार्चत आपोऽजायन्त।।
naiveha kiñcanāgra āsīt । *mṛtyunaivedamāvṛtamāsīt* ।
tanmano'kuruta so'rcannacarat । *tasyārcata āpo'jāyanta* ।
(I. 2.1)

In the beginning there was nothing. The universe was enveloped by death alone. He produced mind. He moved about worshipping himself. As he was worshipping himself, water was produced.

आपो वा अर्कः तद्यदपां शर आसीत्तमहन्यत। सा पृथिव्यभवत्।
āpo vā arkaḥ tadyadapāṁ śara āsīttamahanyata । *sā pṛthivyabhavat* ।
(I.2.2)

Water verily is *arka*. What was there as froth of water hardened and it became earth (the cosmic egg, embryonic state of the Universe).

KṚṢṆA YAJURVEDA

The *Taittirīyopaniṣad* says:

असद्वा इदमग्र आसीत्। ततो वै सदजायत।
तदात्मानः स्वयमकुरुत। तस्मात्तत्सुकृतमुच्यत इति।।
asadvā idamagra āsīt । tato vai sadajāyata ।
tadātmānaṁ svayamakuruta । tasmāttatsukṛtamucyata iti ।।
(II.vii.1)

In the beginning all this was unmanifested. From that emerged the manifested. The *Brahman* created Itself by Itself. Therefore it is called the self-creator.

The *Kaṭhopaniṣad* says:

न तत्र सूर्यो भाति न चन्द्रतारकं नेमा विद्युतो भान्ति कुतोऽयमग्निः।
तमेवभान्तमनुभाति सर्वं तस्यभासा सर्वमिदं विभाति।।
na tatra sūryo bhāti na candratārakaṁ nemā vidyuto bhānti kuto'yamagniḥ ।
tamevabhāntamanubhāti sarvaṁ tasyabhāsā sarvamidaṁ vibhāti ।।
(II. ii.15)

There the sun does not shine, neither do the moon and the stars; nor do these flashes of lightning shine. How can fire? He shining all these shine; through his lustre all these are variously illuminated.

Atharva Veda

यार्णवेऽधिं सलिलमग्र आसीत्।
yārṇave'dhiṁ salilamagra āsīt ।
(*Kāṇḍa*; XII. 8)

Earth was formerly water upon the ocean of space.

रोहितो द्यावा जजान। . . . . अज एकपादोऽहहद्द्यावा पृथिवी बलेन . . . .
rohito dyāvā jajāna । . . . . aja ekapādo' hahaddyāvā pṛthivī balena . . . .
(XIII. 6)

Rohita produced heaven and earth. The one footed goat, the sun made firm the heavens and earth with his strength.

The *Muṇḍaka Upaniṣad* (II.ii.10) reiterates the words of *Kaṭhopaniṣad* (II.ii.15) न तत्र सूर्यो भाति . . .

> एतस्माज्जायते प्राणो मनः सर्वेन्द्रियाणि च।
> खं वायुर्ज्योतिरापः पृथिवी विश्वस्य धारिणी।।
> *etasmājjāyate prāṇo manaḥ sarvendriyāṇi ca* ।
> *khaṁ vāyurjyotirāpaḥ pṛthivī viśvasya dhāriṇī* ।।
> (II.1.3)
>
> From him originate — vital force, mind, all senses, space, air, fire, water and earth that support everything.
>
> तस्मादग्निः समिधयो यस्य सूर्यः।
> *tasmādagniḥ samidhayo yasya sūryaḥ* ।
> (II.1.5).
>
> From him emerges the fire (heaven) of which the sun is the fuel.

The *Māṇḍūkya Kārikās* say:

> स्वप्नमाये यथा दृष्टे गन्धर्वनगरं यथा।
> तथा विश्वमिदं दृष्टं वेदान्तेषु, विचक्षणैः।।
> *svapnamāye yathā dṛṣṭe gandharvanagaraṁ yathā* ।
> *tathā viśvamidaṁ dṛṣṭaṁ vedānteṣu vicakṣanaiḥ* ।।
> (II. 3.1)
>
> Just as dream and magic are seen to be unreal, or as is a city in the sky, the whole universe is known to be unreal.

The *Praśna Upaniṣad* (III.8) equates the Sun with *prāṇa*, Earth with *apāna*, Space with *samāna*, Air with *vyāna* and Luminosity with *udāna*.

> प्राणाच्छ्रद्धां खं वायुर्ज्योतिरापःपृथिवीन्द्रियं मनः।
> *prāṇācchraddhāṁ khaṁ vāyurjyotirāpaḥpṛthivīndriyaṁ manaḥ* ।
> (VI.4.)
>
> From *prāṇa*, Space, Air, Fire, Water, Earth were created.

In addition to these traditional four *Vedas*, the *Pañcama Veda Mahābhārata* also has important observations on cosmogony:

> आकाशादभवद्वारि सलिलादग्निमारुतौ।
> अग्निमारुतसंयोगाततस्सम्भवन्मही।।
> *ākāśādabhavadvāri salilādagnimārutau* ।
> *agnimārutasaṁyogātatassambhavanmahī* ।।
> (*Śāntiparvan*, 180.16)

> Water was formed from the space; from water, fire and wind, and from their reaction the earth was formed.
>
> अग्निपवनसंयुक्तखात् समुक्षिपते जलम्।
> सोऽग्निमारुत संयोगात् घनत्वमुपपद्यते।।
> तस्याकाशान्निपातः स्नेहात्तिष्ठति योऽपरः।
> स संघत्वमापात्तो भूमित्वमनुगच्छति।।
>
> *agnipavana saṁyukta khāt samukṣipate jalam* ।
> *so' gnimāruta saṁyogāt ghanatvamupapadyate* ।।
> *tasyākāśānnipātaḥ snehāttiṣṭhati yo'paraḥ* ।
> *sa saṁghatvāmāpātto bhūmitvamanugacchati* ।।
> (*Śāntiparvan*, 180.15)
>
> The water produced in the sky by fire and wind attains solid state owing to the reaction of fire and wind. The oily quality of the water produced from the sky takes the form of the earth.

The *Sāṁkhya* system of *Darśana* considers the origin of the *pañcamahābhūtas* in the atomic form by means of combinations of the *tanmātrās*:

> कृष्णपादाचार्याः (तत्त्वत्रयविवरणम्) अत्रायं क्रमः — भूतादेः शब्दतन्मात्रं जायते, शब्दतन्मात्रं भूतादिरावृणोति, तत आकाशो जायते, ततोऽस्मात् शब्दतन्मात्रात् स्पर्शतन्मात्रं जायते, स्पर्शतन्मात्रं शब्दतन्मात्रमावृणोति, एवं शब्दतन्मात्रावृताद् आकाशसहायकात् स्पर्शतन्मात्राद् वायुर्जायते, ततोऽस्मात् स्पर्शतन्मात्रात् रूपतन्मात्रं जायते, रूपतन्मात्रं स्पर्शतन्मात्रमावृणोति, एवं स्पर्शतन्मात्रावृताद् वायुसहायकात् रूपतन्मात्राद् तेजो जायते। एवमादि।
>
> *kṛṣṇapādācārya (tattvatrayavivaraṇam) atrāyaṁ kramaḥ— bhūtadeḥ śabdatanmātraṁ jāyate, śabdatanmātraṁ bhūtādirāvṛṇoti, tata ākāśo jāyate, tato'smāt śabdatanmātrāt sparśa tanmātraṁ jāyate, sparśatanmātraṁ śabdatanmātramāvṛṇoti, evaṁ śabdatanmātravṛtād ākāśasahāyakāt sparśatanmātrād vāyurjāyate, tato' smāt sparśatanmātrāt rūpatanmātraṁ jāyate, rūpatanmātraṁ sparśatanmātramāvṛṇoti, evaṁ sparśatanmātrāvṛtād vāyusahāyakāt rūpatanmātrād tejo jāyate* । *evamādi* ।

The *śabdatanmātra* produced the Space and also the *sparśatanmātra* and the combination of the Space with the *sparśatanmātra* produces the Atmosphere (*Vāyu*). The *rūpatanmātra* is produced from the *sparśa tanmātra* and envelopes the *sparśatanmātra.* From the enveloped *sparśatanmātra,* the *rūpatanmātra* with the help of the *Vāyu* produces the fire etc.

The cosmological ideas in *Vedas* can thus be summarised as:

1. In the beginning there was neither the non-existent nor the existent.
2. The Supreme cosmogonic force by the sheer Will to produce the universe first in the form of darkness enveloped in darkness.
3. The cosmological waters *ambhas* got manifested next in the form of undifferentiated fluid in darkness where there was no light whatsoever.
4. From the cosmic waters, combined with the motivation to move and probably as a consequencce of the friction, fire called *arka* got generated.
5. Due to the action of the fire and water, wind was produced and the combination of wind, fire and water produced a froth which got solidified subsequently to form the earth.
6. The Supreme *Brahman* who is like an uplifted thunderbolt, makes the entire universe to emerge and to move. Thus the cosmic fluid originates due to the motion induced by the Will of the Supreme Soul moves the undifferentiated atoms into an undifferentiated cloud of dark fluid which because of the friction of motion attains heat and gives rise to the cosmic earth (the cosmic egg or the embryonic state of the universe), which is the **protostar** of the modern concept of cosmogony. The further motion of the cosmic fluid along with the cosmic earth produced the *ekapada aja*, the sun. The sun is the *Prāṇa* and from this *Prāṇa* the *Pañcabhūtas* originated.

The specific contributions by *Vedas* to the cosmogony, in superiority to the most modern cosmological concepts, thus include: (a) The concept of non-existent and non-non-existent state simultaneously; (b) The Supreme Will which motivated the non-differentiated atoms to combine to get differentiated into various forms like the nebula — *ambhas*; the frictional fire — *arka*; the protostar — **cosmic earth** (*brahmāṇḍa*) and finally the sun which is the *prāṇa* which differentiated the *pañcamahābhūtas*.

In spite of the unprecedented advancements in the science and technology, we are still as enlightened as the Vedic seers and their philosophical idea —

इयं विसृष्टिर्यत आबभूव यदि वा दधे यदि वा न।

योऽस्याध्यक्षः परमे व्योमन् सो अङ्ग वेद यदि वा न वेद।।
iyaṁ visṛṣṭiryata ābabhūva yadi vā dadhe yadi vā na ।
yo'syādhyakṣaḥ parame vyoman so aṅga veda yadi vā na veda ।।
(*ṚV*, X.129)

Where from has this cosmogony come; who is its chief architect? whether he knows or not — is still as valid and as beautiful as when it was composed.

References

Aitareya Upaniṣad : Gambhirananda, *Eight Upaniṣads*, Vol. II pp. 1-76, Ramakrishna Mission Publication.

Atharva Veda: Sattavalekarah, Sripad Damodara, 520 p.

Bṛhadāranyakopaniṣad : Ramakrishna Mission, Madras.

Kaṭhopaniṣad: Gambhirananda, *Eight Upaniṣads*, Vol. I, pp. 91-220, Ramakrishna Mission Publication.

Māṇḍūkyopaniṣad : Gambhirananda, *Eight Upaniṣads*, Vol. II, pp. 173-404, Ramakrishna Mission Publication.

Muṇḍakopaniṣad: Gambhirananda, *Eight Upaniṣads*, Vol. II, pp. 77-172, Ramakrishna Mission Publication.

Ordway, Richard, J., 1971, *Earth Science*, 705p. Affiliated East-West Publication.

Praśnopaniṣad: Gambhirananda, *Eight Upaniṣads*, Vol. II, pp. 405-506, Ramakrishna Mission Publication.

Ṛg Veda: Arthur A. MacDonnel, 1971, *A Vedic Reader*, Oxford Publication.

Śatapatha Brāhmaṇa : Ed., by A. Chinnaswami Sastri, 1984, Chowkambha Publication.

Sāṅkhya: Krishnapadacharya, quoted in Gaur, D. S., and Gupta, L.P., 1970, *Pañcamahābhūta with special reference to Āyurveda*, I.J.H.S., Vol. 5, no.1, pp. 51-67.

Śāntiparvan: Mahābhārata, Ed. by S. Suktankar, Vishnu.

Taittirīyopaniṣad: Gambhirananda, *Eight Upaniṣads*, Vol. I, pp. 221-398, Ramakrishna Mission Publication.

6

Cosmogony and Cosmology in Major Upaniṣads

K. V. Mande

The *Upaniṣads* represent the epitome of philosophical insights provided by ancient India. They have tried to search into the purpose behind the cosmos, and provided a philosophical interpretation regarding the theory of creation. At the same time they are not mere esoteric ideology, but have a practical legitimisation in term of life as lived here and now.

Upaniṣads contain philosophical discussions on different issues relating to man, nature and cosmos. Upaniṣadic seers generally explain these ideas on three levels — *ādhidaivika ādhibhautika* and *ādhyātmika* or waking state, dream state and deep sleep state. According to philosophical point of view the universe originates from Supreme Being. Materialistic (*bhautika*) viewpoint holds that the five elements are the root cause of the world. The third way of interpretation takes help of similes and explains the origin of the world. Now let us take a closer look at these three interpretations regarding the origin of the universe.

Philosophical Interpretation

Just as a physicist would explain the nature of the world with the help of physics, the *Upaniṣads,* give a philosophical interpretation. *Upaniṣad* means the secret knowledge which has all the while philosophical bearing. Therefore, the philosophical interpretation is taken first. As it is observed in *Taittirīya,* the Supreme Being is that from which all the beings come forth, in which they sustain and in which they merge at the time of dissolution.[1] The major *Upaniṣads* have mainly accepted the lord in an unmanifested form, still the superimposition of emotions takes place. Regarding the creation, *Upaniṣads* have accepted two processes, viz. mental and physical. At some places the thinking process is introduced before the actual creation starts. Such as, in *Aitareya* it is said that He foresaw, I should create the worlds,[2] or in *Chāndogya,* He foresaw, I should be many and then He created the lustre,[3] etc. The verb used *aikṣata* is very significant. One can guess that the Lord might have drawn a picture of the whole world before his mind, and then the creation might have started. On the other hand, in *Praśna,* III.3 and in *Taittirīya,* II.1, respectively the direct process is mentioned as 'from that Supreme Being the vital breath is originated'[4] and 'from that *Ātman* the ether is manifested'.[5] Perhaps this may be cosmic creation which ultimately turns into the visible world. It means from that Highest Soul the space is produced. Space creates wind, which means some sort of movement starts. Then the heat which naturally comes out of any sort of action. The water indicates sort of flow, and ultimately the result is earth as a gross element. By keeping in mind the Upaniṣadic device of describing a thing from a subtle point of view to gross, this passage is interpreted in this manner. *Muṇḍaka* also believes that the whole manifestation is due to that Highest Being.[6]

Material Interpretation

Though it is a fact that the whole world is created by the Supreme Being, still, it does not come out at once, but has a certain sequence. This is *Upaniṣad's* scientific method. *Taittirīya* describes this order which is already mentioned above. It starts from the space to the human being.[7] Human being is at the centre. Really speaking it is a human intellect which has discovered the theory of cosmogony and cosmology. Therefore how a human being comes in this world is a basic thought. In this regard *Upaniṣad's* scientific reason is very remarkable. *Bṛ* declares that the pair was produced from the self and the human beings came into existence.[8] *Aitareya* gives a detailed description of the birth of a human being.[9] *Chāndogya* correlates cosmos with human beings in the famous *Pañcāgni vidyā.*[10] Another noteworthy point is that from the symbolic sacrifice a human being is born. *Upaniṣads* think of the inanimate world also, but in terms of animate things, e.g. *sat* and *asat* unite with each other. Then the egg comes forth. After one year it breaks into two. One is silver that is earth and the other is gold that is ether. The outer skin of embryo constitutes the mountains. The clotted portion is cloud. The tubes of human body are rivers. The abdominal water is the sea. From that the Sun is born. After it the melodious noise, all the beings and all desires are born.[11] Theory of threefoldness is Upaniṣadic device (*trivṛtkaraṇa*) which is the source of the theory of fivefoldness of *Advaita Vedānta.* The three entities are lustre, water and food.[12] The conclusion thus made is that there are three categories of beings, viz. those born out of egg, out of embryo and by breaking the earth.[13] *Aitareya* adds one more, viz. those who are born from sweat.[14]

In *Praśna* cosmological viewpoint is very skilfully introduced — Bhāradvāja asked Pippalāda about *Ṣoḍaśakala Puruṣa.* Pippalāda answered that the originator of the sixteen digits dwells in the body. He (the Puruṣa) started thinking, "by whom should I be uplifted and established?" For that reason he created the vital breath. From it *śraddhā*, five gross elements, sense-organs, mind, food, semen, penance, spell, deed, worlds and name manifested. That person has no digit.[15] According to *Upaniṣads*, the presiding deity entered the sense-organ, with a specific task; e.g. in *Aitareya* it is mentioned that fire being speech, entered the mouth; wind being breath, entered the nose[16] and so on.

Literary Interpretation

In spite of deep philosophical insights, the *Upaniṣads* are also important because of their literary significance, being a record of an ancient civilization and culture. As literary pieces, they have great poetic flavour, marked by a curious mixture of classicism and lyricism. Therefore a literary interpretation of cosmology is possible by resorting to the use of similes in the *Upaniṣads*. There are many similes in the *Upaniṣads* but three of them are useful in this regard. Out of them one helps to explain cosmological aspect, while the other two exhort themselves in explaining cosmogonical aspect. The whole universe is originated from that imperishable entity. *Muṇḍaka* interprets this fact with the help of three similes viz. spider, earth and person.[17]

In the case of the earth and person respectively, they are the causes of herbs, plants and hair. But in respect of the spider, the seer points out two types of deeds, viz. origination and dissolution.

Again in the same *Upaniṣad* the seer declares that just as thousands of fire particles come out of the well-kindled fire, in the same manner form that imperishable entity all sorts of beings come forth and again merge into it.[18] The simile in this case should be understood properly. In the case of the fire he uses the term "particles of the same forms", but not in the case of the imperishable entity, for the very reason that the forms differ, their essence does not. Further, the fire particles come out of the fire but nevertheless do not enter again. With regard to the Supreme Being, all beings come out of it and again at the end enter the same entity. So in both these similes, the similarity lies in their difference.

The third simile highlights the cosmological aspect. It is said in *Praśna* that all universe establishes itself in that Highest Soul, just as all birds find stability on the tree where they dwell.[19] The simile is clear and needs no explanation.

Mahābhūta as Deity

The scope of this concept of the *mahābhūta* is wide. As it is divided above on three planes, it can be further divided. There is a unanimous opinion that all these five gross elements come out of that imperishable soul.[20] In *Praśna* it is stated that these are the gods holding the living beings.[21] Neither the word *adhi* precedes there, nor any other explanation of the word *deva* is given. It is an example of *mahābhūtas* being mentioned as *devas.*

Connection with Symbolic Ritual and Meditation

It can be said about this concept that it is rather a popular one. In *Praśna* the deities of the four gross elements are connected with the four vital breaths.[22] It is a basic principle of the *Upaniṣads* that the one which lies in the body can be visualised well in the world. This may be the reason for the equation of vital breaths with the gross elements. Like *Bṛhadāraṇyaka, Chāndogya* is well-known for its symbolic ritual. In the latter regarding *Udgītha,* the earth and the fire are connected with *tha* and the wind with *gī.*[23] Again in *Pañcavidha Sāman* the earth is related with *hiṅkāra* and *nidhana,* the fire with *pratihāra* and *hiṅkāra* and the wind with *prastāva.*[24] In *Bṛhadāraṇyaka,* except the earth, remaining four elements are included in the symbolic meditation.[25] In the same *Upaniṣad* all the five gross elements are present in the famous *madhuvidyā*.[26] Further in that very *Upaniṣad* these five gross elements are declared as embodiments of the highest reality.[27] Symbolic ritual and symbolic meditation are two branches of the Upaniṣadic system, the one leading to religion and the other catering to philosophy. It also shows the gradual development of the *Upaniṣads* from the *Brāhmaṇas,* where the ritual had a primary role to play.

Victory Over *Mahābhūtas*

In *Bṛhadāraṇyaka* the gross elements are stated as the symbols of the Highest reality. *Śvetāśvatara* goes a step further and declares that for one who conquers these five elements there is no disease, no ageing and no death.[28] Further the *Upaniṣad* points out that the omniscient one rules over action which comes into effect including five gross elements.[29]

To sum up, two ways of interpreting the concept of *mahābhūta* have been highlighted here. The previous interpretation involves philosophical, material and literary viewpoints. They hold that the Supreme Being is the creator, sustainer and the destroyer of the universe. Some other sources hold the view that there is a gradual development (as it is in the evolution theory) and in that sequence the world is manifested. Both these views are supported by theories and views pertaining to cosmological and cosmogonic ideas.

In the second interpretation again there are three levels. In the first one, the *mahābhūtas* are treated as the principal agent or the deity, as it is in the *Praśna,*

II.2. At the second level, they are regarded as the embodiment of that Highest Reality, which can be found in *Bṛhadāraṇyaka,* III.7.3,4,7,12 and 14. At the third level they are considered the creator of the world. A specific mention of this can be seen in the *Taitt,* II.1. Keeping in mind all these references it can be said that these gross elements have a foremost position in the major *Upaniṣads.*

Abbreviations

Ait	:	*Aitareya*
Chāndo	:	*Chāndogya*
Taitt	:	*Taittirīya*
Praśna	:	*Praśna*
Bṛ.	:	*Bṛhadāraṇyaka*
Muṇḍ	:	*Muṇḍaka*
Śve	:	*Śvetāśvatara*

Notes

1. यतो वा इमानि भूतानि जायन्ते। येन जातानि जीवन्ति। यत्प्रयन्त्यभिसंविशन्ति। तद्विजिज्ञासस्व। तद् ब्रह्मेति।
   Taitt, III.1.
2. आत्मा वा इदमेवाग्र आसीत्।
   स ईक्षत — लोकान्नु सृजा इति।
   Ait, I.1.1.
3. तदैक्षत — बहु स्यां प्रजायेयेति। तत्तेजोऽसृजत।
   Chāndo, VI. 3.2.
4. आत्मनः एव प्राणः जायते।
   Praśna, III.3.
5. तस्माद्वा एतस्मादात्मनः आकाशः सम्भूतः।
   Taitt, II.I.
6. (पुरुषात्) एतस्माज्जायते प्राणो मनः सर्वेन्द्रियाणि च।
   खं वायुर्ज्योतिरापः पृथिवी विश्वस्य धारिणी।
   Muṇḍ, II. 1.3.
7. तस्माद्वा एतस्मादात्मन आकाशः सम्भूतः। आकाशाद्वायुः। वायोरग्निः अग्नेरापः। अद्भ्यः पृथिवी। पृथिव्या ओषधयः। ओषधीभ्योऽन्नम् अन्नात्पुरुषः।
   Taitt, II.1.
8. (आत्मा) स नैव रेमे। . . .। स द्वितीयमैच्छत्।

स इममेवाऽऽत्मानं द्वेधाऽपातयत्। ततः पतिश्च पत्नी चाभवताम्। . . . ततो मनुष्या अजायन्त।

Br, I.4.3.

9. पुरुषो ह वा अयमादितो गर्भो भवति यदेतद्रेतः।
तदेतत्सर्वेभ्योऽङ्गेभ्यस्तेजः संभूतमात्मन्येवात्मानं बिभर्ति।
तद्यदा स्त्रियां सिञ्चत्यथैनज्जनयति। तदस्य प्रथमं जन्म।
तत्स्त्रिया आत्मभूयं गच्छति यथा स्वमङ्गं तथा। . . .।
सा भावयित्री भावयितव्या भवति। तं स्त्री गर्भं बिभर्ति।
सोऽग्र एव कुमारं जन्मनोऽग्रेऽधि भावयति।
तदस्य द्वितीयं जन्म।

Ait, II.1.2.

10. असौ वाव लोको गौतमाग्निः। तस्याऽऽदित्य एव समित्। रश्मयो धूमः। अहरर्चिः। चन्द्रमा अङ्गाराः। नक्षत्राणि विस्फुलिङ्गाः . . .। तस्या आहुतेः सोमो राजा सम्भवति। पर्जन्यो वाव गौतमाग्निः। तस्य वायुरेव समित्। अभ्रं धूमः। विद्युदर्चिः। अशनिरङ्गाराः। ह्रादुनयो विस्फुलिङ्गाः। . . . तस्या आहुतेर्वर्षं सम्भवति। पृथिवी वाव गौतमाग्निः। तस्याः संवत्सर एव समित्। आकाशो धूमः। रात्रिरर्चिः। दिशोऽङ्गाराः। अवान्तरदिशो विस्फुलिङ्गाः। . . .। तस्या आहुतेरन्नं संभवति। पुरुषो वाव गौतमाग्निः। तस्य वागेव समित्। प्राणो धूमः। जिव्हाऽर्चिः। चक्षुरङ्गाराः। श्रोत्रं विस्फुलिङ्गाः। . . .। तस्या आहुतेः रेतः संभवति। योषा वाव गौतमाग्निः। तस्या आहुतेर्गर्भः संभवति।

Chāndo, V.4.9.

11. असदेवेदमग्र आसीत्। तत्सदासीत्। तत्समभवत्। तदाण्डं निरवर्तत। तत्संवत्सरस्य मात्रामशयत। तन्निरभिद्यत। त आण्डकपाले रजतं च सुवर्णं चाभवताम्। तद्यद्रजतं सेयं पृथिवी। यत्सुवर्णं सा द्यौः। यज्जरायु ते पर्वताः। यदुल्वं स मेघो नीहारः। या धमनयस्ता नद्यः। यद्वास्तेयमुदकं स समुद्रः। अथयत्तदजायत सोऽसावादित्यः। तं जायमानं घोषा अुलूलवोऽनूदतिष्ठन्त्सर्वाणि च भूतानि सर्वे च कामाः।

Chāndo, III.19.1-3.

12. (सत्) तत्तेजोऽसृजत। . . .। तदपोऽसृजत। . . .। (आपः) ता अन्नमसृजन्त।

Chāndo, VI. 3.3-4.

13. तेषां भूतानां त्रीण्येव बीजानि भवन्त्याण्डजं जीवजमुद्भिज्जमिति।

Chāndo, VI.3.1.

14. एष ब्रह्मा। एष इन्द्रः। एष प्रजापतिः। एते सर्वे देवाः। इमानि च पञ्चमहाभूतानि पृथिवी वायुराकाश आपोज्योतींष्येतानीमानि च क्षुद्रमिश्राणीव बीजानीतराणि चेतराणि चाण्डजानि च जरायुजानि च स्वेदजानि चोद्भिज्जानि . . . यच्च स्थावरम्।

Ait, III.3.

15. इहैवान्तः शरीरे सोम्य स पुरुष यस्मिन्नेताः षोडशकलाः प्रभवन्तीति। स इक्षांचक्रे। कस्मिन्नहमुत्क्रान्त उत्क्रान्तो भविष्यामि। कस्मिन्वा प्रतिष्ठिते प्रतिष्ठास्यामीति। स प्राणमसृजत। प्राणाच्छ्रध्दां खं वायुर्ज्योतिराप पृथिवीन्द्रियं मनोऽन्नमन्नाद्वीर्यं तपो मन्त्राः कर्म लोकाः लोकेषु नाम च।

Praśna, VI.2-4.

16. अग्निर्वाग्भूत्वा मुखं प्राविशत्। वायुः प्राणो भूत्वा नासिके प्राविशत्। आदित्यश्चक्षुर्भूत्वाऽक्षिणी प्राविशत्। दिशः श्रोत्रं भूत्वा कर्णौ प्राविशत्। ओषधिवनस्पतयो लोमानिभूत्वा त्वचं प्राविशत्। चन्द्रमा मनो भूत्वा हृदयं प्राविशत्। मृत्युरपानो भूत्वा नाभिं प्राविशत्। आपो रेतो भूत्वा शिश्नं प्राविशत्।

Ait, I. 2.4.

17. यथोर्णनाभिः सृजते गृह्णते च यथा पृथिव्यामोषधयः सम्भवन्ति। यथा सतः पुरुषात् केशलोमानि तथाऽक्षरात् सम्भवतीह

विश्वम्।

Muṇḍ, I.1.7.

18. यथा सुदीप्तात्पावकाद्विस्फुलिंगाः सहस्रशः संभवन्ते सरूपाः। तथाक्षराद्विविधाः सोम्य भावाः प्रजायन्ते तत्र चैवापियन्ति।।

Muṇḍ, II.1.1.

19. स यथा वयांसि वासोवृक्षं संप्रतिष्ठन्ते।
एवं ह वै तत् सर्वं पर आत्मनि संप्रतिष्ठते।।

Praśna, IV.7.

20. See footnotes 6 and 7.

21. अथ हैनं भार्गवो वैदर्भिः पप्रच्छ। भगवन् कत्येव देवाः प्रजां विधारयन्ते। . . .। तस्मै स होवाच। आकाशो ह वा एष देवो वायुरग्निरापः पृथिवी वाङ्मनश्चक्षुः श्रोत्रं च।

Praśna, II.1. 2

22. पृथिव्यां या देवता सैषा पुरुषस्यापानमवष्टभ्य। अन्तरा यदाकाशः स समानः। वायुर्व्यानः तेजो ह वा उदानः।

Praśna, III.8.9.

23. द्यौरेवोत्। अन्तरिक्षं गीः। पृथिवी थम्। आदित्य एवोत्। वायुर्गीः। अग्निस्थम्। . . .। य एतान्येवं विद्वानुद्गीथाक्षराण्युपास्त उद् गी थ इति।

Chāndo, I.3.7.

24. लोकेषु पञ्चविधं सामोपासीत। पृथिवी हिंकारः। अग्निः प्रस्तावः। . . .। इत्यूर्ध्वेषु। अथाऽऽवृत्तेषु। . . .। अग्निः प्रतिहारः। पृथिवी निधनम्।

Chāndo, II.1, 2.

पृथिवी हिंकारः। तताः शक्वर्यो लोकेषु प्रोताः।

Chāndo, II.17.1.

अग्निर्हिंकारः वायुः प्रस्तावः। . . .। एतद्राजनं देवतासु प्रोतम्।

Chāndo, II.20.

25. स होवाच गार्ग्यः — य एवायमाकाशे पुरुष एतमेवाहं ब्रह्मोपास इति। . . .। य एवायं वायौ पुरुष एतमेवाहं ब्रह्मोपास इति। . . .। य एवायमग्नौ पुरुष तमेवाहं ब्रह्मोपास इति। . . .। य एवायमप्सु पुरुष तमेवाहं ब्रह्मोपास इति।

Bṛ, II.1.5-8.

26. इयं पृथिवी सर्वेषां भूतानां मधु। . . .।
इमा आपः सर्वेषां भूतानां मधु। . . . ।
अयमग्निः सर्वेषां भूतानां मधु। . . .।
अयं वायुः सर्वेषां भूतानां मधु। . . .।
अयमाकाशः सर्वेषां भूतनां मधु। . . .।

Ibid., II.5.1-4, 10.

27. यः पृथिव्यां तिष्ठन् पृथिव्या अन्तरो यं पृथिवी न वेद यस्य पृथिवी शरीरं यः पृथिवीमन्तरो यमयत्येष त आत्माऽन्तर्याम्यमृतः।
यः अप्सु तिष्ठन् . . . यस्य आपः शरीरं . . .।
यो वायौ तिष्ठन् . . . यस्य वायुः शरीरं . . .।
य आकाशे तिष्ठन् . . . यस्याकाशः शरीरं . . .।
यस्तेजसि तिष्ठन् . . . यस्य तेजः शरीरं।

यस्तेजसोऽन्तरो यमयत्येष त आत्माऽन्तर्याम्यमृतः। इत्यधिदैवतम्।
Ibid., III.4.3, 4, 7, 12, 14.

28. पृथ्व्यप्तेजोनिलखे समुस्थिते पञ्चात्मके योगगुणे प्रवृत्ते।
न तस्य रोगो न जरा न मृत्युः प्राप्तस्य योगाग्निमयं शरीरम्।।
Śve, II.12.

29. येनाऽऽवृत्तं नित्यमिदं हि सर्वं ज्ञः कालकालो गुणी सर्वविद्यः।
तैनेशितं कर्म विवतति ह पृथिव्यप्तेजोनिलखानि चिन्त्यम्।।
Ibid., VI.2.

Reference

Eighteen Principal Upaniṣads—Vol. I, ed. by V. P. Limaye and R. D. Wadekar. Poona : Vaidika Saṁśodhana Maṇḍala (1958).

7

The Five Mahābhūtas

A Semantic Analysis

A. M. Ghatage

By the word *mahābhūta* we usually understand the elements out of which all the material things in the world are formed or to which all the material things can be reduced. In this sense, these can be considered as the basic physical elements, the building blocks of the material world. The history of Indian Philosophy has given rise to two distinct trends of thought : One of them, which can be described as materialistic, in which the existence of these elements, is admitted as real, is the view of Cārvāka School (also called *Lokāyata*). The other, which is traditionally traced to Bṛhaspati whose postulates are often quoted for corraboration, admits the existence of mental or psychological entities as being equally real, and can be described as idealistic philosophy. These non-material entities may be either considered as having a fleeting existence, as is done by the Buddhist philosophers or they may be considered as permanent, as is done by the majority of Indian philosophical schools. A further trend of thought was developed later in which the mental or spiritual entity alone was regarded as really existing, thereby implying the non-existence of the material things, giving rise to a kind of monism. But the majority of the philosophical schools in India admitted the existence of both the mental and material elements and drew a sharp distinction between the two, and hence may be designated as realistic in nature. Among them a further distinction can be made between those who regarded the psychic element as being inactive, the activity being confined to the material elements as is done by the *Sāṁkhyas*, and those who assigned all the activity to the psychic element only, thinking the material elements as being inactive because of being insentient. The concept of the *mahābhūtas* and their proto-types called the *tanmātras* play a vital role in all philosophical systems of India.

Though these are generally admitted as real elements, the systems differ among themselves as regards their exact number and nature. Five of these are most frequently named, probably under the influence of the analysis to which the microcosm is subjected and wherein the number five plays an important part. Sometimes only four of them are given on the basis of everyday experience and insistence on their concrete form as is done by the Cārvāka, Jain and Buddhist Schools. There are however some indications of an earlier list of only three elements as can be seen from the *Vedānta* doctrine of *trivṛtkaraṇa* as against the later *pañcīkaraṇa.*

Both these views are based upon the supposition that each element has something of the others in its composition. The Ionian Greek philosophers also refer to only three such elements, water, air and fire as the source of all things (Gr. *arkhē*), unless we choose to interpret *épeiron* of Anaximandros as standing for space which is endless. We may choose to consider only two — earth and waters — if we interpret the passage from *Bṛhadāraṇyaka Upaniṣad,* V. 5.1 *āpaevedamagra āsuḥ* । *itā āpaḥ satyamasṛjanta satyaṁ brahma brahma prajāpatim prajāpatirdevān* as giving the whole list in this concept of cosmogony.

This paper attempts to concentrate on the words *mahābhūta* and *bhūta* and assess their nature from three different points of view, which are generally used in the study of ancient literature. As Bruno Snell points out, the study of early Greek philosophy, usually called pre-Socratic, is to be based on the interpretation of the Greek texts with a view to understand them from a mythological point of view, both as literary works and as showing aesthetic values. Another is a semantic analysis, by looking at the development of the meanings of the important words, leading to the history of ideas or concepts; or from a philosophical viewpoint by fixing the context of the complex system of thought which they reveal. Here we can attempt only one of these approaches, viz., the historical development of the concepts associated with words *bhūta* or *mahābhūta* with the hope that we would be able to clarify them a little better. Here the key-words are studied not in the way in which a linguist or a lexicographer studies them, an approach in which emphasis is laid on the form of the words and their usage, but to concentrate on the **idea itself**, trace its origin and follow its development and ramifications.

The method which can be effectively used for this purpose would be to try to ascertain as accurately as possible the etymology of the words pertaining to the ideas in general, then to fix the scope by considering the contexts in which these words are used. Their places in the context of similar words in the same language or a group of closely related languages are also ascertained, so as to build a broad semantic field, and assign a function to the given word. Thus taking up the basic concept one tries to classify it along different scales, which are known as the semantic co-ordinates like concrete or abstract, an individual or a generic type, etc., and build up the history of the meaning of that word. Each of these steps has its own limitations and hence for arriving at a reasonably acceptable conclusion, it is necessary to supplement it with material obtained from what can be tentatively called a comparative study of word-meanings, which attempts to build up a prototype for its use as does the historical linguistics for the form of the word. Our attempt will be confined to the semantics of the given word. For the present, only one aspect or two of *mahābhūta*, namely, its predominant use in the field of cosmogony and cosmology and its numerical scope are taken up.

Let us translate the word *mahābhūta* as 'basic element'. Its use is most conspicuous in speculations on the early cosmogonies and cosmologies in the Indian and Greek traditions. These material elements seem to have grown in number from three to four and then to five and their primitive meanings are preserved in the two well-developed systems of Buddhism and Jainism, the two so-called heterodox systems. In other words, they mark an earlier stage of the concept of the *mahābhūtas* as compared to the other systems of Indian thought, and their primary meaning is better revealed in the growth of these concepts in the early Greek Philosophy.

The traditional list enumerates them as *pṛthivī* (earth); *āpaḥ* (waters); *agni* (fire); *vāyu* (air); and *ākāśa* (sky). In its reverse order we find them at *Taittirīya* (2.1): *"tasmād vā etasmād ātmana ākāśas sambhūtaḥ* ǀ *ākāśāt vāyuḥ* ǀ *vāyoragniḥ* ǀ *agnerāpaḥ* ǀ *adbhyaḥ pṛthivī"*. Originally they were called merely as *bhūtas*. The earliest occurrence of the word *mahābhūta* is found in the *Aitareya Āraṇyaka* (3.4): *imāni ca pañca mahābhūtāni pṛthivī, vāyuḥ ākāśaḥ āpo jyotīṁṣi.* It is again found in the apocryphal 14th chapter of *Nirukta* the meaning of which is not at all clear. Another relatively early use is found in Charaka's *Śarīrasthāna* (1.27.28): *mahābhūtāni khaṁ vāyuragnirāpaḥ kṣitistathā* ǀ In the Pāli literature it is found in the *Sāmaññaphalasuttaṁ* of the *Dīghanikāya: ayaṁ kho me kāyo rūpī cātumahābhūtiko māttāpettikasambhavo odanakummāsūpacayo . . . idaṁ ca pan me viññāṇaṁ ettha sitaṁ ettha paḍibaddhaṁ*; in the *Saṁyuttanikāya*, 22.82 : *cattāro kho bhikkhū mahābhūtā hetu cattāro mahābhūtā pañcayo rūpakkhandhassa pañcāpanāya*; in the *Pañcaskandha Prakaraṇa* of Vasubandhu (as rendered in Sanskrit) *yat kincit rūpaṁ sarvaṁ tat catvāri mahābhūtāni catvāri ca mahābhūtāni upādāya.* Most of the earlier *Upaniṣads* and Jain and Buddhist works use the simpler word *bhūtāni* as in *Taittirīya* 3.1: *yato vā imāni bhūtāni jāyante yena jātāni jīvanti yat prayanti*; *Chandogya*, 1.9.1: *sarvāṇi ha vā imāni bhūtānyākāśādeva samutpadyante ākāśaṁ pratyastaṁ yānti.* (We should note particularly the words *sarvāṇi* "all" and *ākāśa* as the source); *Bṛhadāraṇyaka*, 2.4.2 : *etebhyo bhūtebhyaḥ samutthāya tānyeva amvinaśyati* (referring to *idaṁ mahadbhūtam*), 4.5.13, *Śvetāśvatara*, 1.2 : *kālaḥ svabhāvo niyatiryadṛcchā bhūtāni yoniḥ puruṣa iti cintyam* ।

In all other cases where the word *bhūta* is used in the eighteen *Upaniṣads* it means a creature or a being and not the material element. In the Pāli works, the word, usually used for the material element is not *bhūta* but *dhātu.* It is highly instructive to read Buddhaghoṣa's commentary *Papañcasūdanī* on *Majjhimanikāya* which says : *tatthāyaṁ bhūtasaddo pañcakkhaṁdha-amanussa-dhātu-vijjamāna-khīṇāsava-satta-rukkhādisu dissati.* These seven meanings are explained by him with passages from the Pāli canon as (1) (*pañcasu khaṃdhesu*); (2) 'goblin' (*yānīdha bhūtāni samāgatāni*); (3) the four material elements (*catusu dhātusu*); (4) any inanimate object (*bhūtasmiṃ pācittiyaṁ*); (5) as the predicative use of the verb (*bhū kāladhaso bhūto*); (6) all beings (*sabbe va nikkhipiṃsaṁti bhūtāloke samussayaṃ*); and (7) the vegetable kingdom, particularly the trees or plants (*bhūtagāmapātavyatāyā*).

The conclusion from this evidence can be easily drawn. *Mahābhūta* is the latest term to be used for the physical elements, which are taken collectively and hence mostly used in plural. This should be distinguished from its other use, where it is found without forming a *samāsa* and means the 'great being' *evaṁ vā aré idaṁ mahad bhūtam anantam apāraṁ vijñānaghana eva — Bṛhadāraṇyaka,* 2.4.12, immediately followed by the other use of *bhūta* in *Aitareya: bhūtebhyaḥ samutthāya.* It thus replaces the earlier word *bhūta* in the same sense. The Buddhists found the word *bhūta* in the sense of the material element confusing, because the primary and usual sense of the word was 'living being'. Hence they replaced it with the word *dhātu* which has the required meaning of a material substance. In its turn the word *bhūta* had the meaning of an embodied being, a living creature and incidentally 'a tree' when it is thought to possess life. It may be noted that the use of the word *bhūta* in this sense does not make a distinction between the material body and the animating soul, and thus represents a stage where both were inextricably mixed up, a stage in which these two aspects were not separated.

In the Jain philosophical writings both in Sanskrit and Prākṛt, the word *mahābhūta* is used while referring to the non-Jain systems of philosophy. Thus in the *Sūyagada,* 1.1.1 called the *samayajjhayaṇa* a reference to the *Lokāyata* system is found in the following two verses: *santi pañca mahabbhūyā ihamegesimāhiyā*। *ete pañca mahabbhūyā. . . āyachaddā pujegātu* । all of which refer to the Cārvāka system and again at 2.1.654 : *iha khalu pañca mahabbhūyā jehiṃ no kijjaī kiriyā* । It also uses the word *pañchamahabbhūiye* to refer to an adherent of this system. In all other cases the word *bhūyā* or *bhūyāiṁ* is used to refer to all kinds of living beings, *mettiṃ bhūésu kappaé bhūéhiṃ na virujjhejjhā* and to groups of various grades of living beings *Ṭhāṇaṃga* 3.359: *devāṇāgā jakkhā bhūyā* and the word *bhūyagāma* is used as a collective term. In fact, the phrase *sabbbé pāṇā, sabbé bhūyā sabbe jīvā sabbe sattā* occurs hundreds of times in the Ardhamāgadhī canon. In the later philosophical writings exemplified by the *Gaṇadharavāda* of the *Viśeṣāvaśyakabhāṣya* of Jinabhadra the words *pañcabhūya* or *bhūya* are used to remove the doubts of the fourth, *Gaṇadharaṁ Viyatta: kim maṇṇe pañcabhūyā atthi va nathitti sansao tujjha (1649); pañcakkhesu ṇa jutte tuha bhūmijalāṇalesu saṅdeho* । *aṇilāgāsesu bhave so viṇa kajjoṇumāṇāo* (1748). We may note in passing that Jinabhadra appears to believe that while the earth, water and fire are directly observable, wind and sky are only to be inferred being not perceptible. What he means can only be clarified in the context of the atomic theory of the Jain philosophers.

The usually accepted five material elements are rubricated in the classical philosophy of the Jains and are elaborated in the famous authoritative work, the *Tattvārthasūtra* of Umāswāti in a peculiar way thus differing from all other philosophical systems. Four of them are included in the concept of *pudgala* which stands for matter in general and the last one called *ākāśa* gets its place along with two other elements called *dharma* and *adharma* as non-sentient entities and coupled with the sentient living beings, *jīvas,* they form the group of five *astikāyas.* This group is then opposed to *kāla* (time) which is regarded as an immaterial non-living thing. Altogether they make up the six *dravyas* and constitute the whole universe called *loka tattvārtha, tatra lokaḥ kaḥ katividho vā kiṃ saṃstho vā* । *atrocyate pañcāstikāyasamudayo lokaḥ* (3-6). The space beyond the *loka* is called *alokākāśa* which is said to be completely void, which makes the place of *ākāśa* incompatible with the other four material elements. The latter forms a group by themselves to be contrasted with the living elements on the basis of their atomic structure. The current word used for them is *astikāya* 'having body'. Kundakunda, in his *Pañcāstikāya* points out that the *aṇu* or *paramāṇu* is the cause of the four *dhātus* (another term for the four material elements) and explains that they are constituted by the molecular units formed of the atoms. Each atom is supposed to possess one of the tastes *tikta, kaṭuka, kaṣāya, āmla* and *madhura,* one of the five colours *śveta, pīta, harita, aruṇa* and *kṛṣṇa,* one of the two smells *sugandha* and *durgandha* and at least two pairs of touch, *karkaśa, mṛdu, guru, laghu, śītoṣṇa, snigdharūkṣa* the last two pairs being compatible with each other, which means that a *paramāṇu* can be either cold or hot, wet or dry. It is also credited with various shapes like *parimaṇḍala, trikoṇa, caturasra, āyata* etc. This description of the atom appears to have a close resemblance with the description given by Leukippos and elaborated by Demokritos. In their view an atom is round and warm, white and rough, black and smooth, sour and angular, and sweet and large, round. This can hardly be an accident. This stage of thought is nearer the concept of animatism than animism, the first and second stages of the semantic development.

This complex theory of the atoms was not known to the earlier Jain writings, and they used the material elements as a part of their doctrine of *Chajjīvanikāya* the standard description of which is found in the 4th chapter of *Dasaveyāliya*, a *mūlasūtra.* The text says these six are *puḍhavikāiyā, āḍakāiyā, teḍakāiyā, vaṇassaikāiyā* and *tasakāiyā.* This view is completely animistic in nature. The elements are conceived as animated beings and only as an afterthought the body is thought to be made of the various elements. The *Vaiśeṣika* theory that all the elements have a threefold form viz. *śarīra-indriya-viṣaya-bhedāt* and the view that the earth-body is what we find here, while the bodies of other elements are located in the *Varuṇaloka,* the *Ādityaloka* and the *Vāyuloka* is a result of this secondary interpretation. *Ākāśa* being incorporeal is excluded from this scheme. The interrelation between the views of the Cārvākas, Buddhists, the Jains and the Vaiśeṣikas is not yet fully worked out in detail.

Before we are able to decide the exact stage of semantic development of these elements called *bhūtas* it is necessary to fix the earliest meaning of this word. It occurs in all Indian philosophical systems and in the so-called scientific cosmogonies of the pre-Socratic philosophers in Greece. It may be pointed out that there is no common word found in Greek to cover all the elements together and they are considered as having their own *phúsis.* The surest example of the reconstruction of a root in IE period is supplied by the equation Gr. *phúsis* and Skt. *bhūta* and a number of verbal and adjectival forms derived from this root. These can be listed as follows:

> Skt. *abhūta,* Gr. *éphū* aorist 3rd sg., Skt. *Bhūyāt,* Gr. *phuiē* benedictive, Skt. *babhūvān,* Gr. *pephuōs* perfect part., and its fem. Skt. *babhūvúṣī,* Gr. *pephunēa.* From these forms it is easy to set up the equation IE *bheə* — Skt *bhū,* Gr. *phúō.* There is a minor point of sound change in this, because the vowel is long in Sanskrit but short in Greek. The most likely explanation for it is to consider the root as having a dissyllabic structure. The root vowel was originally short, which has been set up as a long *ū* in Skt., for purely technical reasons that the root is to be given in the form in which it occurs in the past passive participle. That the vowel was originally short is reflected in the *sūtra* of Pāṇini *bhūvādayo dhātavaḥ,* 1.3.1. where, in spite of Patañjali, the V-sound was a mere glide between *bhū* and *ādi.*

The main purpose of this comparison is to find out the original meaning of this root. Without going into details I am inclined to think that the suppletion between the two Indo-European roots *bheə* and *es* tell us their semantic relationship.

While *as* — has the meaning of a verb of existence, the root *bhe ∂* — expresses the idea of growth, development, change. This is reflected in the Pāṇini's *Sūtra* 2.4.52 *asterbhūḥ* by which the root *bhū* replaces the root *as* in all non-conjugational tenses, which can be explained only on the assumption that *as* has a stative aspect, confirming the fact as it is, while *bhe ∂* has a progressive aspect, stating what the thing is growing or developing into. The first is static while the second is dynamic. This is quite clear in Sanskrit where *bhavati* means 'it grows', while *asti* means 'it exists'. Prof. Burnel appears to think that the corresponding root in Greek and its noun form *phúsis* means 'the stuff out of which a thing is made', thus having nearly the same meaning which *arkhē* has. Most linguists however believe that the root means 'to grow', and the noun means 'growth'. The meaning of *phúsis* as 'nature of a thing' is a later development due to its contrast with the other word *thésis* which means what is attributed or assigned to a thing, in fact, the association of a word with its meaning which corresponds to the Sanskrit concept of *vṛtti* or *saṁketa.* Its exact Skt. correspondence is *bhūti* which never has the meaning of existence but that of growth and hence prosperity. On the other hand, the passive participle of the root *bhe ∂* gives us in Sanskrit *bhūta* which has been all along used to refer to living beings. Only on this suffixation can we explain the meaning 'a tree' of this word as attested by Buddhaghoṣa in Pāli and the meaning of the Greek word *phúton* to mean a plant or tree as can be seen from its use in words like *zoophyte* — 'a plant resembling an animal' and *phyto*-graphy which means descriptive botany. This original meaning plays an important role in the context of cosmogony both in India and Greece where we are told that one thing gives birth to another or one thing merges into another, which are the basic concepts of the cosmogony of the elements.

The speculations of a cosmological nature which are found scattered in the major *Upaniṣads* have been clearly summarised by Prof. R.D. Ranade in his well-known work, *A Constructive Survey of Upanisadic Philosophy,* in which he has also drawn attention to similar ideas found in early Ionian philosophers from the seventh century onwards. Thales the earliest among them considered that all things came out of water. Anaximenes thought that air is the primary substance out of which arose all others by the process of *manósis* 'thinning' and *púllnosis* 'the process of thickening'. Anaximander considered the primary substance to be infinite or indeterminate, calling it *a-peiron* 'endless', which was intermediate between earth and water on the one side and air and fire on the other, from which developed all these four elements.

Heracleitos of Ephesos championed the claim of fire as the source of the other elements by saying that fire first transformed itself into sea and this changed partly into earth and partly into air (*prēstḗr*) as can be seen from his fragments 20 to 26. With these can be compared *Bṛhadāraṇyaka,* V.5.1: *āpevedamagre āsuḥ* । *tā āpaḥ satyamasṛjanta. Chāndogya,* IV.3.1: *vāyurvāva saṁvargo* । *yadā vā agnirudvāyati vāyumeva apyeti* । *yadā āpaḥ ucchuṣyanti vāyumeva apiyanti.* We find in *Chāndogya,* VI. 8.4 the suggestion that the first evolute was fire from which came water and food (which stands for the earth) on the analogy of the root and the shoot of a tree: *evameva khalu somya annena śuṅgena āpomūlamanviccha, adbhiḥ somya śuṅgena tejomūlamanviccha tejasā somya śuṅgena sanmūlamanviccha.* There are a couple of passages where *ākāśa* (is it sky? heaven, or space?) is considered as the source of all the other elements. *Chāndogya* 1.9.1: *sarvāṇi ha vā imāni bhūtāni ākāśādeva samutpadyante ākāśaṁ pratyastaṁ yanti.* As thought progressed, the *Upaniṣads* suggested some abstract or psychological objects as the real source of all these elements. Like Anaximander's *á-peiron ākāśa* is taken as the source of all. Similarly *asat* (Gr. *mē ón*), *sat* (Gr. *ón*), *prāṇa, ātman* and still later a creator was taken as the original point of departure. All these speculations suggest some further progress of thought, but do not explain or clarify the older ideas of taking the elements as basic, which certainly was the earlier stage.

To understand the conceptual background of these earlier cosmogonies, we have to look at the history of the meanings of the words used for the elements. In other words, we have to fix the original meanings of the names of these elements. A few facts about them may be stated without much discussion. The words *pṛthivī, ap, tejas, vāyu* and *ākāśa* appear to be their original designations. Only at a later stage, when these words lost their cosmological affiliations are they replaced by other words having the same meaning. From being of specific connotations, they acquired more generalised meaning and then it became unimportant which word could be used for them. One can compare the original words with the words used in a text like *Caraka Saṁhitā*: *kha, ap, vāyu, agni, kṣiti, mahī* and *bhūmi* are used only in the *Jaiminīyopaniṣad,* 1.10.10, while *kṣiti* is found in the older *Upaniṣads. Maitrāyaṇī* has the list in the form *ākāśavāyvagnyudaka bhūmyādayaḥ* 6.4; *vāta* is not used in this context, as also *udaka.* In *Muṇḍaka,* 2.1.3 we read: *etasmāt (puruṣāt) jāyate prāṇo manaḥ sarvendriyāṇi ca* । *khaṁ vāyurjyotirāpaḥ pṛthivī viśvasya dhāriṇī* । which is a very late form of cosmogony and these things never play the role of a source. Long ago Meillet showed that while *udaka* means water in a secular sense, *āpaḥ* has religious and cosmological associations. Of the two IE words for fire, *agni* (IE *ognis*) and *púr,* the first is the older being found in the marginal areas while *púr* (e.g. fire) is an innovation.

The situation is very similar to this in Greek as well. For earth both *gē* and *khthōn* are used but the first gets a place in the cosmology as one member of the primeval pair, and is used as an element. *Khthōn* cognate with Skt. *kṣmā* mostly refers to the surface of the earth, as a place of habitation. In the *Iliad*, XIX-259 it is associated with the seen and the Erinys and occurs in the utterance of an imprecation (*gē te Kái hèlios Kāi Evinéies*). For wind *áveimos* (root — *ave*— to blow) is used which suggests its origin in breathing, while Sanskrit *vāyu* corresponds to *aēr* and originally meant mist, or lower atmosphere, as against the upper vault or firmament, which corresponds to Sanskrit *ākāśa* 'the shining one'. The word used in the building up of the Greek mythology is however *Ouranós* 'heaven'. *Aithér* is used as a feminine noun to refer to the upper air or heaven. Thus air and sky did not occur as different elements in Greek cosmogony. Here either one or other element is taken as the original substance which in the Greek mythology is concerned as a living thing, and in no way different from the anthropomorphic gods.

The situation is slightly different in the Upaniṣadic cosmogonies. While commenting upon *Chāndogya*, III.14.1: *tajjalāniti śānta upāsīta* the cryptic word *tajjalān* is explained by Śaṅkara with the words, *katham sarvasya brahmatvam-ityata āha tajjalāniti* । *tasmād brahmaṇo jātaṁ tejo' bannādikrameṇa sarvam* । *atastajjam* । *tathā tenaiva jananakrameṇa pratilomatayā tasminneva brahmaṇi līyate tadātmatayā ślişyate iti tallam* । *tathā tasminneva sthitikāle'niti prāṇiti ceṣṭate iti* ।

Whatever the value of such an explanation, taking the word-element *ja* from *jāta*, *la* from *līyate* and *an* from *aniti*, it is obvious that the cosmogonies use two methods of evolution and involution to describe the process of creation or dissolution, which is only partly true of the Greek cosmogonies. Obviously the process is built on the model of the birth, existence, and death of a man or a living being. A close scrutiny of the wording of the cosmogonies reveals the fact that in all of them, the process of birth and also that of absorption or end on the part of these basic elements is used in the active sense, as something which they do. This means they are animate things acting on their own. In this context we should consider expressions like: *tā āpaḥ satyamasṛjanta tadaikṣata bahu syāṁ prajāyeyeti, tattejo'sṛjata* while creating and *apyeti, prayanti, abhisaṁviśanti* while merging, which attribute to them conscious acts of origination and dissolution.

Let us summarise the semantic development discussed so far. The four elements or *mahābhūtas* were originally considered as living objects like men and animals, and hence could do all the activities which were expected of them as living beings. This stage of thought is given the name of animatism by the anthropologists while dealing with the origins of religion. At this stage no distinction was drawn between the living and lifeless. This was the stage at which these four or five *mahābhūtas* were conceived.

In the next stage occurred a differentiation between those who were endowed with the power of conscious activity which gave rise to anthropomorphism and there emerged mythological stories when these elements, particularly the earth, water, air and sky were personified to produce the stories of creation. This marked the second stage of thought where a distinction was drawn between the sentient element and the non-sentient part which was conceived as the bodies of these elements. This gave rise to what are known as the scientific cosmogonies of the early Greek thinkers, and also some of the early cosmogonies found in the *Upaniṣads.*

The third stage of development further emphasized the part played by the psychic element in creation and the cosmologies were so adjusted as to give to these elements the real activity of production, while their bodies were regarded as inanimate by nature. This completed the distinction between living and lifeless things. Further growth of thought centred round the ephemeral or permanent nature of the psychic element called the soul. The semantic history of the Greek word *psūkhe* epitomises this development in its three successive meanings breath, life and soul, while others like *gē, herdór, púr, ánemos, aithēr* or *ouranós* became fixed in their meanings at the end of the second stage of development.

8

The Mahābhūtas

The Buddhist Approach

Pratibha Pingle

While considering the concept of *mahābhūtas* in the Buddhist context, normally attention is drawn to Pāli commentaries, but the present discussion is based not on the Pāli sources,[1] but on Sanskrit sources and to be very precise, on a later work, the *Abhidharmakoṣa* of Vasubandhu. This is because of the fact that although late (i.e. fourth century AD) the *Abhidharmakoṣa* is a systematized exposition of a much earlier work, the *Abhidharma-Vibhāṣā Śāstra*, which is a commentary on the *Abhidharma* of the *Sarvāstivāda* school. And this school is one of the earliest of the Buddhist sects. The age of Vasubandhu is about the same as that of the Pāli commentaries. Moreover, the *Abhidharmakoṣa* is accepted as an authority by all the schools of Buddhism, though it is written from the standpoint of the *Sarvāstivāda*. And that is why *Abhidharmakoṣa* will be the main source for this discussion about the *bhūtas*.

The terms *mahābhūta* (the gross elements of matter) and *aṇu* are not specifically Buddhist, though the terms *pṛthivī* etc., have lost their original meaning completely in the Buddhist context. This is the characteristic example of the Buddhist terms, which in the beginning were definitely a physical phenomenon, and acquired psychological character subsequently. In the field of the Buddhist theory of the *dharmas*, which explains the existence of consciousness-stream, it is not easy to explain the terms like *bhūta* and *aṇu* which have obviously a material meaning. To the Buddhist, the universal elements of Matter are more energies than the substances. And this is indicated by the fact that air (*vāyu*), the fourth gross element is characterised by motion.

Now let us see the place of the *mahābhūtas* in the context of Buddhist philosophy. The simplest classification of all the elements of existence is represented by a division into five groups of elements. The first of them is matter — *Rūpaskandha*. The physical elements of personality, including its outer world, i.e., the external objects, are represented by this one item — matter. If we use the old pre-Buddhistic term *nāma-rūpa,* this matter, the first of the five *skandhas*— is *rūpa* and the rest of the four *skandhas— vedanā* (feelings), *samjñā* (ideas). *Saṁskāra* (volition) and *vijñāna* (pure sensation) come under the category of *nāma. Abhidharmakoṣa* explains this *rūpa* —

> रूपं पञ्चेन्द्रियाण्यर्थाः पञ्चाविज्ञप्तिरेव च।
> *rupaṁ pañcendriyāṇyarthāḥ pañcāvijñaptireva ca* ।
> *Abhi.* 1.9.
>
> The *rūpa-skandha* consists of five senseorgans (*indriyas*), their five objects (*arthas*) and the unmanifested Act (*avijñapti*).

Thus it is elevenfold. The five sense -organs are the eye, the ear, the nose, the tongue and the tactile organ. And the five objects are the objects of these very sense-organs, namely the visible, the sound, the odour, the taste and the tangible. It is further said —

> तद्विज्ञानाश्रया रूपप्रसादाश्चक्षुरादयः।
> *tadvijñānāśrayā rūpaprasādāścakṣurādayaḥ* ।
> *Abhi.*, 1.9
>
> The subtle material elements (*rūpaprasāda*) (conveying visual and other sensations), which are the points of support (*āśraya*) for the respective consciousness of the visual etc. (or the eye etc.) are the five sense-organs the eye etc.

Vasubandhu quotes from the *Prakaraṇa-grantha* —

> चक्षुः कतमत्। चक्षुर्विज्ञानाश्रयो रूपप्रसादः
> *cakṣuḥ katamat* । *cakṣurvijñānāśrayo rūpaprasādaḥ*
>
> What is *cakṣu.* It is subtle material element (*rūpaprasāda*) which is a point of support for the eye consciousness etc.

Similar is the case with the rest of the sense-organs. And this *rūpaprasāda* or the subtle material element is derived (*upādāya*) from *mahābhūta,* the gross elements. "O Monk, the eye is the internal base of cognition of the subtle element of matter, which is derived from the four gross elements. This is the explanation". Thus the five sense-organs and their five external objects (and of course *avijñapti*) is the Matter. In other words matter is nothing but sense-data. It is broadly divided into two categories. Objective sense-data (*artha* or *viṣaya*) constituting external objects and the sense-organs conceived as a kind of translucent subtle matter (*rūpaprasāda*) which is "like the shining of the jewel, it cannot be cut into two. And it disappears without a residue at death". It covers the body when it is living. This division is similar to the *Sāṁkhya* view that matter developed along two different lines, the one with predominance of the translucent intelligence-stuff (*sattva*) resulting in sense-organs, the other with predominance of dead matter (*tamas*) resulting in sense-objects in their subtle (*tanmātra*) and gross (*mahābhūta*) forms. The concept of *tanmātra* comes very near to the Buddhist conception of an element of matter. But the fundamental difference between the two conceptions is that in the *Sāṁkhya* system these elements are modifications of an eternal substance. In Buddhism they are mere sense-data without any substance in them.

After explaining the nature of these sense-organs the *Koṣa* describes the external objects.

> The visible is two-fold and twentyfold.
> The sound is eightfold.
> The taste is sixfold.
> The odour is fourfold.
> The tangibles are elevenfold.
>
> (For details please see the Appendix)

When we say that *rūpa* consists of the sense-organs and their external object, we have to see what the term *rūpa* means : *rūpyate bādhyate iti rūpam.* Matter is what materializes. According to Prof. Th. Stcherbatsky, matter is what materializes. Different meanings are given of this materializing — as pressure, pain, disappearance or change. Thus matter is something that disappears. The real meaning is impenetrability (*sapratighatva*) which is further expressed variously. The impenetrability is defined as the fact that space occupied by one of them cannot at the same time be occupied by another. This *rūpa* or matter is atomic.

When it is said that both the types of matter is derived from the *mahābhūtas*, which are these *bhūtas* —

> भूतानि पृथिवीधातुरप्तेजोवायुधातवः . . . महत्त्वमेषां
> सर्वान्यरूपाश्रयत्वेनौदारिकत्वात्।
>
> *bhūtāni pṛthivīdhāturaptejovāyudhātavaḥ . . mahattvameṣāṁ*
> *sarvānyarūpāśrayatvenaudārikatvat* ।
>
> The gross material elements (*bhūtas*) are the primary substances (*dhātu*) of earth, water, fire and air. Their grossness is because of their greatness and because of their being the support of all other forms.[2]

And again in which these primary substances — (*dhātus*) are established. What is their nature?

> ते पुनरेते धातवः कस्मिन् कर्मणि संसिद्धा
> किं स्वभावाश्चेत्याह धृत्यादिकर्मसंसिद्धाः।
> *te punarete dhātavaḥ kasmin karmaṇi saṁsiddhā* ।
> *kim svabhāvāścetyāha dhṛtyādikarmasaṁsiddhā* ।।
> *Abhi.*, 1.12.

> They are established through their (respective) functions like supporting etc.

These primary substances — the earth, water, fire and air — are established through their respective functions as follows :

earth — *dhṛti* or holding together,
water — *saṁgraha* or cohesion or striking.
fire — *pakti*, ripening, maturing or transformation
and
air — *vyūhana* movement.

Vyūhana should be understood as expansion, *vṛddhi* or *prasarpaṇa*.

Their natures are respectively

> खरस्नेहोष्णतेरणाः। खरः पृथिवीधातुः। स्नेहोऽब्धातुः। उष्णता तेजोधातुः।
> ईरणा वायुधातुः।
> *kharasnehoṣṇateraṇāḥ* । *kharaḥ pṛthivīdhātuḥ* । *sneho'bdhātuḥ* ।
> *uṣṇatā tejodhātuḥ* । *īraṇā vāyudhātuḥ* ।

> Hardness is the earth element.
> Adhesion is the water element
> Heat is the fire element.
> Motion is the air element.

The *Abhidharmakoṣa* also explains the different meaning of the word *pṛithivī* in the sense of a *bhūta* and in the common usage. This peculiarity of the Buddhist terms is already mentioned in the beginning.

The *Koṣa* says —

> कः पुनः पृथिव्यादीनां पृथिवीधात्वादीनां च विशेषः ?
> *kaḥ punaḥ pṛthivyādīnāṁ pṛthivīdhātvādīnāṁ ca viśeṣaḥ* ?

> What is the distinction between the earth and the earth element.

पृथिवी वर्णसंस्थानमुच्यते लोकसंज्ञया।
pṛthivī varṇasaṁsthānamucyate lokasaṁjñayā ।

In common parlance what is designated as earth is colour (*varṇa*) and shape (*saṁsthāna*).

Now what is *pṛthivīdhātu*? We have already seen that the matter is atomic. These are simple atoms (*dravyaparamāṇu*) and combined atoms (*saṅghātaparamāṇu*). The *dravyaparamāṇus* do not appear separately. The combined ones include four atoms of 'universal elements' (*mahābhūtas*) conventionally termed as earth, water, fire, air. But it is expressly stated that these are only conventional names, they denote respectively a hard stuff, a coagulating stuff, heat and motion. They are called universal because they are present everywhere, in every piece of matter, always in the same proportion; but in some combinations one or the other energy may get greater intensity and we accordingly get hard and liquid stuffs, warm and moving bodies. There is as much element of heat in a blazing flame as there is in wood or in water and *vice versa*. The difference is only in their intensity, e.g. the tactile sensation may have a different degree of intensity as the touch by the bunch of steel needles is more intensely felt than the touch of a painter's brush although the quantity may be the same. It is also said that the existence of cohesion, i.e., of the element water in a flame is proved by its keeping a shape. The pressure of repulsion of hardness, i.e., of the element of earth, in water is proved by the fact of its supporting a ship etc. Yaśomitra's *Sphuṭārthā* — the *Adhidharmakoṣabhāṣya* — explains many such examples in II. 22.[3] The *Koṣa* says:

रूप्यते बाध्यते इत्यर्थः
rūpyate bādhyate ityarthaḥ

Rūpa is that which obstructs.

What is that obstruction

रूपस्य पुनः का बाधना ? विपरिणामोत्पादना
rūpasya punaḥ kā bādhanā ? vipariṇāmotpādanā

What is the nature of that impress or obstruction created by *rūpa*. It brings about some change, creation of transformation.

न वै परमाणुरूपं एकं पृथग् भूतमस्ति। संघातस्थं तु तद् रूप्यत एव।
na vai paramāṇurūpaṁ ekaṁ pṛthag bhūtamasti ।
saṅghātasthaṁ tu tad rūpyata eva ।

> The separate atom does not have any form. But in collected form it impresses or obstructs.[4] Every combined atom includes four atoms of the four *mahābhūtas* or universal elements and at least four secondary atoms, what may be termed as atoms or quality (*bhautika*) — of colour, of smell, of taste and of touch, one of each. Consequently a combined atom consists at least of eight simple atoms in *Kāmadhātu.* When matter resounds, an atom of sound becomes present in every combined atom, it then consists of nine parts. The number increases in organic matter, the organs of sense being also a special atomic matter. Each secondary atom always has as its support a combination of four universal ones. According to other authorities the number of primary atoms supporting each atom of quality must be eight, two of each element. So (in reality) a combined atom has many more parts, but it is usually spoken of as consisting of eight kinds of matter at least. And this only is the sphere of defiled matter (*kāmadhātu*). In the higher regions of pure matter (*rūpadhātu*) smells and tastes are absent and the combined atom changes accordingly.

We have already seen that the subtle or translucent organic matter is also atomic. It is represented by five different kinds of atoms. The *Kośa* gives the description and the arrangement of these atoms.[5]

The atoms of the eye the organ of sight (*cakṣurindriya*) cover in concentric circles the pupil of the eye; these look like the small jar flowing. The atoms of the ear are arranged inside the conch or the outer ear. The atoms of the nose, the olfactory organ — are located inside the nostrils. These look like cone-shaped and remain arranged like the garland in the same way as the atoms of the eye and ear are arranged. The atoms of the organ of taste, or precisely, that matter which is supposed to convey the sensation of taste or the gestatory organ are like a half moon. They are scarcely spread over the centre of the tongue. The atoms of the tactile organ are pervasive in character as the organ itself. It is said that all the atoms of the organ of sight and the tactile organ are not *sabhāga* (or function only in their own field). Some of them are *tatsambhāga* (not confined to their own field). The atoms of other organs are *sabhāga* only. The atoms of *pumindriya* (the faculty of masculinity) look like the thumb (*aṅguṣṭha*) and of *strīndriya* (faculty of femininity) are like the horn (*bherī*) or vessel (*kaṭāha*). These two organs are placed in some parts of *kāyendriya* but these are distinctly different both in structure and function. That is why their atoms are separately mentioned.

The Buddhists explain their atom-theory as parallel to the *kṣaṇavāda.* Atom is the smallest unit of so-called matter.[6] Moment is the smallest unit of so-called time. And all atoms are momentary existences having no duration.

So far we have discussed the ten aspects of the elevenfold Buddhist matter. The subtle, internal fivefold organic matter and the five external objects. Now let us come to the eleventh aspect — *avijñapti,* which is not discussed in Pāli Commentaries so elaborately.

The *Koṣa* says :

> विक्षिप्ताचित्तकस्यापि योऽनुबन्धः शुभाशुभः।
> महाभूतान्युपादाय स ह्यविज्ञप्तिरुच्यते।
> *vikṣiptācittakasyāpi yo'nubandhaḥ śubhāśubhaḥ* ।
> *mahābhūtānyupādāya sa hyavijñaptirucyate* ।
> *Abhi.,* 1.11

> *Avijñapti* is that stream of actions which being morally either good or bad, is present even in the mind of a distracted or unconscious person and which is essentially a product of material element.

The term *avijñapti* implies that this particular kind of physical element cannot be revealed to others. Unlike the other ten elements of *rūpaskandha,* it is unmanifested and undiscoverable. When we promise to do something and then fulfil the promise after some time, the interval between the promise and the overt action of its fulfilment represent the period, when the physical action remains unexpressed as *avijñaptirūpa.* The folding of one's hands in prayer and an accidental, unintentional folding of the hands are two different kinds of actions, the former being accompanied by concealed form of moral activity — *avijñaptirūpa.* Obviously *avijñaptirūpa* has a twofold character. It is not merely a *rūpa* like the visible etc., because unmanifested as it is, it always implies some kind of activity (*kriyā*); nor is it mere activity, because, it is essentially a product of the material elements and therefore shares the nature of *rūpa.*

This idea of *avijñapti* is a special concept recognised by only the *Sarvāstivādins.*[7]

In Indian tradition the *mahābhūtas* are counted as five, the fifth being *ākāśa.* In the *Koṣa, ākāśa* is included in the *asaṁskṛta dharmas* :

> अनास्रवा मार्गसत्यं त्रिविधं चाप्यसंस्कृतम्।
> आकाशं द्वौ निरोधौ च तत्राकाशमनावृतिः।।
> *anāsravā mārgasatyaṁ trividhaṁ cāpyasaṅskṛtam* ।

ākāśaṁ dvau nirodhau ca tatrākāśamanāvṛtiḥ ||
Abhi., 1.5

> Undefined *dharmas* (*anāsrava*) consist of truth of the path of salvation and the threefold unconditioned *dharmas* — space and two types of cessation. Space means absence of covering (where matter can penetrate).

Thus contrary to the matter, it is of the nature of non-obstruction. It is *arūpī, anidarśana, apratigha, anāsrava* and *asaṁskṛta.* But when *ākāśa* is counted in the list of *dhātus* or the elements of existence it is exactly the opposite, i.e., *rūpī, sanidarśana, sapratigha, sāsrava* and *saṁskṛta. Abhidharma* defines local space as a hole or cavity in which there are no material objects but which like a mouth or gate is near them and can be perceived. It is described as the gaps or holes which occur between visible objects. This local space is described to be two-fold. The cavities in doors and windows etc. is external *ākāśadhātu.* And the cavities in the mouth or nose is internal *ākāśadhātu.*

Thus according to *Koṣa, ākāśa* is not included in the list of the *mahābhūtas.*

Generally speaking the Buddhists do not show much interest in what the *bhūtas* are and what they do. This absence could be because of two reasons :

1. Keeping in mind the goal of the Buddhists there was no incentive to do any serious thinking about the non-human and non-moral universe.
2. Secondly, the Buddhists attributed moral function to the law of cause and effect. They did not accept cosmic activity as impersonal and inevitable but explained it in the light of their belief in the *karma* theory. However, the concept of the *mahābhūtas* is discussed in detail in the *Abhidharma* texts.

APPENDIX

I. The Visible (*Rūpa*) is twofold — colour and form.

The colour is fourfold — blue, yellow, red, white, other colours are the varieties of these four. The form is eightfold — odd etc.

(In other words) the same *Rūpāyatana* is twentyfold:

1.	*nīla*	—	blue
2.	*pīta*	—	yellow
3.	*lohita*	—	red
4.	*avadāta*	—	white
5.	*dīrgha*	—	long
6.	*hrasva*	—	short

7. *vṛtta*	—	round
8. *parimaṇḍala*	—	circle
9. *unnata*	—	high
10. *avanata*	—	low
11. *sāta*	—	even
12. *visata*	—	odd
13. *abhra*	—	of the colour of the cloud
14. *dhūma*	—	of the colour of the smoke
15. *rajas*	—	of the colour of the dust
16. *mahika*	—	of the colour of the mist
17. *chāyā*	—	of the colour of the shadow
18. *ātapa*	—	of the colour of the sun
19. *āloka*	—	of the colour of the moon
20. *andhakāra*	—	of the colour of the darkness

II. The audible is eightfold:

1. *upāttamahābhūta* — produced artificially by four gross elements.
2. *anupāttamahābhūta* — produced non-artificially by four gross elements.
3. *sattvākhya* — produced by living beings.
4. *asattvākhya*—produced by non-living being. Each of these forms is further divided into harmonious (*manojña*) and discordant (*amanojña*).

III. The taste is sixfold:

1. *madhura*	—	sweet
2. *āmla*	—	sour
3. *lavaṇa*	—	salty
4. *kaṭuka*	—	bitter
5. *tikta*	—	pungent
6. *kaṣāya*	—	astringent

IV. The odour is fourfold.

mild and strong smell of good and bad odour.

sugandhadurgandhayoḥ samaviṣama-gandhatvāt

V. The tangibles are elevenfold:

Four gross elements, smoothness

(*ślakṣṇatva*), harshness (*karkaśatva*),

heaviness (*gurutva*), lightness

(laghutva), coldness (*śītam*)

hunger (*jighatsā*), thirst (*pipāsā*)

Notes

1. The concept of the *mahābhūtas* is discussed in detail in the Pāli commentaries — the

Dhammasaṁgaṇī, the *Aṭṭhasālinī* etc.

2. The Pāli commentaries discuss in detail why the elements of existence are called *mahā* (gross).
3. सूचीतूलीकलापस्पर्शवत् सक्तुलवणचूर्ण रसवत् च। अग्निभूते सति कठिनस्य लोहस्य द्रवणम् तेन ज्ञायते लोहेऽब्धातुरस्तीति। तथा द्रवस्य शैत्यादिप्रत्ययलाभे काठिन्यं तेन ज्ञायते पृथ्वीधातोरत्रास्तित्वमिति। तथा कठिनसंघर्षादौष्ण्यमुपलभ्यते। तेन तेजोधातोरत्रास्तित्वं गम्यते।
4. For more explanation, see *The Buddhist Nirvāṇa* by Th. Stcherbatsky.
5. श्रोत्रेन्द्रियपरमाणवो भूर्जाभ्यन्तरावस्थिताः। घ्राणेन्द्रियपरमाणवो घटाभ्यन्तरेण शलाकावत्। आद्यानि त्रीणीन्द्रियाणि मालावदवस्थितानि। जिह्वेन्द्रियपरमाणवोऽर्धचन्द्रवत्। वालाग्रमात्रं किल मध्यजिह्वायां जिह्वेन्द्रियपरमाणुरभिस्फुटम्। कायेन्द्रियपरमाणवः कायवदवस्थिताः। स्त्रीन्द्रियपरमाणवो भेरीकटाहवत्। पुरुषेन्द्रियपरमाणवोऽङ्गुष्ठवत्। तत्र चक्षुरिन्द्रियपरमाणवः कदाचित्सर्वे सभागा भवन्ति। कदाचित्तत्सभागाः काचिदेके सभागाः एके तत्सभागाः। एवं यावत् जिह्वेन्द्रियपरमाणवः *Bhāṣya* on 1.44.
6. परमाण्वक्षरक्षणाः। रूपनामाध्वपर्यन्तः। *Abhi.*, 3.85. *bhāṣya* — रूपस्यापचीयमानस्य पर्यन्तः परमाणुः कालस्य पर्यन्तः क्षणो नाम्नः पर्यन्तो क्षणम्।
7. 'What is Avijñaptirūpa' by Prof. V.V. Gokhale, In *Ñew Indian Antiquary*, Vol. 1.

References

The Abhidharmakoṣa with Bhāṣya, ed. by P. Pradhan.

The Sphuṭārtha-Abhidharmakoṣavyākhyā, ed. by Dvarikadasa Sastri.

Th. Stcherbatsky, "The Central Conception of Buddhim" and "The Soul Theory of the Buddhists".

Conze, *Buddhist Thought in India.*

'What is Avijñaptirūpa' by Prof. V.V. Gokhale, In *New Indian Antiquary,* Vol. 1.

Dic Probleme der Buddhistischen Philosophie, by O. Rosenberg.

9

Concept of Bhūta in Early Buddhist Philosophy

Mahesh Tiwary

Early Buddhist Philosophy, generally understood as *Abhidhamma* philosophy, is a well-integrated system of thought which accepts the existence of thirtyone world-systems, situated in vacuum in an ascending order. They are broadly divided in three main spheres, namely *kāma-dhātu, rūpa-dhātu*, and *arūpa-dhātu.* There are eleven world-systems in the *kāma-dhātu,* sixteen in *rūpa-dhātu,* and four in *arūpa-dhātu,* making the total number thirtyone. According to Buddhist thought, the beings of the *kāma-dhātu* and *rūpa-dhātu* are the psycho-physical manifestations and those of the *arūpa-dhātu* are in possession of the psychic personality alone.

The structural exposition of the beings has been made with two reals, namely, *nāma* and *rūpa.* The term *nāma* stands for the inner personality, expressing itself through the *citta* (consciousness) and *cetasika* (psychic factors). *Rūpa* refers to the physical personality, within and without, gross in nature and material in character with all its varieties of manifestations. The concept of *bhūtas* in *Abhidhamma* philosophy is thus closely related to the notion of *rūpa,* for it is the generic name for material elements.

Many insights have been thrown on both the *nāma* and *rūpa* in canonical (*Piṭaka*), non-canonical (*Aṇu-piṭaka*), commentarial (*Aṭṭhakathā*), sub-commentarial (*Ṭīkā*) and miscellaneous (*Pakiṇṇa*) Pāli literature in general, and in all the seven texts of the *Abhidhamma-Piṭaka* in particular. The issue has further been taken up in the philosophical treatises, appearing as independent texts, commentaries and manuals like *Visuddhimagga, Aṭṭhasālinī, Sammoha-vinodini, Pañcapakaraṇa-Aṭṭhakathā, Abhidhammāvatāra, Abhidhammatthasaṅgaha, Nāmarūpa-pariccheda, Paramattha-vinicchaya* etc.

There is detailed discussion on the concept of *rūpa* in the second chapter of the *Dhammasangaṇī,* the first book of the *Abhidhamma-piṭaka,* in a catechetical way. The question has been raised such as — "What is that which is called *rūpa* in totality?"[1] The answer follows that "The four *mahābhūtas* (basic material elements) and the *upādā-rūpas* (generated material elements) constitute the *rūpa* in totality."

According to early Buddhist thought, *mahābhūtas* are four in number. They are: *paṭhavī-dhātu* (earth-element), *āpo-dhātu* (water-element), *tejo-dhātu* (fire element) and *vāyo-dhātu* (air-element). They form the basic material elements or the primary non-psychic Real (*paramatha*). The material creations related to beings, internal (*ajjhatika*) and external (*bahira*), and the surroundings all around them in both the spheres of *kāma-dhātu* and *rūpa-dhātu* are their creations and manifestations. They take variegated forms in the process of evolution and play a vital role in smooth functioning of the universal psycho-physical order. They are vital components in creation in the *kāma-dhātu* and *rūpa-dhātu*. It is for this reson that they are called *mahābhūta*.

Early Buddhist heritage attributes five basic reasons for referring to the basic material elements as *mahābhūtas*. These reasons, which also provide a broad understanding of the concept of *bhūtas* are enumerated as follows:

Mahantapātubhāvato (Manifestation of Greatness)

They are called *mahābhūta* because of manifestation of greatness. It means they manifest with immense vastness with respect to phenomena 'grasped at' (*upādinnasantati*) and to those of un-grasped at (*ana-upādinna-santati*). In case of the former, they appear as the material forms, as the bodies of various kinds of beings like men, gods, demons, animals, birds, etc. In latter case, they appear into a world system, tremendously vast, traditionally calculated as 1203450 *yojanas* in circumference containing big waters, mountains (like Sineru, Isadhara, Karavīka, Sudassana, Nemidhara, Vinataka, Himavā etc.), as well as the grandeurous trees like *jambu*-tree in the Jambu-dīpa, *citta-pātalī*-tree (trumpet flower) in the kingdom of demon; *simbalī*-tree (silk-cotton) in the land of Garulas, *kadambas*-tree in Aparagoyāna, *kappa*-tree in Uttarakura, and *sirisa*-tree (acacis) in *pubba-videha* and the *paricchattaka*-tree (coral) in the divine kingdom of Tāvatiṃsa etc.[2]

Mahābhūta-sāmaññato (Showing illusory Resemblances in Phenomena)

They are called *mahābhūta* because of their appearance as illusory resemblances in variegated forms of deceitful manifestations. They are not in their being, possessing any colour but they manifest as blue, yellow, red, white, black etc. They are illusory objects appearing as real and continuing to develop the impression of being real, just like the juggler showing water which is not water, a gem, stone or gold which is not real. Marking their such illusory resemblances to the juggler's counterfeiting, they are called *mahābhūtas.*

They are again explained with the simile of ogresses. As ogresses seductively transform their external appearances, and hide their own terrible forms, so the *mahābhūtas* conceal their true nature and present an illusion to the people. This characteristic of concealing the true identity being a similar trait they share with ogresses, they are called *mahābhūtas.*

Mahā-pariharato (Immensity of their Maintenance)

They are called *mahābhūta* because of immensity of their maintenance. It has its reference to the moment to moment generational changes in material structure of the beings due to fourfold food (*āhāra*) and factors like *kamma, citta, utu* and *āhāra.* Thus, it is said that — "these mateial forms, being daily maintained occur as essentials through abundance of food, covering etc., hence there is the name *mahābhūta*".

Maha-vikārato (Immensity of Metamorphoses)

Again they are called *mahābhūta* because of the immensity of their metamorphoses. It refers to the tremendous changes undergone by the elements in material forms, both in derived and 'un-derived' phenomena. Of these, the vastness of changes in the 'underived' is manifested on the occasion of the destruction of the world-cycle. Similar changes are manifested with respect to 'derived ones', when there is the disturbance of the elements within.

At the time of the destruction of the world-cycle, all the four basic material elements become furious and manifest in their devastating forms. The Fire-element turns into blazing flames embracing the world system up to the *Brahmaloka,* consuming the entire phenomena and turning the universe as the heap of ash. The water-element, on such occasions, also take the form of overwhelming watery uproar and the world of ten myriad *koṭis* is made overpowered and reduced to nothing within it. Similar becomes the form of air-element which blows away the entire phenomena and reduce them to the dust particles.

Vast changes are brought when there is the disturbance of the element in the 'derived phenomena'. When there is disturbance in the earth-element, the bodies become stiff as if they enter the mouth of *kaṭṭhamuka.* Due to the disturbance in the water-element, the bodies go putrid and become rotten as if entered into the mouth of *pūtimukha.* The bodies become hot and turn into wax as entered in the mouth of *aggimukha* due to disturbance in the fire-element. Further, when there is the disturbance in the air-element, the bodies are turned into pieces as if they have entered the mouth of the *satthamukha*. Such mighty and devastating changes take place in the basic material elements with reference to 'underived' and 'derived' phenomena and as such they are called *mahā-bhūta.*[3]

Mahanta-bhūtata (Vast elementality)

They are called *mahābhūta* because of their vast elementality. It means that they exist as very powerful force and do not come under the process of *dassana* or *bhāvanā* for their elimination. Mighty efforts are required to cope with them. Specially in *kāma-dhātu,* where there is the existence of a being, there is the existence of the *mahābhūtas.* One cannot have even the idea of the beings without them.

In this way, a set of five reasons are seen in the tradition to explain the name *mahābhūta.*

Depending on these four basic material elements, there arise the *upādā-rūpa. Upādā* means generated, derived, dependent etc. The material elements which come into being depending upon the four *mahābhūtas* are called *upādā-rūpa.* This may be understood with the simile of the earth and tree. Like the earth are the *mahābhūtas,* and the *upādā-rūpas* are just like trees which spring therefrom. It is for this reason they are called 'derived material elements'. They have been stated to be twenty-three in earlier texts. Later on, their number becomes twenty-four with the inclusion of the *hadaya-vatthu.*

A number of attributes have been introduced to unfold the intrinsic nature of the material elements as a whole. Firstly, they are unconscious. They are neither the consciousness (*citta*) nor the psychic factors (*cetasika*), nor the roots (*hetu*). They are devoid of both the moral (*kusala-hetu*) and immoral (*akusala-hetu*) roots. They are *abyākata,* neither moral or immoral in character. They come into being depending upon some causes of conditions (*sapaccaya*), and stand as composite (*sankhata*), made of other elements. Thus, they themselves are not the defiling forces but become the object of pollution (*sāsava*). They are knowable by the six types of consciousness, namely, eye-consciousness (*cakhu-viññāṇa*), ear-consciousness (*sata-viññāṇa*), nose-consciousness (*ghāna-viññāṇa*), tongue-consciousness (*jihvā-viññāṇa*), body-consciousness (*kāya-viññāṇa*) and Mind-consciousness (*mano-viññāṇa*). They, by nature, are impermanent (*anicca*) and subject of destruction (*jarābhibhūta*).

The material elements are grasped in the form of **Qualities** or the **Qualitative energies**. A piece of stone in our hand is heavy, hard, rough, brown and of triangular shape. Apart from these qualities like — heaviness, hardness, roughness, brownness and triangularness, there is nothing like stone. Analysis of other similar material object also reveal the same truth. In this background the term *rūpa* may correctly be rendered into English as Material qualities and not the matter or material elements.

Reaching this stage, it seems desirable to append a brief note on each of the twenty-eight types of material qualities. For the sake of their easy communication, they are studied under eleven heads in later Abhidhammic texts. The same is being followed here too.[4]

Bhūta-rūpa

They are the *paṭhavī-dhātu* (earth-element), *āpo-dhātu* (water element), *tejo-dhātu* (fire-element) and *vāyo-dhātu* (air-element).

PAṬHAVĪ-DHĀTU

The term *paṭhavī* is derived from the root *puttha* which means 'to expand' to 'extend', to 'grant support' etc. *Dhātu* means that which bears its own characteristic marks — (*attano sabhāvaṃ dhāretiti dhātu*). Thus the literal as well as nearer meaning of the term is — "the element of Extension".

Intrinsically, the earth-element is that — "which is hard (*kakkhalaṃ*), rough (*khara-gataṃ*), hardness (*kakkhalattaṃ*), rigidity (*kakkhal abhāvo*) both internal and external.

It has the characteristic of hardness; its function is to become the base of co-existing elements; and receiving them is its manifestation. In this way, it is understood by touch, appearing as a tangible object of the body-sense-organ (*kāya*). It provides base for the existence of co-existing material elements and it is due to that are received as such and such. The various objects occupy space for existence due to presence of this element. Finally, it is the material energy of extension, manifesting as amalgam of a number of qualities.

ĀPO-DHĀTU

The derivation of the term *āpo* is traced from the root *apa*, which means 'to arrive' or from *paya* means to grow, to increase, to hold, to bind together etc. In this sense, it is called 'the element of cohesion'. It makes the different material particles cohere and prevents them from being scattered. It acts as a binding force of the material elements. The *Dhammasanganī* explains it as fluid (*āpo*) belonging to fluid (*āpogatam*), viscid (*sineho*) belonging to what is viscid (*sinehagataṃ*) and the cohesiveness of matter (*bandhanattaṃ rūpassa*). It is further analysed in the commentary as — "the water-element has trickling as its characteristic (*paggharaṇa-lakkhaṇa*), breeding of co-existing states as function (*brūhaṇa-rasa*) and gathering them together as manifestation (*saṅgahapaccupaṭṭhāna*). In short, it is a material energy which manifest in binding the things together. The formations of any kind is possible by its association.

TEJO-DHĀTU

It is generally rendered as the element of heat or 'Fire element'. Literally, it is derived from the root *tija* which means to sharpen, to 'mature'. From it, vivacity and maturity are understood due to its presence. In reality it is the 'heat' itself or the material energy of heat or **Fruition.** Or it may be said that the fire-element is that which is flame (*tejo*) belonging to flame (*tejogatam*), heat (*usmā*) belonging to heat (*usmagataṃ*) hot (*usumaṃ*), belonging to what is hot (*usumagataṃ*).

Further, the fire-element has the characteristic of heat, maturing as function, and the gift of softening of co-existing states as manifestation. Both heat and cold are its properties. It means the intense *tejo* is heat and the mild *tejo* is cold. It helps the maturity and fruition of the things within and without.

VĀYO-DHĀTU

It is understood as the air-element or the element of motion. The word *vāyo* is formed from the root *vāya* which means to move, to vibrate. In this word, it is understood as motion, vibration, oscillation and pressure. It is a material energy to keep the things in a particular position by generating pressure all around.

It is defined as the air (*vāya*), that which belongs to air (*vāyogataṃ*), fluctuation; and the inflation of form (*thambhitattaṃ rūpassa*). Its characteristic is strengthening (*vitthambana*), impelling as function (*samudīraṇa*) and bringing near and over as manifestations (*abhinihāra*).[5] The things get motion because of its presence. It is the universal carrier of the subtle material elements.

These four basic material elements are studied separately simply for the sake of understanding. Really speaking they are inseparable. One cannot identify and exhibit in idividually as earth, water, fire and air. They exist depending upon each other by the force created by the relation known as *Aññamaññapaccaya.* They serve as the originating ground of the generated material qualities.

Pasāda-rūpa

It is the name of sensitive material qualitites, generated by the four basic material elements. It refers to the five sense-organs, namely; *Cakkhu* (eye), *Sota* (ear), *Ghāṇa* (nose), *Jivhā* (tongue) and *Kāya* (body). Each one of them is a sensitive material quality, functioning as reflecting the object which appear in their respective ranges (*apātha*). They also serve as the base (*vatthu*) of the five *viññāṇas*.

It should be clarified here the five sense-organs, as referred to above, do not signify the perceptible organs. They refer to the sensitive part of each of them. It means that each sense-organ should be understood in its two forms; the perceptible form (*Sasambhāra-rūpa*) and sensitive form (*pasāda-rūpa*). The external form is the manifested mode of appearance (*santthāna*) and within it, there is the sensitive part, known as the *Pasāda-rūpa*. Such *Pasāda-rūpa* are the six senses.

For instance, the perceptible eye-ball, eye-brow, etc. are not the eye but the sensitive part which is within, in the centre of the retina, which enables one to see the visible objects, is the *cakkhu-pasāda*, the real eye. It is a type of sensitive material energy which has the capacity of reflecting the object, may meaningfully be called *Dassana-samatthatā*. Similarly the ear is the *sota-pasāda*, having potentiality to hear the audible objects (*savana-samatthatā*); nose is the *ghāna-pasāda*, to smell the odorous objects; (*ghāyana-samatthatā*); tongue is the *jihvā-pasāsa* to relish the sapid objects (*sāyana-samatthatā*), and the body is the *kāya-pasāda* to touch the tangible objects (*phusana-samatthatā*). Each of them serves as the base of respective consciousness (*viññāṇa*) in maintaining the thought-processes (*citta-vīthi*) at different doors.

Gocara-Rūpa

Literally, the word *gocara* means a place where there is the smooth way-faring of the senses. Technically, it stands for the object. The material qualities which function as the object of the senses are called *Gocara-rūpa*. They are four in number namely; *Rūpa* (visible object), *Sadda* (audible object), *Gandha* (odorous object) and *Rasa* (sapid object). The object of *Kāya* (*phatabha*) has been included in *paṭhavī*, *tejo* and *vāyo* and, therefore, with a view to avoid duplications, not included here in the present context:

(a) *Rūpa*, the object of the eye, stands for the colour and shape. It manifests as red, blue, white, black, etc. in colour, and triangular, rectangular, square, circular etc. in shape. It is visible (*sannidassana*) and impinging (*sapaṭigha*).

(b) *Sadda* means sound. The sounds of the drum (*bheri-sadda*), conches (*saṅkha*), song (*gīta*), cymbals, clapping hands, of the people, of the non-human beings, of splitting bamboos, tearing of the clothes etc. are included here. Each of them is audible and impinging.

(c) *Gandha* refers to odour. It includes the odours of roots, barks, vegitables, fish, shell fish, stale butter, flowers, fruits etc. It appears as desirable smell (*sugandha*) or undesirable smell (*dugandha*). All the odours have the characteristic of striking the sense of smell.

(d) *Rasa* is the taste. It includes all the various types of tastes like sour, sweet, bitter, pungent, alkaline, acid etc. They have the characteristics of striking the tongue.

Bhāva-rūpa

It expresses the sense of the material qualities of sex. It is of two types, namely; femininity (*itthindriya*) and masculinity (*purisindriya*). It is due to these two types of material qualities, the distinction between the physical structure of a male and that of a female is marked. With the presence of *itthindriya*, there is a different type of development in the body of a woman. She is markedly different from a man in respect of her appearance, occupation, deportment and other feminine conditions. She is in possession of different types of physical properties which distinguish her from those of a man. It is not the object of visual cognition alone but can be understood by mind-cognition also. It has the characteristic of knowing the state of a woman, the function of showing 'this is woman', and the manifestation is the cause of femininity in feature, mark, occupation as well as deportment.

Again the *purisindriya* (masculinity) is a material quality due to which there is a different type of physical development of the body of a man. In generic sense, masculine features, mark, occupation, deportment etc. should be understood as the opposite of the feminine. The shape of the hands, feet, neck, breast etc. of a man is unlike the shape of those of a woman. It is also not the object of mere vision. It can be understood through mind alone. Expressing the state of a man, is its charactersitic, and showing 'this is a man' is its function. Its manifestation is the cause of masculinity in features, mark, occupation, deportment etc.

Hadaya-rūpa

It is the name of the base of consciousness, technically called *hadaya-vatthu*. Like the base of functioning of other senses, the base of mind has also been indicated through it. It is said that at the time of *Paṭisandhi* (birth) of a human being, the *viññāṇa* enters into the womb of a mother. Simultaneously, there is the appearance of the *hadaya-vatthu* as a material base, on which the conscious stream rests. It is very small in size, perhaps, the subtlest particle of material qualities.

Jīvita-rūpa

It is the name of vitality or the life-force of material qualities, *Jīvitindriya* by its name. A material form remains sound, compact, solid etc., due to its presence. A thing becomes old because of relative loss of *jīvitindriya*. The body of a man receives expressions like young, adult, old, extremely broken due to relative appearance and disappearance of this force. Here the term *jīvita* is qualified by *indriya* because it exercises dominating influence over other co-existing material qualities in vivifying them from the moment of *patisandhi*.

Ahāra-rūpa

It literally means the food material qualities. In technical sense, it refers to the nourishing quality or the nutritive essence which sustains the body. In generic sense, it is the name of the *Kabalīkāra-āhāra* or the gross food that one takes morsel by morsel. They are the rice (*odana*), curry (*kummāsa*), fish (*maccha*), meat (*mansa*), gram powder (*sattu*) etc.

Pariccheda-rūpa

It is the name of *Ākāsa-dhātu* or space-material quality. Here it should be understood that *āvāsa* has been included in the *mahābhūtas* in some of the systems of Indian philosophy. They are commonly known as *pañca mahābhūta*. In the Buddhist system, it is a generated material quality, basically dependent on the four *mahābhūtas*. The reason is obvious that it has relative existence.

Ākāsa means space which provides place for existence of other material qualities. Thus the space-element is that which is not 'scratched', 'not scratched off', not possible to break or cut. At the same time, it takes shape according to the existence of the material qualities. It has the characteristic of delimiting material objects. Its function is the showing of their boundaries and the manifestation is marked as showing their limits.

Viññatti-rūpa

It is the name of intimating material qualities. It is through this medium that an idea is intimated, conveyed and understood by others. It is done by actions and speech. Accordingly, the intimation through the physical actions is *kāya-viññatti* and that through the speech is *vacī-viññatti.* To be more clear, it may be said that each physical as well as the vocal action has the peculiarity of its own, and such peculiarity, distinguishes one action from the other. For instance, sitting has its own peculiarity due to which it is sitting and it is not understood, as standing, running, etc. Similarly, standing, running, lying down have their own peculiarities existing with each of them and due to which one is distinguished from the other. Such peculiarities, associated with physical actions are collectively called *kāya-viññatti* or physical intimation. As regards the vocal actions, it is marked in day-to-day life, like teaching, singing, rebuking, crying etc. which are distinct from one another. These distinct actions associated with vocal action are *vācī-viññatti.* Thus it may be stated that the "intimating material quality is that due to which an idea related to a particular action is rightly communicated and understood by others with full background of awareness of various types of physical and vocal actions".

Vikāra-rūpa

It means the material qualities of changing modes in material elements. They are of three types, namely; lightness (*lahutā*), mildness (*mudutā*) and adaptability (*kammaññatā*) associated with material qualities. On experiential base, the lightness existing with the physical body is *lahutā,* mildness existing with it is *mudutā,* and the adaptability of the body towards the action in the moment is *kammaññatā.* In absence of *lahutā,* one feels heaviness in discharging the physical performances. In absence of *mudutā* there is disinterestedness and in the state of non-presence of *kammaññatā,* there is no lively leaning towards the activities to be performed in a particular unit of time. The three material qualities are experienced with body within and also may be understood with reference to the material surroundings.

Lakkhana-rūpa

It is material quality or rather the natural characteristics of material elements in general, manifesting in four ways as *upacaya* (coming into being), *santati* (continuity), *jaratā* (decay) and *aniccatā* (destruction). It is seen that a thing comes to exist, it continues, gradually starts growing old and in the end suffers destruction. A seed comes to be a sprout, continues to exist as a plant, gradually starts decaying and in one fine moment turns into the dust particles. The coming into being, existing, decaying and finally destroying are the natural characteristics of things existing within and without. Because of their such a nature, they are called *lakkhana-rūpa.*

In this way, the four *mahābhūtas* and the twenty-four types of the *upādā-rūpas* have briefly been presented. Collectively they are called *rūpa* or the *bhūta* in early Buddhist tradition.

The Buddhist philosophy does not believe in a **Creating Agency** as the first in the beginning of creation. It proceeds with the statement that the beginning of the *sansāra* is not known. It is not known whether it started during the reign of such and such a king, in the *sāsana* of such and such a Buddha — *anamataggo, ayaṃ saṁsāro, purimākoṭi assa na paññāyati.* Nevertheless the processes of *sansāra* is an ongoing one. If it is so, then there should be some **Law** governing it. As answer to this, it may be said that there is **Law of Dependent Origination** (*Paticca-samuppāda*) taking care of the systematic revolving of the *Saṃsāra* with the help of twelve links, known as *nidānas.* The coming into existence of *nāma* and *rūpa* has meaningfully been illustrated therein.

In the process of explaining the generation of the material elements, a set of four factors are systematically at work. They are *kamma, citta, utu* and *āhāra.*

The first factor is *kamma.* It refers to the resultants of the moral and immoral actions done in the past. Here the action should be understood in the sense of consciousness. There are the twenty-five types of consciousness of the *kāmāvacāra* and *rūpāvacāra* spheres. They are the twelve types of *kamavacara* — immoral consciousness, eight types of *kāmāvacāra* — moral consciousness and five types of *rūpāvacāra* — moral consciousness. They arise in different units of time in our practical life and we express as performance of moral and immoral actions. These twenty-five types of consciousness yield their resultants. Such resultants are technically called *kamma.* It has its bearing in generating the material elements. The process of generation starts from the moment of the beginning of life known as *paṭisandhi.*

The second factor is *citta* or consciousness. It refers to the seventy-five types of consciousness as — *kāmāvacāra-akusala-citta* (12), *ahetuka-citta* (8), *kāmāvacara-sahehana-citta* (24), *rūpāvacāra-sobhana-citta* (15), *arūpāvacāra-sobhana citta* (8), *lokuttara-sobhana-citta* (8). They start generating material elements from the moment of beginning of the life process of the life of the being. The moment of starting the process is called *bhavaṅga.*

Utu is the third generating factor. It means weather. It manifests as hot or cold — and effects the material elements accordingly. Its heating or cooling effect starts from the moment the being comes into existence and being experienced accordingly in the process of life.

The fourth factor in this context is *āhāra.* The literal meaning of the term is food. In a generic sense, it refers to the food taken by one in morsels. But it also signifies of the nutritive quality of food. It has its effect on the body, internally and externally, from the moment one starts taking food.

Those four factors are the four types of generating forces acting continuously with the life of beings as well as with the things associated with the life-process remaining within or without. They function individually or in association. Some material elements are generated by one particular factor and some are generated with their collective efforts. It may be illustrated firstly as which types of material elements are generated by which types of generating forces and secondly as which type of generating factor individually or collectively generates which types of material elements.

In the former case, it is stated as below:

(a) The eight types of *indriya-rūpas* and the *hadaya-vatthu* are directly generated by *kamma.* Here the five types of sensitive material elments (*cakkhu, sota, ghāna, jīhvā,* and *kāya*), the two types of sex material elements (*itthindriya* and *purisindriya*) and one type of life-force material element (*jīvitindriya*) are the eight *indriya-rūpas,* while *hadaya-vatthu* is the seat of consciouseness. These nine material elements are the products of the *kamma* as an individual force. It also functions in association with other forces and produce nine more material elements. They are the eight types of inseparable material elements (*abbinibhoga-rūpa*) and one space-material elements (*ākāsa-dhātu*). *Paṭhavī, apo, tejo, vāyo, yaṇṇa, gandha, rasa,* and *oja* are always available as one inseparable unit and, therefore, they are called 'Inseparable material element'. These nine are the collective products.

(b) The two type of *viññatti-rūpas,* namely, *kāya-viññatti* (physical intimation) and *vacī-viññatti* (vocal intimation) are produced by *citta* (consciousness).

(c) *Sadda* (sound) is produced by the joint effort of *citta* and *utu.*

(d) The three material elements, namely, *lahutā, mudutā* and *kammaññatā* are produced by the three factors, namely, *citta, utu* and *āhāra.*

(e) The eight types of *abbinibhoga-rūpas* and *ākāsa-dhātus* are produced by the combined efforts of all the four factors: *kamma, citta, utu* and *āhāra.*

(f) The four types of *lakkhaṇa-rūpas,* namely, *upasaya, santati, jaratā* and *aniccatā* are not produced by any factors. The reason is obvious that they are the nature of material elements.

In this way, the twenty-eight types of material elements are produced by the four generating factors.

Further, analysing the generation of material elements as stated above, the role of each generating factor may be illustrated as below:

(i) *Kamma* generates nine material elements individually and nine in association with the other factors. It makes a total of eighteen material elements which are understood as *kamma*-products.

(ii) *Citta* generates two material elements individually and thirteen in association with others. In this way, there are fifteen material elements which are regarded as *citta*-products.

(iii) *Utu* has no independent generation of material elements. It functions in association with others and generates thirteen material elements. They are the *utu*-products.

(iv) *Āhāra* has also its collective but important role in generating the material elements which are thirteen in number. It is in this way, that the four generating factors are seen at work in producing the natural elements in the process of existence in the fluxional nature of existence.[6]

Coming to this stage, now, it seems desirable to state how the different material elements come to be in the process of life and how they disappear when the life-continuum comes to an end in the present state.

The first moment in the present state of existence is called *paṭisandhi.* It is rather the rising of a *paṭisandhi-citta* or the birth consciousness. From the moment of its existence there starts the function of *kamma,* and with this, *kammaja-rūpas* appear.

The second moment in this process is called *bhavaṅga.* It is also the rising of a consciousness which functions as preparing a base of the present state of existence with the accumulation of the resultants of all the past activities done by a particular being. With the rising of this consciousness there starts the generation of material elements by the *citta.*

Gradually the being has its initial physio-psychic amalgam which in common parlance is stated as "coming into existence". From this moment there is the generation of material elements produced by *utu.*

Further, *āhāraja-rūpas* start coming into being from the moment one starts taking food and it is assimilated. The process continues till the being exists.

There is also a process of degeneration or disappearance of the material elements when the life-process has a state of conventional cessation which we name **death**. It is the rising of a *cuti-citta* or death consciousness. From the moment of its rising the process of the material elements produced by *kamma* has a stop. Thereafter, there is the cutting off between the *cittaja* and *āhāraja-rūpas*. The *utuja-rūpas*, in some form or other, continues till the dead body exists. With gradual disappearance of the dead body they also disappear.

Notes

1. *katamaṃ sabbam rūpaṃ iti? cattāro ca mahābhūtā, catunnam ca mahābhūtānam upādāya rūpaṃ, idaṃ vuccati sabbaṃ rūpam.*
   — *D.S.*, 147.

2. *pātalī-simbali-jambu, devānaṃ păricchattako.*
   kadambo kapparukkhoca, sirisena bhavati sattamo.
   — *A.S.*, 242.

3. *bhūmi to vitthitā yāva, brahma-lokā vidhavati,*
   acci, accimato loke, dayhamanamhi tejaso.
   kotisatsahassekam, cakkhvalaṃ viteyuti,
   kupitena yadā loko, salilena vinassati.
   koṭisatasahassekam, cakkavalaṃ vikirati,
   vāyodhātuppakopena, yadāloko vinassati.

   patthaddho bhavati kāyo, daṭtho kaṭṭhamukhene va,
   paṭhavidhatukopena, hoti kaṭṭhamukhe va so.
   putiko bhavati kāyo, daṭṭho putimukhene vā,
   apodhātuppakopena, hoti putimukhe va so.
   santatto bhavati kāyo. daṭṭho aggimukhena vā.
   tejo-dhātuppakopena, hoti aggimukhe va so.
   sanchinnobhavati kāyo, dattho saṭṭhamukhena vā.
   vāyo-dhatuppakopena, hoti satthamukhe vaso.
   — *A.S.*, 243

4. *bhūtappasādavisayā, bhāvo hadayamiccapi,*
   jīvitahārarūpehi, aṭṭhārasavidhaṃ tathā,
   paricchedo ca viññatti, vikāro lakhaṇamti ca,
   anipphanna desa cuti, aṭṭhavisa vidham bhava.
   — *A. San.*, 286.

5. *D.S.*, 256; *A.S.*, 267.

6. *atthāvasa pannarasa, terasa dvadasāti ca,*
   kammacittotukāharājaṃ honti yathakkamaṃ.
   — *A. San.*, 174.

10

The Concept of Great Elements in Jain Cosmology

Mangala Mirasdar

All philosophical systems aim at a quest for Supreme Truth or Reality, based upon the concept of Universe. All of them try to explain the creation and existence of the Universe from their own points of view.

According to Umāswāti, the author of the renowned Jain philosophical text *Tattvārthādhigama-sūtra,* the definition of Reality is *sat,* i.e., existence. He uses the word *dravya* or substance for Reality. In the process of the creation of the world, various philosophies mention the role of the well-known five great elements viz. *pṛthivī, ap, tejas, vāyu* and *ākāśa.* Jain philosophy also mentions these elements but in different contexts. The first four, except *ākāśa* are included by them in the *pudgala dravya. Ākāśa* is considered to be a different *dravya* in Jain thought. To point out this difference of substances from the five great elements in other systems, it is necessary to see in brief the *Ṣaḍdravyas* in Jainism. Jain system has divided the universe in two main categories, *jīva* and *ajīva,* which comprise of six substances (*dravyas*). This *ajīva* category is a positive variety standing opposed to *jīva.* It is not merely of the form of negation. *Ajīva* consists of five substances — *ākāśa* (space); *dharma,* i.e., medium of motion; *adharma* (medium of rest), *kāla* (Time) and *pudgala* (matter). Excluding *kāla,* all other substances are of the nature of *astikāyas. Astikāya* means a combination or collection of areas or aspects. Because they exist, they are called *asti* and because they have many *pradeśas* like bodies, they are called *kāyas.* These *astikāyas* or extensive substances are *jīvāstikāya, ākāśāstikāya, dharmāstikāya, adharmāstikāya* and *pudgalāstikāya. Jīva* also is called *astikāya* because, according to Jainism each *jīva* has innumerable *pradeśas.* By contraction and expansion of its *pradeśas,* the *jīva* occupies different proportions. It is just like the flame of a lamp whose light can fill a small room as well a big hall.[1] So a *jīva* can occupy a smallest body of a bacterium or the biggest body of a great fish.

These five fundamental substances in the form of five *astikāyas* are eternal (*nitya*); immutable (*avasthita*) and devoid of form (*arūpin*). They are not externally created, but are evident by their own nature.

The *pudgalas* are possessed of *rūpa*. The properties are capable of being grasped through the sense-organs. So they are *mūrta* or *rūpin*. Though the atoms on account of being supra-sensuous, are not grasped through the sense-organs, but under some specific transformation they do develop the capacity to be grasped through the sense-organs. Generally it is defined that *ajīva* is that which has no consciousness, but which can be touched, tasted, seen and smelt; but according to Jainism, these four characteristics belong to *pudgala* or matter which can be touched, tasted, seen and smelt because matter has gross forms. It shows that the scope of the *ajīva* category of Jainism comprises not only *pudgala* or matter but something more, that is, *dharma, adharma, ākāśa* and *kāla*.

According to the Jain system, *ākāśa* is not included among the well-known five great elements, i.e., *pṛthivī, ap, tejas, vāyu* and *ākāśa. Ākāśa* is a substance which allows *dharma, adharma, kāla, pudgala* and *jīva* to remain within itself and which allows them to enter itself. It means that *ākāśa* acts as a support for the remaining substances which act as occupants. It is self-supporting. The Jain concept of space is unique in its originality, for it holds space as positional quality of the world of material objects and space as the container of material objects and other substances.

The seed of the Jain concept of space is embodied in the Jain *āgamas* like the *Bhagavatī Sūtra* etc. In the post-*āgama* age, Umāswātī had sown the seed of its metaphysical aspects on the basis of its āgamic conception. The Jain thinkers retained the substantial existence of space as conceived by the *Nyāya Vaiśeṣikas*;[2] but they had discarded the elemental concept of space of the *Sāṁkhyas. Sāṁkhyas* in their *Prakṛtivāda*, i.e., the doctrine of the fundamental cause of the material universe, mention *ākāśa* as produced from *tanmātras*. It is also stated to have originated out of the Mass or Inertia (*tamas*) in the *Prakṛti* as a result of its transformation, when the original equilibrium comes to an end. So in *Sāṁkhya, ākāśa* is *janyapadārtha* of an evolved entity or element; but not an independent absolute substance. The *Nyāya-Vaiśeṣikas* conceive *ākāśa* as one of the categories of *dravya* and the fundamental principle of creation. The *Vedāntin* also maintains the view that *ākāśa* is *Brahman* as the characteristic marks are mentioned.[3] As all the prominent characteristics of *Brahman* are ascribed to *ākāśa* it cannot be the etheral *ākāśa* but *Brahman*. But according to Jainism, in the purest form, this objectively real entity *ākāśa* does one function only, i.e., to accommodate other substances of the universe. The function of the other *dravyas* is to attain room and the function of the space is to give room to them.[4]

The aphorism in *Tattvārthādhigamasūtra* (*lokākāśe avagāhah*) (V.12) implies the division of space into *lokākāśa* and *alokākāśa*. The five fundamental substances are accommodated in *lokākāśa*. So the differentiation of space is to accommodate other substances.

Another substance *pudgalāstikāya*, goes under the *ajīva* category. This term *pudgala* is used in Buddhist literature also, but there it is used in the sense of soul. In Jainism *jīva* and *pudgala* are totally different categories. *Pudgala* generally means Matter. It has two parts *pud* and *gala*. The first part means 'to combine' and second part *gala* means 'to dissociate'. So the etymological meaning of *pudgala* is that substance which undergoes modifications by combination and dissolutions. The definition is significant because this process of combination and dissolution does not occur in other substances.

Pudgala is of two types — *aṇu* and *skandha* or atoms and aggregates or molecules. An indivisible material particle is called atom. It is the smallest possible form of *pudgala*. *Skandha* means an aggregate or something tied together. It is significant that each and every atom possesses touch, taste, smell and colour and is potentially capable of forming earth, water, fire and air. These are no distinct and different kinds of atoms of earth etc., i.e., the atoms are ultimately not different. For example, airy atoms can be converted into water, watery atoms can be converted into fire and so on. Ultimately all the atoms belong to one and the same class of *pudgala*. Sometimes they form earth, sometimes they form water and so on. Thus according to Jainism, earth, water, fire and air are not ultimately separate and independent entities but only different forms of *pudgala*. There are no qualitative difference among them. The school of *Nyāya-Vaiśeṣika* does not agree to this view of Jain as seen before that regards earth, water, fire and air as absolutely different and independent substances and so their atoms are also ultimately distinct and different.

The function of *pudgala* is to form the basis of the body and organs of speech, mind and respiration. Pleasure, pain, life, death also are the benefits due to *pudgala*.

Though we call *pudgala* as synonymous with matter, *pudgala* is not pure matter untouched from consciousness like the insentient matter of the *Sāṁkhya*. The *pudgala skandha* has also an element of consciousness. The *jīva* and *ajīva* categories of Jainism are not empirical abstractions of consciousness and non-consciousness. In the following characteristics of the conception of the gross elements in Jainism this point will be very clear.

The gross elements excluding *ākāśa* are included in *pudgala*. It is interesting to know that unlike the gross elements in *Sāṁkhya* and *Vedānta*, the gross elements contained in *pudgala* are not totally insentient. But they are sentient as well as insentient also. Among the twofold classification of *jīvas* as *trasa* and *sthāvara* the *sthāvara jīvas* are of five kinds — *pṛthivīkāya, apkāya, tejaskāya, vāyukāya* and *vanaspatikāya.* Thus *jīvas* whose body consists of *pṛthivī* is called *pṛthivīkāya,* the *jīva* whose body consists of *ap* is called *āpkāya.* These are sentient and non-sentient. Earth is the body of the sentient being as well as sentient body itself. These are elemental souls, which live and die and are born again in the same or other elemental bodies. Their sentient part increases. To explain further, a metallic stone drawn from the mine in its natural condition is sentient but as soon as we make some chemical reaction on it, it becomes non-sentient. Earth which has not suffered the blow of friction is sentient, but once there is friction it becomes insentient. In a similar way, the water which is flowing through a river is sentient but as soon as water is boiled it becomes non-sentient. All these are *ekendriya jīvas* or *jīvas* having only one sense. In the case of *vanaspatikāya,* the plants are the *jīvas* of one sense. Each plant may be the body of one soul or may possess a multitude of embodied souls. Thus, the doctrine of the gross elements having the sentient and non-sentient aspects, and the theory that there are souls even in inorganic objects like metals, stones, water, etc. are special features of the Jain system of thought.

According to the *Vaiśeṣika* system air or *vāyu* contains only the quality of touch. The other qualities colour, taste and smell are absent in air, but according to Jainism, colour, taste, touch and smell are found invariably together and therefore whenever there is touch, form, taste and smell will necessarily be there. This Jain theory is validated by the modern science, according to which air can be converted into bluish liquid by continuous cooling, as steam can be converted into water, and the liquid contains all the four qualities of touch, colour, taste and smell. So the gross elements excluding *ākāśa* possess not only the specific qualities but, as these elements are included in *pudgala,* all the qualities of *pudgala* as touch, form, taste and smell are present in each element.

These six *dravyas* together are called universe. In their original state, they are stable and firm but on account of their mutual relation, new things emerge and old things perish. The working of universe is nothing but the substances experiencing the power of production, destruction, duration and transformation in respect of their forms and status. According to *Vedānta* and the *Nyāya-Vaiśeṣika* system, *sattā* is absolutely permanent having no change whatsoever. But the Jain philosopher Umāswāti decrees that "the thing which is characterized by origination, destruction and permanence is 'real'".[5] During the period of taking new forms and leaving old ones, the substance does not leave its essence.

In both origination and decay, it remains as it is. This immutable nature is called permanence. For example, a thing, say clay, assumes various shapes and undergoes diverse changes such as jug, pan etc. As illustrated by *Chāndogya Upaniṣad,*

वाचारम्भणं विकारो नामधेयं मृत्तिकेत्येव सत्यम्।
vācārambhaṇaṁ vikaro nāmadheyaṁ mṛttiketyeva satyam ।

the unchangeable substance, i.e., clay alone is true and the changing forms are more illustrations of senses or mere objects of names. But Jainas do not suppose that substances alone are true and the qualities are false and illusory appearences. They argue, that in actual experience in all changes there are three processes: (1) some qualities remain unchanged, (2) some new qualities are generated, (3) some old qualities are destroyed. For example, when a jug is made, the lump-clay is destroyed, the jug is generated and the clay is permanent. Due to these unchanged qualities a thing is said to be permanent though it undergoes change. When a lump of gold is turned into a rod or a ring, all the specific qualities which connote the word 'gold' are seen to continue, though the forms are successively changed and with each change some of its qualities are lost and some new ones are acquired.

Due to the interaction of the six *dravyas,* new things emerge and old things perish. Through the interaction of soul and matter, the Universe rolls. Matter is the cause of making bodies. It forms the physical basis for the body, speech, mind, respiration of the worldly souls. When the worldly career of the beings is over, they give up the gross body and accompany the subtle body and again receive physical particles appropriate for the gross body in the next birth.

In short, the Jain system refuses to attribute either absolute permanence or absolute transience to anything, but treats everything as either permanent or transitory. This system retains the elemental nature of the gross elements to some extent but at the same time it gives its own interpretation to the term *ākāśa.*

Notes

1. *Tattvā.,* V.16 — प्रदेश संहारविसर्गाभ्यां प्रदीपवत्।
2. *Vaiśeṣika Sūtra,* I.15 — पृथिव्यापस्तेजो वायुराकाशं कालो दिगात्मा मन इति।
3. *Br., Sū.* I.1.22 — आकाशस्तल्लिङ्गात्।
4. *Tattvā.* — आकाशस्यावगाहः।
5. *Tattvārthādhigama Sūtra,* — उत्पादव्ययध्रौव्ययुक्तं सत्।

11

Mahābhūtas in Jyotiṣa Śāstra

S. D. Sharma

Ancient sages had insight into the cosmogonical and cosmological aspects of the universe. Through the advanced stages of thought experimentations (*Yogic pratyakṣa* as you may call these) they inferred the existence of subtle stages of matter in the evolution process and correlated the same with the gross elements. They had a constant dialogue with nature and in this process they correlated the microcosm with the macrocosm. Interestingly, their inferences have many fundamental affinities with the insights of modern Astrophysicists.

In the cosmogonical evolution process from subtle stages of matter, the ancients arrived at the notion of *pañcamahābhūtas* the gross elements, considered to be the building blocks of the macroworld around us. It may be pointed out that this categorization should not be confused with the present-day periodic table classification of elements. The former is the categorisation based on *indriyagrāhyatā* (faculty perceptibility) of materials in the world. Sir John Ballantyne in his *Nyāya Kaumudī* (Litho print 1885 AD) has confused the two categorisations and states:

> भूतान्युपषष्टि संख्यानि
> *bhūtānyupaṣaṣṭi saṅkhyāni*

i.e., there are *bhūtas* about 60 in number. He is referring to Hydrogen, Helium, Oxygen, iron and other elements as *mahābhūtas.* Note that at the time of Prof. Ballantyne, there were only sixty elements known to scientists. Needless to say, this statement is erroneous, for *mahābhūtas* are not the same as basic elements of physics. It may be noted that *pañcamahābhūtas* of *Sāṁkhya* philosophy result as a consequence of *pañcīkaraṇa* process on *pañcatanmātras,* which are subtle stages in the evolution process and on the other hand are connected with the senses of perception. The concepts based on *mahābhūta* classification prevail all the branches of philosophy and religion, but *Āyurveda* has used these concepts for practical applications. *Jyotiṣa Śāstra* too being a discipline of experimental verifications must have used these concepts for developing the laws of nature and in understanding the cosmic genesis. *Jyotiṣa Śāstra* and *Āyurveda* have put the philosophical concepts on experimental verification tests. Here the attempt of this paper is to study the concept of *pañcamahābhūtas* in relation to *Jyotiṣa Śāstra*. What ideas were developed by ancient *Jyotiṣācāryas* regarding cosmogonical evolution? How far did their findings tally with those of philosophers, and to what extent they had advanced further through their observational verifications? This paper seeks to address these questions and explore possible answers.

Jyotiṣa Śāstra deals mainly with time and space. The former is not in the list of *pañcamahābhūtas*. But space is the *ākāśa* of the *mahābhūtas*. In fact in modern philosophy, time and space are so correlated that their unison is referred to as "space-time continuum". *Jyotiṣa Śāstra* takes into account *pṛthivī* (earth) and other elements. The *Pṛthivī* of *Jyotisa Śāstra* should not be confused with the *pṛthivī mahābhūta*, as the latter is the most generalised term to represent anything perceptible. Similar are the cases with other *mahābhūtas*. *Jyotiṣa Śastra* talks of *mahābhautika* entities in the cosmos and these terms should not be confused with the general terms of *mahābhūtas* philosophy. The *bhautika* entities as individual units are studied in *Jyotiṣa Śāstra*. This *śāstra* discusses the properties of the *bhautika* entities like earth, planets, water, *tejas* bodies, stars, suns, etc. and goes to the maximum extent to explore the very nature of space. Some aspects are dealt within *siddhānta Jyotiṣa* and some of them are studied under the heading of 'Astrology'. Any way in this exposition we should like to explore the references to the concepts of *mahābhūtas* in *Jyotiṣa* through the studies of *bhautika* entities without confusing the terminologies of the two disciplines. Here we have tried to survey the literature as far as possible in a chronological fashion, starting from *Vedāṅga Jyotiṣam* and up to the *Saiddhāntika Jyotiṣa* traditions. As such in *Vedāṅga Jyotiṣam* of Lagadha, which is exclusively a text of *Jyotiṣa*, we do not find reference to *mahābhūtas* but earlier and later Vedic *vāṅgmaya* has important notions which paved the basis for cosmogony. So here we will deal first with the cosmogony and then having discussed the genesis and the evolution, will go over to the properties of *mahābhūtas* as inferred in *Jyotiṣa Śāstra* and then see if some universal laws have been formulated in *Jyotiṣa* tradition on the basis of philosophical grounds.

It may be remarked that in addition to cosmogony etc., *Jyotiṣa Śāstra* deals also with cosmography and cosmology, the sciences of form and age of the universe. Hindu, Jaina and Buddhist traditions discuss the geometrical models of the universe and the terrestrial earth, (ref. *Cosmography of Hindus, Buddhists and Jainas* by Nerifil). All these models are indicative of their philosophical notions. Even modern astrophysicists talk of cosmology models which are based on highly complex mathematical exercises. Concerning the age of universe, Jainas talk of very big cycles like *utsarpiṇi, apasarpiṇi, kāla* etc. The *Siddhānta Jyotiṣa* texts talk of big life spans of Brahmā, Viṣṇu, Maheśa and *Yuga* systems which are of much importance for astronomical computations. Here we do not discuss these in detail but will elaborate the more interesting philosophical ideas of the ancients regarding the cosmogonical process.

Cosmogony

The concepts about creation of the world, consisting of all stars, sun, planets and the animate and inanimate world, are found in the Vedic and later Sanskrit literature. The oldest strata of *Vedas* and allied literature have deep philosophical notions about cosmogony. In these very notions we find astronomical and astrophysical concepts of ancient sages. We discuss here few references from Vedic literature and then will come to *Jyotiṣa* texts later.

In *Ṛgveda* we find *Bhāvita Sūkta* describing all void in the world and darkness engulfing all around. The cosmos came into existence through *kāma* (desire) which was the primal seed or germ of the spirit. We will not give all details of the text material of the *Sūkta* but may point out that the notions as expounded in this *Sūkta* are quite similar to the ones put forward in modern cosmogonical hypotheses. An Astrophysicist from U.S.A compared the *Bhāvita Sūkta* notions with the origin of world out of the Black Hole state of the matter. The ancients seem to have arrived at these notions through yogic *pratyakṣa* which is just an advanced stage of thought experimentations, while the modern astrophysicists inferred somewhat similar, through analyses of observable data.

In *ṚV*, 10.190.1.3 we have the following hymns:

> *ṛtam ca satyaṁ cābhīddhāt tapaso'dhyajāyata*
> *tato rātryajāyata tataḥ samudro arṇavaḥ.* (1)
> *samudrādarṇavādadhi saṁvatsaro ajāyata*
> *ahorātrāṇi vidadhāt viśvasya miṣato vaśī.* (2)
> *sūryā-candramasau dhātā yathā pūrvamakalpayat*
> *divañca pṛthivīñ cāntarikṣamatho svaḥ.* (3)
>
> Truth and truthfulness were born from intense penance. Hence was darkness born hence the watery ocean. (1)
>
> From the watery ocean was born the year ordaining days and nights the controller of every living moment. (2)
>
> The creator then created in due order Sun, the Moon, the sky, the

earth and the regions of the air and light. (3)

tasmādvā etasmādātmana ākāśaḥ saṁbhūtaḥ, ākāśādvāyuḥ
vāyoragniḥ agnerāpaḥ, adbhyaḥ pṛthivī, pṛthivyā oṣadhayaḥ.
oṣadhībhyo'nnaṁ, annāt puruṣah. (*Tait. Up. Brahmavallī*). (1)

Verily from this soul, space arose; from space arose air; from air fire; from fire, the waters; from waters, the earth; from earth vegetation; from vegetation, the food; and from food, the man.

There is one more from *ṚV*, describing creation of the Sun, Moon, *mahābhūtas*

candramā manaso jātas'cakṣoḥ sūryo'jāyata.
mukhādindraś cāgniśca prāṇād vāyurajāyata. (13)
nābhyā āsīdantarikṣam śirṣno dyauḥsamavartata
padbhyāṁ bhūmir diśaḥ śrotrāt tathā lokamakalpayat. (14)
(*ṚV*, 10.190-13,14)

The moon was gendered from his mind and from his eyes the sun had birth; Indra and *agni* from his mouth were born and *Vāyu* from his breath. (13)

Forth from his navel came mid air, the Sky was fashioned from his feet and from his ear the regions. Thus they formed the worlds. (14)

Now we come to *jyotiṣa* texts and see what the later astronomers contemplated about cosmogony. The *Bhūgolādhyāya* of *Sūryasiddhānta* discusses the creation of the universe, including the earth, and the evolution of *pañcamahābhūtas*. The relevant text stanzas are the following:

vāsudevaḥ param brahma, tanmūrtiḥ puruṣaḥ paraḥ.
avyakto nirgunaḥ śāntah pañcaviṁśāt paro'vyayaḥ. (1)
prakṛtyantargato devo bahirantas'ca sarvagaḥ.
saṅkarṣaṇo'paḥ sṛṣṭyādau tāsu vīryamavāsṛjat. (2)
tadaṇḍamabhavaddhaimam sarvatra tamasāvṛtam
tatrāniruddhaḥ prathamam vyaktībhūtaḥ sanātanaḥ. (3)
hiraṇyagarbho bhagavāneṣacchandasi paṭhyate.
ādityo hyādibhūtatvāt prasūtyā sūrya ucyate. (4)
paraṁ jyotistamaḥ, pāre sūryo'yaṁ saviteti ca.
paryeti bhuvanānyeṣa bhāvayan bhūta-bhāvanaḥ. (5)
prakāśātmā tamohantā mahānityeṣa viśrutaḥ.
ṛco'sya maṇḍalam sāmānyusrā mūrtiryajūṁṣi ca. (6)
trayīmayo'yaṁ bhagavān kālātmā kālakṛd-vibhuḥ.
sarvātmā sarvagaḥ sūkṣmaḥ sarvamasmin pratiṣṭhitam. (7)

rathe visvamaye cakraṁ kṛtvā saṁvatsarātmakaṁ.
chandāṅsyaśvāḥ saptayuktāḥ paryaṭatyeṣa sarvadā. (8)
tripādamamṛtam guhyam pādo'yaṁ prakaṭo'bhavat.
so 'hankāram jagatsṛṣṭyai brahmāṇamasṛjat prabhuḥ. (9)
tasmai vedānvarāndattvā sarvalokapitāmahaṁ.
pratiṣṭhāpyāṇḍa-madhye'tha swayaṁ paryeti bhāvayan. (10)
atha sṛṣṭyām manascakre brahmāhankāra-mūrtibhṛt.
manasascandramā jajñe suryo'kṣṇostejasāṁ nidhiḥ. (11)
manasaḥkhaṁ tato vāyuragnirāpo dharā kramāt.
gunaika-vṛddhyā pañcaiva mahābhūtani jajñire. (12)
agnīṣomau bhānu-candrau tatastvaṅgārakādayaḥ.
tejo bhūkhāmbuvātebhyaḥ kramaśaḥ pañca jajñire. (13)

Parambrahma is Vāsudeva. His form is *parama puruṣa* who is *avyakta* (unmanifested), *nirguṇa* (devoid of *sattva, rajas* and *tamas*), *śānta* (undisturbed), *avyaya* (non-changing) and is beyond the twenty-five *tattvas* of *Sāṁkhya* philosophy. (1)

This internally and externally omnipresent *Deva* having entered the *Prakṛti* in the form of *Saṅkarṣaṇa* created waters and saw the seed (of the universe). (2)

This became a golden egg which was surrounded by darkness all around, out of the same, first appeared *sanātana* (everlasting) *aniruddha.* (3)

This is referred to as *hiraṇyagarbha* in *Vedas.* Having appeared first, it is called *āditya* which because of having created all the animate and inanimate world is referred to as *sūrya.* (4)

Being in the form of most intense light and because of having dispersed all the darkness it is referred to as *savitā.* This *bhūtabhāvana,* i.e., the creator, preserver and destroyer of the whole world traverses the worlds dispersing the darkness. (5)

The same in the form of light, disperser of all darkness is known as *mahattattva.* His *maṇḍala* is *Ṛgveda, karṇa* is *Sāmaveda* and *mūrti* is *Yajurveda.* (6)

Thus this is *trayīmaya,* i.e., in the form of three *Vedas* and this is also in the form of 'Time' as this is the one who creates time and is omnipotent. He is the soul of all and is omnipresent. He is subtle and whole of the world rests in him. (7)

> He always travels in the world-cart with the year wheel having *saptac chandas* as seven horses. (8)
>
> His three *caraṇas* being immortal are obscure, i.e., they are beyond comprehension, only the fourth *caraṇa* is manifested. The same *Prabhu*, the omnipotent, created Brahmā in the form of *ahaṁkāra,* i.e., the *ahaṁtattva* of *Sāṁkhya* philosophy. (9)
>
> Having handed over the desired *Vedas* to the Grand father of the world (the Brahmā) and having made him sit in the egg *aniruddha* travels illuminating the whole world. (10)
>
> Brahmā in the form of *ahaṁtattva* first created *manas* and from *manas*; the moon appeared and from the eyes appeared the ocean of *tejas,* the 'Sun'. (11)
>
> From *manas* appeared *ākāśa* , from *ākāśa* came *vāyu* (the air), from air, *agni*; from *agni,* the water; and from waters appeared *pṛthivī.* Thus five *mahābhūtas* appeared with the increase of each *guṇa* (qualities, sound, *rūpa* (form), *rasa* (taste), touch and smell at each step of manifestation. (12)
>
> After the creation of fiery Sun and Soma Moon, Mars was created from *tejas,* Mercury from *pṛthivī,* Jupiter, from *ākāśa,* Venus, from water, Saturn from air. (13)

It may be remarked that the above stanzas are the replies to the questions of Mayāsura, by the Sūryāṅśa *puruṣa.* This cosmogonic descritpion is an admixture of *sṛṣṭikramas* from *Sāṁkhya Vedānta* and *Śrīmadbhagavatam.* The parable of Saṅkarṣaṇa and Aniruddha is somewhat different from the one in *Bhāgavatadharma.* According to the latter, from Vāsudeva Parameśvara, manifested the *Jīva* Saṅkarṣaṇa; from Saṅkarṣaṇa, Pradyumna was born and from Pradyumna, Aniruddha (i.e., the *ahaṁtattva*). Some schools do not mention Pradyumna in the sequence. Note that in the above stanzas *pañcatanmātras* are not categorically mentioned but these are automatically understood in right order in the sequence because the text refers to the Vāsudeva to be beyond twenty-five *tattvas* of *Sāṁkhya* philosophy.

Now we come to other texts which exclusively deal with *Jyotiṣa Śāstra.* In *Jyotiṣa Vedāṅgam* of Ṛṣi Lagadha we do not find as such any reference to any of the *pañca- mahābhūtas* except to the Sun and Moon which are *tejas bhautika* bodies. In *Purāṇas,* (like *Mārkaṇḍeya Purāṇa)* we do have exclusive sections dealing with *jyotiṣa,* but these have mostly the same contents as the proper *Jyotiṣa Śāstra* texts like *Jyotiṣa Vedāṅgam, Sūrya Prajñapti, Candra Prajñapti, Jambūdvīpa*

Prajñapti and *Jyotiṣa-Karaṇḍaka* in *Prākṛta* (of Jaina Tradition), *Śārdūla Karnāvadana* of Buddhist tradition. So it is worthwhile to discuss here only the references to *mahābhūtas* or *bhautika* entities as found in proper *Jyotiṣa* texts.

Bṛhat-saṁhitā of Varāhamihira (6th century AD) has many chapters exclusively on various aspects of astronomy. It talks of cosmic evolution as follows:

> *āsittamah kiledaṁ tatrāpām taijasebhavaddhaime.*
> *svarbhūśakale brahmā viśvakṛdaṇḍārka-śaśinayanaḥ.* (6)
> (Varāha *BṛS.* 1.6)
>
> Before creation, there was nothing but darkness everywhere. Then water came into being, wherefrom sprang a golden egg consisting of two parts of the shell, i.e., the earth and the heavens. There arose the creator of the universe Brahmā with Sun and Moon as his eyes. (6)

Note that here Sun and Moon are said to have born simultaneously with Brahmā (in a lyrical simile in the language) while *Sūrya Siddhānta* talks of creation of Sun and Moon after Brahmā's appearance in the genesis sequence.

The Concepts About *Bhautika* Entities in *Jyotiṣa* Texts

Earth (one entity in the big assembly of *pañcamahābhautika* world in infinite space) is described in detail by Indian astronomers in their respective treatises. Varāhamihira in *Pañca-siddhāntikā* describes the earth as a *pañcamahābhautika* body standing in space without support, like an iron ball in a cage of magnets. See diagram 8.1.

The Notions predecessor of law of gravitation on the basis of symmetry property of space (*ākāśa*)

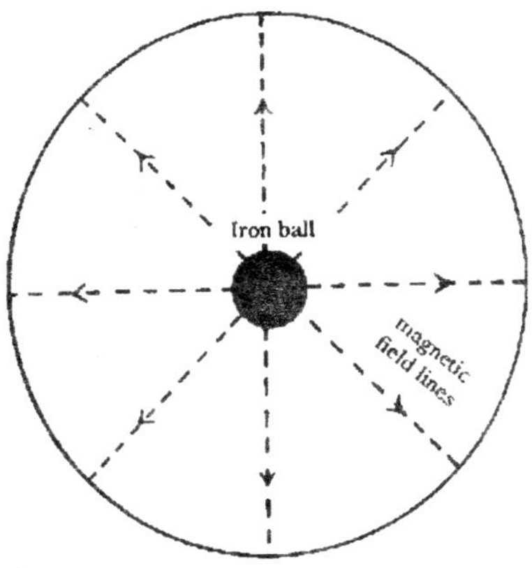

Magnetic cage Earth in space

Diagram 8.1 Magnetic cage Earth in space

panca-mahābhūtamayastārāgaṇapañjare mahīgolaḥ.
khe'yaskāntastho loha ivāvasthito vṛttaḥ. (1)
(Varāha. *Bṛ. S.* 13.1)

It may be noted that in *Jyotiṣa* mostly Sopādhīkṛta *mahābhūtas* are discussed.

Varāhamihira gives the simile with the iron ball held at the centre of a magnetic cage, while some thought of the supporting power of *Brahman* responsible for the **Earth's held up** position in space.

Earlier the rotation of earth was not conceived, the revolutions of heavens during day and night were considered to be caused due to *Pravāha Vāyu.* Since very old days of the *saiddhāntika* astronomy, Lalla's *Siṣyadhī vṛddhida tantra* discusses the seven types of air in seven shells around the earth. The atmospheric air enveloped around the earth is known as *āvaha.* Its radius is said to be 537 *yojanas.* But it is interesting to note that Āryabhaṭa about five hundred years earlier than Lalla, claimed the rotation of earth about its own axis, but the hypothesis was not accepted and was much criticised by Lalla. It may be remarked that the basic unit of time is defined using the rotation of earth as standard. This definition stands even now when atomic watches are invented for use in scientific works. The other units of time are defined on the bases of motion of the sun and the moon. The time so defined is *sopādhika* while in *Nyāya* philosophy this is absolute but gets into use when defined in relation to the motion of a body in space (*ākāśa*). This way it is rendered *sopādhika.* Time and space are one and the same in Eiensteinian frame-work of the theory of relativity. But astronomers like Newton took space and time as absolute and considered these to be different *padārthas.* We discuss the implication of these concepts as used by our exponents of *Jyotiṣa.*

Absoluteness of Space and Law of Gravitation

It may be noted that *Jyotiṣa Śāstra* is a discipline, where the theories are evolved and hypotheses are supported or rejected through the mathematical arguments based on observations. *Jyotiṣa Śāstra* texts describe the methods of determining the direction(s) in space. The directions (*dik*) are nothing but *sopādhika* space. The directions are always relative to a particular point in space and thus will have no meaning in absolute sense. Thus *dik* is just the *sopādhikīkaraṇa* of space. Although *Jyotiṣācāryas* developed mathematical techniques to determine Directions/Subdirections or any relative orientation of a system, yet they were aware of the absolute nature of space. Using this concept they arrived at the concept of law of gravitation qualitatively (of course Newton treated the problem mathematically.) Before we discuss the notion about force of attraction of earth and planets in ancient or medieval Indian traditions, it is desirable to point out how the ancient seers thought of causes of planetary motions.

It is interesting to note that in ancient *Jyotiṣa Śāstra* tradition, the notions on causes of planetary motions were based on the philosophical concepts regarding time and space. *Sūrya Siddhānta* talks of the agents of planetary motion as the invisible personified **Time Gods** standing at the cardinal points (Apogee, perigee and the nodes) on the orbit. These Gods were indentified mathematically with ***manda kendra*** (anomaly) ***śighra kendra*** (the elongation argument) and *pāta* (the orbital nodes). It was conjectured that these Gods stand at their specific positions and drag the planets by their left and right hands on both the sides.

The notions predecessor of law of gravitation based on the symmetry property of space (*ākāśa*).

As *ākāśa* is all around symmetric or directionless, how the planets can move? There must be some force?

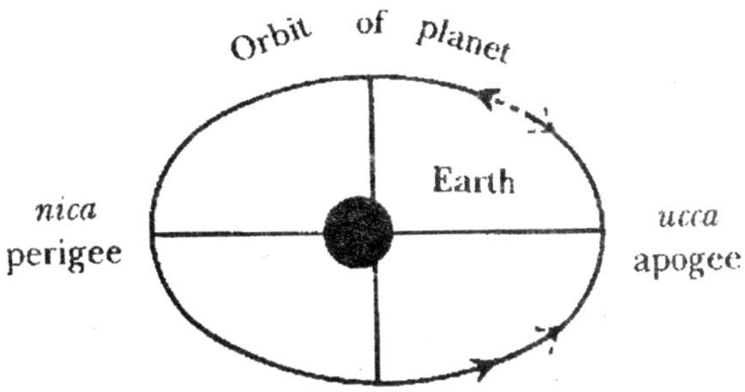

Diagram 8.2

Broken arrowheads show the direction of the force due to the divine agent at *ucca* (Full arrowheads show the direction of velocity vector of the planet) *Sūryasiddhānta* (*SS*) talks of Divine agents of force (Representative of Compelling Time harmonicities) which are responsible for changes in velocity through invisible air ropes (The action at a distance).

Broken arrowheads indicate just the directions of action of force agent, located at *ucca*. The velocity increases on one side and decreases on the other side of *ucca*.

(See the diagrams 8.2, 8.3 which show the details of this model of drag-hypothesis). On the basis of this model they explained the variations in speeds of planets (and even argued to have proper signs for their accelerations). Even comparing the velocities of Moon and Mars etc., they attributed their relative velocity magnitudes to their sizes and masses while under the force of drag by the invisible Time Gods. Motion towards the north and south of ecliptic were explained on the basis of the dragging force due to Gods at the *pātas*. Mercury and Venus are said to be under the faster attractive drag force due to the God at *śīghra kendra*. It may be remarked that on the basis of this model they could not explain the *vakra gati* (Retrograde motions) of planets. Note that they did study the different types of possible velocities but just reported these types without explaining. These are the earliest notions about force of attraction and it may be pointed out that in these notions time is considered to be the compelling force, which causes changes in velocitites and keeps planets moving along the curved space but no force of attraction responsible for keeping the planets in orbits could be assigned. There is no doubt that the notion similar to the above one is quite natural because Time binding on the motion is likely to be taken as a compulsion on the moving body and the cardinal points are the points from where the change in velocity starts developing. Even in the framework of the law of gravitation, the motion is represented by Sin(nt), (where nt = anomaly), the acceleration starts developing from the cardinal point (velocity = n radians per unit of time).

The Notions Predecessor of law of Gravitation, based on the symmetry property of space (*Ākāśa*)

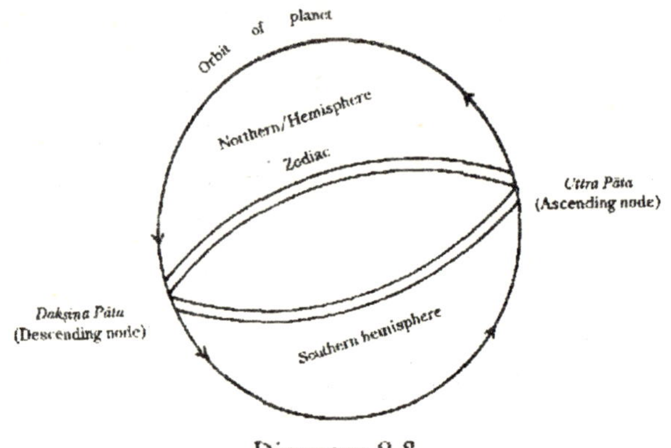

Diagram 8.3

The *S.S.* talks of divine agents of force also at the nodes which drag the planets towards northern or southern hemispheres.

Bhāskarācārya studying the motion of Mars, Jupiter etc. found that in case these are behind the Sun, they get accelerated and when Sun is behind any planet the latter is retarded. In fact Bhāskarācārya had almost arrived at the conclusion that Sun attracts the planets but he missed the point without the necessary elaborations. On the other hand, he could arrive at the most important conclusion about earth's gravity using absoluteness (leading to the all round symmetry) of space. How was the concept of the absolute or relative nature of space used in arguments by Bhāskarācārya in arriving at the hypothesis about the law of gravitation in case of earth? This would be clear from the following paragraph.

Symmetry of Space (*ākāśa*) is a property which could be easily inferred. In fact Newton's first law of motion, that nothing can move unless some force is applied, is a notion conceived by man since the beginning of creation. Newton just postulated the same in categoric statements and developed the laws of motion mathematically. Note that this law is just a mathematical translation of the fact that space is all around symmetric. It has no direction downward, upward or north, east, south or west. All the directions in space lack any preference for any directivity if there is no object at a point (which is negation of space at that point). If you suppose that the body will move in a particular direction defined with respect to a point in open space (without any other body) one can counter-argue, "what is space with that direction?" "Why should the body not move in another direction?" Thus on simple logical grounds even the primitive man might have had familiarity with the first law of motion qualitatively. In addition to this, so naturally accepted inference, the spherical shape of the earth helped a lot in arriving at the notion of the force of gravitation. This fact will be clear in the following discussion.

When it was clear to man that the earth is a figure like a ball and he knew that there are habitants all over the earth, it helped to conclude about gravitation due to the earth. *Sūrya Siddhānta* describes the symmetry of space in a good philosophical way as follows:

> *sarvatraiva mahīgolé svasthānamupari sthitam.*
> *manyante khe yato golāstasya kvordhvam kva vāpyadhaḥ.*
> (*S.S. Bhūgolādhyāya*, Stanza 53)

i.e., Everywhere on the spherical earth, the observer's place is above (i.e., his head points towards upward direction), because this sphere (earth) is (held) in space. So which direction is upward and which direction is downwards? The directions have no meaning in space. Bhāskarācārya advanced further to infer about gravitation of the earth. His statement is :

> *ākrṣṭaśaktiśca mahī tayā yat*
> *khasthaṁ guru svābhimukhaṁ svāsaktyā*
> *ākrṣyate tat patatīva bhāti*
> *same samantāt kva patatviyam khe?*
>
> The earth has capability to attract and due to this very property, in fact, this attracts any heavy object in space and the latter appears as if 'falling'. In the space which is symmetric all around, where it can fall?

It is clear that Bhāskarācārya arrived at the notion about gravitational force on the very basis of the principle of the 'Falling apple' about five hundred years earlier that Newton. There is no doubt that the credit to Newton is for all mathematical developments regarding motion which led kinematical studies to dynamical treatments, but Bhāskarācārya was the first to state categorically about existence of gravitational force of earth and argued more beautifully on the basis of symmetry of space and the spherical figure of the earth. As the earth is populated all around, for a man at a certain place (say 'A', see diagram 8.4) on the globe there is one 'B' just below on the other side of the earth, like a shadow in water. There are other people too whose positions are along directions inclined with respect to the position of the first one. There are also along 90^0 away (i.e., along perpendicular directioon (S)), but none falls away from earth's surface. Everyone thinks of himself standing above or towards-upwards direction. In this diagram are shown stones thrown by men at A and B falling to the earth from opposite directions. Thus one concludes that there exists force of attraction which is responsible for the "fall of bodies in space". So in fact the 'falling apple' theory is explained by Bhāskarācārya.

The Physical laws derived from the fact that *Ākāśa* is all around symmetric

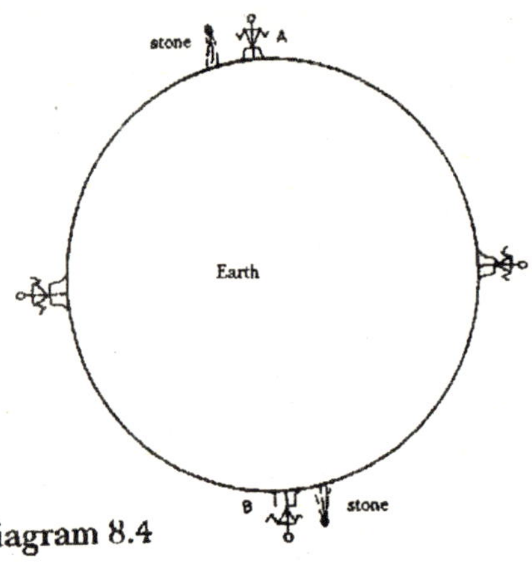

Diagram 8.4

(Falling stone Syndrome in Bhāskarācārya's *Siddhānta Śiromaṇi*)

It also talks of the directionlessness of *ākāśa* as inferred from the spherical shape of the earth which is all around populated by human beings (on the one side (**above**) and on the other side in *Pātāla* (or **just below**). But Bhāskarācārya advanced further to infer that **Earth attracts** the heavy things (say a stone) left in space and the latter appears "as if falling". He argues, where can the stone fall? *Ākāśa* is all around symmetric whichever direction is **above** or just below (like the shadow of a man in water) as the earth has spherical shape. This falling stone principle of Bhāskarācārya (1150 AD) came about five centuries earlier than Newton (1676 AD).

There is no doubt that for mathematicians space is symmetric and infinite, and they use the former property to arrive at the law of gravitation but we find in *Jyotiṣa* texts like *Sūrya Siddhānta*, Bhāskarācārya's *Siddhānta Śiromaṇi* etc., the dimensions of *ākāśa kakṣā* (the orbit of space) which in fact is defined as the limit up to which point Sun's rays reach. Thus it is limited to *ākāśa*. Yet for them too, *ākāśa* is *vibhu* (all around and hence symmetric) and infinite, but unlike in qualitative philosophy they could go ahead and conclude about the laws of motion and universal gravitation functioning in nature by translating symmetry of space in mathematical language.

Conclusion

The references to *Jyotiṣa* in Vedic *vāṅgmaya* and later texts give details of cosmogonic evolution leading to the creation of *pañcamahābhūtas* from *tāmasa bhūtādi ahaṁkāra*. The stars and planets have evolved out of these *mahābhūtas*. Astronomical and astrological texts make use of the concept of *mahābhūtas* in their working principles. They used the *sopādhika ākāśa* in determining the directions/subdirections in two-dimensional and three-dimensional space, which helped in specifying the positions of terrestrial and celestial objects. They also made use of the *vibhu* absolute and infinite nature of space in inferring the existence of law of gravitation functioning in nature and derived the laws of conservation of momenta from its symmetry properties. The development of the laws of motion and gravitation are the most interesting developments in the hands of astronomers, which grew out of the philosophic concepts of *mahābhūtas*. They attributed the reasons for the gravitational forces to the very nature of matter, for example Bhāskarācārya gives the simile of a natural phenomenon like the heat in fire, hardness in stones etc. for the gravity of the earth. These modern studies in space science and other disciplines of study of *mahābhautika* entities have advanced to remarkable extents, which have served the causes of human conveniences all over the world.

It may be pointed out that *Hayata*, an Arabic astronomical text (translated into Sanskrit) talks of bodies (*Vasita, Falaki, Unsāri*, etc.) with one, two or more *mahābhūtas* but excluding *ākāśa*. (The Graeco-Arabic philosophy does not include *ākāśa* in the list of *mahābhūtas*. There are only four *mahābhūtas* in this system of philosophy) *Nyāya* philosophy too talks of bodies made up of specific *mahābhūtas* taken each individually but Śaṅkarācārya's *Pañcīkaraṇa* (a process claiming mixtures of *tanmātras* in the gross *mahābhūta* elements) has no provision for pure single *mahābhūta* elements. *Sūrya siddhānta* the astronomical text talks of five star planets out of five *mahābhūtas* taken individually. Thus there are differences in various schools of philosophy. But there is no doubt that the

Jyotiṣācāryas went ahead to use the properties of the *mahābhūtas* to arrive at laws of motion and the gravitational law working in the universe which served the cause of scientific development.

References

A comprehensive and scientific study of vaiśeṣika concepts applied to Caraka Saṁhitā., Ph.D. thesis by Dr. Narmada Prasad under coguidance of the author of this paper and Dr. Jyotirmitra of B.H.U. (1982).

A source book of Indian Astronomy comp. by B.V. Subbarayappa and K.V. Sharma, published by Nehru Centre Worlie, Bombay.

Āryabhaṭīyam of Āryabhaṭa, comm. by Sh. K.S. Shukla and B.V. Subbarayappa. Published by Indian National Science Academy, New Delhi.

Atharva Vedīya Jyotiṣa (*Atharva Vedāṅga Jyotiṣam*) Published by Pītāmbarā Peeṭh Pariṣad Datia (N.P) (1965).

Bhāratīya Jyotiṣa by Dixit in Marāṭhī, tr. into Hindi by Śrī Śivanātha Jhārkhandi.

Bharatiyeṣu Darśaneṣu Paramāṇu Pudgala Vādaḥ, A Vidyā Vāridhi (Ph.D.) thesis under guidence of the author (1981).

Brahmasphuṭasiddhānta, Ed. by Pt. Ramswarup Shastri, Karol Bagh, Delhi.

Bṛhat Saṁhitā of Varāhamihira, comm. by Bhaṭṭotpala.

Cosmography of Hindus, Buddhists and Jainas by Nerfil (in German).

Hayata, An Arabic text of *Jyotiṣa* in Sanskrit, ed. by Vibhūti Bhūṣaṇa Bhaṭṭācārya, Sanskrit Saraswati Bhavanagranth Mālā Vol. 96 Varanasi. (1967).

Jyotiṣkaraṇḍaka comm. by Ācārya Malaya Giri. Published by Indore Pipali Bazar Sh. Jaina Bandhu Press.

Mahābhāskarīyam, Govinda Swāmi's Bhāṣya and super-commentary Siddhānta Dīpikā by Parameśvara. Published by Govt. Oriental Manuscript Library Madras (1957).

Mathematical Analysis of Presiddhāntic. Post Vedāṅga Jain Astronomy, Ph.D Thesis under supervision of the author of this paper (1975).

Pañcasiddhāntikā of Varāhamihira, ed. by David Pingree. Brown University Providence Rhode Islands U.S.A.

Ṛgveda Saṁhitā, commentary by Sāyaṇa.

Samrāṭ Siddhānta by Paṇḍita-Samrāṭ Jagannāth, ed. and Published by Pt. Ramswarup Shastri Jyotiṣa Kendra, Karol Bagh, Delhi.

Śārdūlakarṇāvadāna, Ed. by Sujitkumar Mukhyopādhyāya. Published by Viśvabhāratī Śāntiniketana (1954). A. Buddhist traditional Astronomical text.

Siddhānta Sārvabhauma of Shri Munisvara.

Siddhānta Śiromaṇi of Bhāskarācārya, *Golādhyāya,* comm. by Pt. Girijā Prasād Dwivedī, Published by Munshi Nand Kishor Press (C.I.E.) Lucknow.

Siddhānta Tattva Viveka of Ācārya Kamalākara.

Sūrya Prajñapti in Prākrit. comm. in Sanskrit by Acharya Malaya Giri (Jaina Canonical text).

A commentary in Sanskrit and English by the author of this paper will be published soon.

Sūrya Siddhānta Vijñāna Bhāṣya by Mahaveer Shrivasta, Published by Vijñāna Pariṣad. Allahabad (1940 AD.)

Taittirīya Upaniṣad

Vedāṅga Jyotiṣa of Ṛṣi Lagadha, comm. by Sudhakar Dwivedi (1908) and of Somākara, tr. by Weber (Berlin 1862).

List of Contributors

Usha R. Bhise	C - 20 Ganesh Prasad Naurshir Bharucha Road Bombay - 400 007
N. S. Devanathachariar	S. Navalakappam Village Vandavasi - 604 408 N. A District, Tamilnadu
T. N. Dharmadhikari	Adiparna 42-43/63 United Western Society Karve Nagar Pune - 411 052
A. M. Ghatage	Hon. Secretary Bhandarkar Oriental Research Institute Pune - 411 004
S. K. Lal	Centre of Advanced Study in Sanskrit University of Poona Pune - 411 007
Srinivas Madabhushi	F6 B4 Prince Apartments Vishakhapatnam - 530 017
K. V. Mande	S.P. College Pune
Mangala Mirasdar	Department of Sanskrit and Prakrit University of Poona Pune - 411 007

Sampat Narayan	Indira Gandhi National Centre for the Arts New Delhi - 110 001
Pratibha Pingle	Dictionary Deptt. Deccan College and Post-Graduate Research Institute Pune
S. D. Sharma	Department of Physics Panjabi University Patiala - 147 002 Punjab
Mahesh Tiwary	45, Uttaranchal Patparganj Delhi - 110 052
Kapila Vatsyayan	Indira Gandhi National Centre for the Arts New Delhi - 110 001

Index